The Broadview Pocket Guide to Writing

to Writing

A Handbook for Students

fifth Canadian edition

A Note on the Cover

For thousands of years humans have been likening the
process of writing to the ways in which we interact with
the land—ploughing and digging, sowing and reaping.
In the early seventh century CE Isadore of Seville tells
of how the Romans for their writing used styluses that
were at first made of iron, later of bone, and quotes
from a now-lost Roman play by the now-unknown
playwright Atta: "we shall turn the ploughshares upon
wax, and plough with a bone point." Around 1400 the
German poet Johannes von Tepl begins his long poem
The Ploughman of Bohemia with a reference to what he
refers to as a well-known maxim of scribes: "the quill is
my plough." In some sense the quill or pen is of course
like a plough in that it digs into the writing surface.
But the digging can also be likened more broadly to
what writing does—as Seamus Heaney famously likens
it in a 1964 poem about his father's digging and what
Heaney himself will do with his "squat pen."

The Broadview Pocket Guide to Writing

A Handbook for Students
fifth Canadian edition

Doug Babington, Corey Frost, Don LePan,
Maureen Okun, Nora Ruddock, and Karen Weingarten

Contributing Editor: *Laura Buzzard*

broadview press

Founded in 1985, Broadview Press remains a wholly independent publishing house. Broadview's focus is on academic publishing; our titles are accessible to university and college students as well as scholars and general readers. With over 800 titles in print, Broadview has become a leading international publisher in the humanities, with world-wide distribution. Broadview is committed to environmentally responsible publishing and fair business practices.

Library and Archives Canada Cataloguing in Publication

Title: The Broadview pocket guide to writing : a concise handbook for students / Doug Babington, Corey Frost, Don LePan, Maureen Okun, Nora Ruddock, and Karen Weingarten ; contributing editor: Laura Buzzard.
Other titles: Pocket guide to writing
Names: Babington, Doug, author. | Frost, Corey, author. | LePan, Don, 1954- author. | Okun, Maureen, 1961- author. | Ruddock, Nora, 1978- author. | Weingarten, Karen, 1980- author. | Buzzard, Laura, editor.
Description: Fifth Canadian edition. | Includes bibliographical references and index.
Identifiers: Canadiana (print) 20220469008 | Canadiana (ebook) 20220469032 | ISBN 9781554815425 (spiral bound) | ISBN 9781770488144 (PDF) | ISBN 9781460407639 (EPUB)
Subjects: LCSH: English language—Rhetoric—Textbooks. | LCSH: English language—Grammar—Textbooks. | LCSH: Report writing—Textbooks. | LCSH: Bibliographical citations—Standards—Textbooks. | LCGFT: Textbooks.
Classification: LCC LB2369 .B24 2023 | DDC 808/.042—dc23

Broadview Press handles its own distribution in North America:
PO Box 1243, Peterborough, Ontario K9J 7H5, Canada
555 Riverwalk Parkway, Tonawanda, NY 14150, USA
Tel: (705) 743-8990; Fax: (705) 743-8353
email: customerservice@broadviewpress.com

For all territories outside of North America, distribution is handled by Eurospan Group.

Broadview Press acknowledges the financial support of the Government of Canada for our publishing activities.

Canadä

Cover Design: Lisa Brawn
Managing Editor: Tara Lowes
Design and Typesetting: Eileen Eckert

PRINTED IN CANADA

HOW TO USE THIS BOOK AND ITS COMPANION WEBSITE

The goal of *The Broadview Pocket Guide to Writing* is to provide a concise reference text that is easy to use in every respect. We've made the book easy to carry around, and easy to use lying flat on a desk. We've also tried to keep the organization simple so that the book will be easy for you to find your way round in. There are three ways to locate information in the text:

- *index:* Go to the index at the back of the book to find the location in the book for any topic, large or small.
- *page headers:* These list section headings on the left and chapter headings on the right.
- *table of contents:* The detailed table of contents at the beginning of the book sets out the sections, chapters, and headings within chapters.

The purchase price of this book includes free access to *The Broadview Guide to Writing* website, where you will find various sorts of material related to this book. (If you have purchased a used rather than a new copy, you may purchase a passcode online through the main Broadview Press website.) Perhaps most importantly, the companion website includes a wide range of exercises relating to almost every aspect of grammar and usage. Many of these are interactive; you can check immediately if you have answered correctly, and—if you haven't—find an explanation. (Instructors may of course ask that you complete particular exercises, but we encourage you to try the exercises on your own as well—especially in areas that the Diagnostic and Review Exercises suggest may not be areas of strength for you.)

You will also find several other sorts of material on *The Broadview Guide to Writing* companion website:

- a selection of expository essays, ranging from Montaigne to the present day, each accompanied by questions and topics for discussion.

- links to a variety of other helpful sites.
- complete sample essays in MLA, APA, Chicago, and CSE formats.

This book does *not* provide certain features that you will find in most other writing guides and handbooks: glossy paper that is both expensive and environmentally unfriendly, and highlighting in many different colours throughout the book. We have added one accent colour, but we have no desire to add more—or to move away from our long-standing policy of using plain (and, as much as possible, recycled) paper stock. That's a choice that's good for the environment—and also one that helps us keep the price of this book at a level little more than half that of most other writing guides or handbooks.

If you have questions or comments about *The Broadview Guide* (or suggestions as to what else we should consider including for future editions, whether on the website or in the bound book), we'd like to hear from you. Just email

customerservice@broadviewpress.com

Thank you!

CONTENTS

STYLES OF WRITING

1. CHOOSING THE BEST WORDS

1a. Be as Clear and Specific as Possible

In most contexts it is best to use language that communicates your ideas to the reader as clearly as possible. (For more on specific issues relating to academic jargon see the section below on "The Language of Academic Writing" [6a].)

needs checking Several key components of this issue will be identified in this essay, and various facets of each will be discussed.

revised This essay will look at three things.

needs checking They wanted the plan to be optimally functional.

revised They wanted the plan to work well.

needs checking In an economic slowdown the economy declines.

revised In an economic slowdown the rate of growth in the economy declines.

1b. Watch for Redundancy

Redundancies are words or expressions that repeat in another way a meaning already expressed. Sometimes they may be useful to add emphasis; usually they should be avoided.

needs checking The house is very large in size.

revised The house is very large.

needs checking It would be mutually beneficial for both countries.

revised It would be beneficial for both countries.

1c. Avoid Wordiness

In groping for ideas at the rough draft stage, writers often latch on to unnecessarily complex or wordy sentence structures.

needs checking As regards the trend in interest rates, it is likely to continue to be upward.

revised   Interest rates are likely to continue to rise.

needs checking   There are many historians who accept this thesis.
revised   Many historians accept this thesis.

needs checking   Due to the fact that each member of the UN Security Council has a veto, the Council is not infrequently unable to take decisive action.
revised   Since each member of the UN Security Council has a veto, decisive action is rare.

Some specifics:

actual/actually: Usually redundant.

as regards: Use *about*, or rephrase. (See example above.)

as stated earlier: If so, why state it again?

as you know, as we all know: Usually better omitted.

aspect: Often a pointer to an entire phrase or clause that can be cut.

needs checking   The logging industry is a troubled one at the present time. One of the aspects of this industry that is a cause for concern is the increased production of cheaper timber in South America.
revised   The logging industry is now a troubled one. Increased production of cheaper timber in South America has reduced the market for North American wood.

at a later date: *Later*.

at the present time: *Now*, or nothing.

attention: *It has come to our attention* that this expression is almost always unnecessarily wordy.

basis/basically: Both are often pointers to wordiness.

needs checking   On the basis of the information we now possess it is possible to see that William Bligh was not the ogre he was once thought to be. Basically, he was no harsher than most captains of the time.

revised   Recent research suggests that William Bligh was not the ogre he was once thought to be. He was no harsher than most captains of the time.

because of the fact that: *Because.*

close proximity to: *Near.*

due to the fact that: *Because, since.* (See example above.)

factor: Heavily overused, and a frequent cause of wordiness.

needs checking   An important factor contributing to the French Revolution was the poverty of the peasantry.

        revised   The poverty of the peasantry was a major cause of the French Revolution.

for the reason that: *Because.*

from my point of view / according to my point of view / in my opinion: All three expressions are usually redundant.

point in time: *Now* or *then.*

situation: By avoiding this word you will usually make your sentence shorter and better.

needs checking   This treaty created a situation in which individual countries ceded some powers to the European Union.

        revised   Through this treaty individual countries ceded some powers to the European Union.

there is / are / was / were: These constructions often produce sentences that are needlessly long.

needs checking   There are many historians who accept this thesis.

        revised   Many historians accept this thesis.

1d. Watch for Missing Parts

It is easy to omit a word or a link in an argument.

needs checking   She told Felicity and about the accident.

        revised   She told Felicity and me about the accident.

needs checking   She reminded the conference that just one inter-continental ballistic missile could plant 200 million trees.

revised   She reminded the conference that the money spent on just one intercontinental ballistic missile could be used to plant 200 million trees.

The word *that* should always be included if its omission might lead to confusion.

needs checking   Darwin believed biblical texts such as those dealing with human origins should not be read literally.

revised   Darwin believed that biblical texts such as those dealing with human origins should not be read literally.

Phrases such as *that of* and *those of* must be included in many sentences for the sake of logical clarity.

needs checking   The drives of golfer Mike Weir have never been as long as Tiger Woods or Rory McIlroy.

revised   The drives of golfer Mike Weir have never been as long as those of Tiger Woods or Rory McIlroy.

1e. Choose the Best Verb: Active or Passive Voice?

(For definitions see 9f in the Grammar section of this book.)

In his famous essay "Politics and the English Language," George Orwell shows that using the passive voice can encourage wordiness and be a form of political duplicity, and suggests that we should use the active voice wherever possible. He's partly right.

As background here, it is essential to appreciate that the distinction between active and passive voice is not relevant to all verbs, but only to transitive verbs. The active voice/passive voice distinction is relevant to the transitive verb *to hit*, for example; you can hit someone or something, and someone or something can be hit by you. Disguising agency by using the passive voice of such verbs (*The protestors were knocked to the ground* rather than *The soldiers knocked the protestors to the ground*) can indeed be a form of political duplicity. But you cannot sleep someone or something, or be slept by someone or something; the active voice/passive voice distinction is not relevant to an intransitive verb such as *to sleep*. Nor is it relevant to that most common of verbs, the verb *to be*.

With verbs that allow for both active and passive voices, either construction may often be used to disguise agency. Such, for example, is the case with the verb *to violate*, which may be used with the agent as the subject but may also be used with the action itself as the grammatical subject:

> The detention of the suspect without any charges violated her constitutional rights.

> The suspect's constitutional rights were violated by her detention without any charges.

Who detained the subject? Agency is as much disguised in the first of these sentences as in the second, though the first is in the active voice, the second in the passive voice.

Here's another example of disguised agency. The sentence *I knocked the vase off the shelf* uses the past tense *knocked* in the active voice. Switching to the passive voice gives us *The vase was knocked off the shelf*, and of course allows for the option of omitting *by me*; this is one way of disguising agency. But if I wanted to disguise agency in such a situation I would be more likely to choose a different verb entirely, perhaps an intransitive verb such as *to fall* for which the active voice/passive voice distinction is not relevant: *That vase fell off the shelf*.

Many verbal stratagems that disguise agency use the pronoun *it* as the grammatical subject. If someone has just dumped a girlfriend or boyfriend, for example, the "dumper" is not always keen to say *I dumped her* or *I dumped him*. But nor is it likely that the speaker will shift to the passive voice and say *she was dumped by me/he was dumped by me*. Much more likely would be a shift to the use of *it* as the subject, together with intransitive verbs such as *to be* or *to work*: *It is over between us*, for example, or *It just didn't work out*.

It is important to recognize that there is nothing pernicious *in itself* in the passive voice. If you want to keep the focus on the recipient of an action rather than on its agent, the passive voice is useful. But in other situations, the active voice is usually less wordy and more direct, and is to be preferred on those grounds.

needs checking   The election was lost by Le Pen.
        (Passive voice—6 words)
revised   Le Pen lost the election.
        (Active voice—4 words)

needs checking   The protestor was killed with a single baton blow to the head.
        [Who is responsible for the killing? If the information is known it should generally be given.]
revised   One of the soldiers killed the protestor with a single baton blow to the head.

2. CONNECT YOUR IDEAS CLEARLY

The order in which you make your ideas appear and the ways in which you connect them—and show your reader how they connect—are as important to good writing as the ideas themselves.

2a. Paragraphing

There is a degree of flexibility when it comes to the matter of where and how often to start new paragraphs. Sometimes a subtle point in an argument will require a paragraph of almost an entire page to elaborate; occasionally a single sentence can form an effective paragraph. Yet separating ideas into paragraphs remains an important aid to the processes of both reading and writing. Following are some guidelines as to when it is appropriate to begin a new paragraph.

i) In narration:

- whenever the story changes direction ("This was the moment the governor had been waiting for ...," "When Napoleon left Elba he ...")
- when there is a gap in time in the story ("Two weeks later the issue was raised again in cabinet ...")

ii) In description:

- whenever you switch from describing one place, person, or thing to describing another ("Even such a brief description as this is enough to give some sense of the city and its pretensions. Much more interesting in many ways are some of the nearby smaller cities and towns ...")

iii) In persuasion or argument:

- when a new topic is introduced ("There can be little doubt that Austen's asides on the literary conventions of her time provide an amusing counterpoint to her story. But does this running commentary detract from the primary imaginative experience of *Northanger Abbey*?")
- when there is a change in direction of the argument ("To this point we have been looking only at the advantages of a guaranteed annual income. We should also ask, however, whether or not it would be practical to implement.")

iv) When changing from one mode to another:

- Description, narration, and argument are commonly blended together in writing. If, for example, a text moves from describing an experiment to analyzing its significance, it's a good time to start a new paragraph. If it moves from telling where Napoleon went and what he did to discussing why events unravelled in this way, the same holds true.

For more on paragraphing, see 5c, "Argument Structure and Paragraphing," below.

2b. Joining Words

The art of combining correct clauses and sentences logically and coherently is as much dependent on taking the time to think through what we are writing as it is on knowledge of correct usage. It is important to use appropriate joining words to help the reader see how ideas are linked—and important as well not to give too many or contradictory cues to the reader. Almost no writer manages these things (let alone perfect grammar and spelling!) the first time. Good writers typically write at least two or three drafts of any piece of writing before considering it finished.

needs checking   At the end of World War II there was substantial optimism that the application of Keynesian analysis would lead to economic stability and security. Over the post-war period optimistic rationalism weakened in the face of reality.

This passage gives the reader too few cues. It is not immediately clear how the idea of the first sentence is connected to that of the second. The problem is readily solved by the addition of a single word:

revised   At the end of World War II there was substantial optimism that the application of Keynesian analysis would lead to economic stability and security. Over the post-war period, however, optimistic rationalism weakened in the face of reality.

needs checking   A short report in which you request an increase in your department's budget should be written in the persuasive mode. Most reports, however, do not have persuasion as their main objective. Persuasion, though, will often be one of their secondary objectives. In reports like these, some parts will be written in the persuasive mode.

Here, the use of *however* and *though* in consecutive sentences gives the reader the sense of twisting back and forth without any clear sense of direction. This sort of difficulty can be removed by rewording or rearranging the ideas:

revised   A short report in which you request an increase in your department's budget should be written in the persuasive mode. Most reports, however, do not have persuasion as their main objective. Persuasion will thus be at most a secondary objective.

The use of joining words is complicated by grammar; certain joining words are used to show how the ideas of one sentence connect to those of the previous sentence, while others are used to connect ideas in the same sentence. Words commonly used to connect the ideas of different sentences:

as a result,	further,
however,	furthermore,
in addition,	nevertheless,

Words commonly used to connect ideas within the same sentence:

although	though
and	whereas
because	while

(NB These lists are far from exhaustive.)

needs checking   There will not be regular delivery service this Friday, however, regular service will resume Monday.

revised   There will not be regular delivery service this Friday. However, regular service will resume Monday.

or   There will not be regular delivery service this Friday, but regular service will resume Monday.

Because: The joining word *because* is a particularly troublesome one. It is easy to become turned around and use *because* to introduce a result or an example rather than a cause.

needs checking   He had been struck by a car because he lay bleeding in the road.

revised   We could infer that he had been struck by a car because we saw him lying bleeding in the road.

    [This follows the causal connections of the writer's thought processes, but is wordy and cumbersome.]

revised   He lay bleeding on the road; evidently he had been struck by a car.

or   He had been struck by a car and lay bleeding on the road.

needs checking   The Suharto regime detained people in jail without trial because it had little respect for the law.

revised   We may conclude that the Suharto regime had little respect for the law because we know it detained people in jail without trial.

[Again, this follows the causal connections of the writer's thought processes, but is wordy and cumbersome.]

revised   The fact that the Suharto regime detained people for long periods without ever bringing them to trial shows that it had little respect for the law.

or   The Suharto regime in Indonesia showed little respect for the law. It detained people for long periods, for example, without ever bringing them to trial.

or   The Suharto regime in Indonesia had little respect for the law; it detained people for long periods without ever bringing them to trial.

2c. Order and Weight Your Ideas According to Their Importance

The order in which ideas appear in any piece of writing, and the space that is devoted to them, will inevitably send signals to the reader as to their relative importance. For this reason, it is wise to avoid long discussions of matters you consider to be of less importance—or else to relegate them to a note outside

Additional Material Online
Exercises on joining words may be found at
sites.broadviewpress.com/writingcdn.
Click on **Exercises** and go to **M2.9**,
"Putting Ideas Together."

the main body of the text. Similarly, it is wise to signal through the amount of space you give to your main ideas your sense of their importance. (Obviously you may also signal this through the use of words and phrases such as *most importantly* ..., *crucially*....) You should be sure as well to give the reader a clear sense in the opening and closing paragraphs of the direction of the piece of writing.

2d. Watch for Ambiguity

Inappropriate word order may often cause confusion as to how ideas are connected.

needs checking	In a 101-foot mine shaft, abandoned for almost fifty years, two injured men were rescued over the weekend after they lit a fire to attract the attention of passers-by.
revised	Two injured men were trapped in a 101-foot mine shaft that had been abandoned for almost fifty years; they were rescued over the weekend after they lit a fire to attract the attention of passers-by.

For more examples, see 1d above and the box below.

2e. Illogical or Confused Connections

Certain words and phrases are particularly likely to lead writers into illogical or confused connections in their writing.

because of the following reasons/the reason is because: The word *because* makes it clear that a cause or reason is being introduced. The addition of a phrase such as *of the following reasons* is redundant. Either use *because* on its own, or use *for the following reasons/many reasons*, etc.

needs checking	During her first few years in New York, Susanna was unhappy because of several reasons.
revised	During her first few years in New York, Susanna was unhappy for several reasons.

Red Tape Holds Up New Bridge

The following are all examples of ambiguity in newspaper headlines. In some cases it may take several moments to decipher the intended meaning.

> Man held over giant L.A. brush fire
>
> Illegal aliens cut in half by new law
>
> Passerby injured by post office
>
> Red tape holds up new bridge
>
> Village water holds up well
>
> Jerk injures neck, wins award
>
> Bishop thanks god for calling

(The above examples come courtesy of columnist Bob Swift of Knight-Ridder Newspapers, and Prof. A. Levey of the University of Calgary.)

Here are two gems provided by editor Beth Humphries:

> The fossils were found by scientists
> embedded in red sandstone.
>
> She walked into the bathroom tiled in
> sea-green marble.

Here's one final example—intended to be a weather prediction for both coasts:

> "On the west coast tomorrow, they're going to see the sun,
> as well as the Atlantic seaboard."

Similarly, the phrase *the reason is because* involves repetition; use *that* instead of *because*, or eliminate the phrase completely.

needs checking	The reason ice floats is because it is lighter than water.
revised	The reason ice floats is that it is lighter than water.
or	Ice floats because it is lighter than water.

needs checking	The reason I have come is because I want to apply for a job.
revised	I have come to apply for a job.

is when/is where: Many people use these phrases erroneously when attempting to define something.

needs checking	Osmosis is when a fluid moves through a porous partition into another fluid.
revised	Osmosis occurs when a fluid moves through a porous partition into another fluid.
or	Osmosis is the movement of a fluid through a porous partition into another fluid.

numbers and things: In any sentence about things and numbers associated with those things, it is easy to become tangled up between the things themselves and the measure of number. Always have this question in the back of your mind: what is the subject of the verb? Here's an example:

needs checking	Delays in new product launches have hammered the company's share price, which started the year at about $60 and now trades at less than $30.
	[This sentence may seem fine at first glance; look again. What is the subject of the verb *trades*? It's the noun *price*. But is it in fact the price that trades at under $30? No; it's the shares that trade at less than $30.]
revised	Delays in new product launches have hammered the company's share price, which started the year at about $60 and is now less than $30.

or   Delays in new product launches have hammered the company's shares, which started the year at about $60; now the stock trades at less than $30.

Here are other examples of the same sort of problem:

needs checking   Many people have said that the price of the Tesla is too expensive.

revised   Many people have said that the price of the Tesla is too high.

or   Many people have said that the Tesla is too expensive.

needs checking   The height of the Shanghai Tower rises more than 2,000 feet.

revised   The Shanghai Tower rises more than 2,000 feet.

or   The height of the Shanghai Tower is more than 2,000 feet.

needs checking   The speed of the Sopwith Camel flew at just over 100 miles per hour during WWI.

revised   The Sopwith Camel flew at just over 100 miles per hour during WWI.

or   The maximum speed of the WWI Sopwith Camel was just over 100 miles per hour.

3. MAKING YOUR WRITING CONSISTENT

3a. Agreement among the Grammatical Parts of Your Writing

In order to be consistent, the various parts of your writing must be in agreement grammatically. Fuller treatment of this subject appears below in the section on grammar; here are a few examples of the sorts of problems that can arise:

needs checking   The state of Afghanistan's roads reflect the chaotic situation.

revised   The state of Afghanistan's roads reflects the chaotic situation.

> [Here the writer has made the mental error of thinking of *roads* as the subject of the verb *reflect*, whereas in fact the subject is the singular noun *state*.]

needs checking   A diplomat represents his or her country in its dealings with other countries. They often help to negotiate treaties and other agreements.

revised   Diplomats represent their country in its dealings with other countries. They often help to negotiate treaties and other agreements.

> [The pronoun *they* at the beginning of the second sentence needs to agree grammatically with the noun to which it refers.]

needs checking   We went over to the woman lying on the pavement; she looked either dead or asleep. Suddenly she sits bolt upright.

revised   We went over to the woman lying on the pavement; she looked either dead or asleep. Suddenly she sat bolt upright.

> [The revised passage is written consistently in the past tense.]

needs checking   Unlike the first version of the novel, which appeared in a weekly newspaper, Stowe had a chance to review the galley proofs of the 1852 edition.

revised   Whereas Stowe did not have a chance to proof the first version of the novel, which appeared in a weekly newspaper, she was able to review the galley proofs of the 1852 edition.

> [The grammatical structure of the first of these sentences suggests that a novel can read itself.]

> **Additional Material Online**
> For more on consistency when it comes to
> the grammatical parts of your writing, see
> **sites.broadviewpress.com/writingcdn**.
> Click on **Exercises** and go to
> **M2.1, "Verbs and Verb Issues."**

3b. Watch for Mixed Metaphors

Using metaphors can help to convey your ideas more clearly to
the reader—and help to make your writing more interesting.
A mixed metaphor occurs when we are not really thinking of
the meaning of the words we use. "If we bite the bullet we
have to be careful not to throw the baby out with the bathwater." "We will leave no stone unturned as we search for an
avenue through which the issue may be resolved." As soon as
one really thinks about such sentences one realizes that the
bullet is really better off out of the baby's bathwater, and that
the best way to search for an avenue is not to turn stones over.

needs checking	Now the President is out on a limb, and some of his colleagues are pulling the rug out from under him.
revised	Now the President is out on a limb, and some of his colleagues are preparing to saw it off.

4. RHYTHM, VARIETY, BALANCE, AND PARALLELISM

The most predictable syntax in the grammar of English is
SUBJECT–PREDICATE, as in the sentence "The effects are dis-
turbing." Upend that predictability, and you are on your way
to rhythmical distinctiveness: "Less obvious, but equally dis-
turbing, are the effects this work could have in...."

An important element in rhythmical distinctiveness is balance. Sometimes a pleasing effect may be achieved simply by
repeating grammatical structures: "We may not wish to deny
Rushton the right to publish such research. Nor can we deny

the harm that it causes." Sometimes balance may be achieved by placing words or phrases in apposition: "Cheney was Bush's closest confidante, his most influential advisor."

Often paired connectives ("if ... then," "either ... or," "not only ... but also") can help in achieving balance. As always, the writer must be careful to put the words in the right places.

needs checking   Hardy was not only a prolific novelist but wrote poetry too, and also several plays.

revised   Hardy was not only a prolific novelist but also a poet and a dramatist.

needs checking   The experiment can either be performed with hydrogen or with oxygen.

revised   The experiment can be performed with either hydrogen or oxygen.

   [The choice is between the two gases, not between performing and some other thing.]

needs checking   To subdue Iraq through sanctions, he felt, was better than using force.

revised   To subdue Iraq through sanctions, he felt, was better than to use force.

   [The infinitive *to subdue* is balanced by the infinitive *to use*.]

The pairing *both ... and* can also help in achieving balance. But here too, difficulties in getting all the words in the right order can easily arise.

needs checking   As a critic she is both fully aware of the tricks used by popular novelists to score easy successes with readers through stylized depictions of sex and violence, as well as realizing that "serious" novelists are sometimes not above resorting to the very same tricks.

revised   As a critic she is fully aware both of the tricks used by popular novelists to score easy successes with readers through stylized depictions of sex and violence, and of the fact that "serious" novelists are sometimes not above resorting to the very same tricks.

We tend to think of constructions involving words such as *both ... and* and *not only ... but also* when we think of balance and parallelism in written work. But the principles involved extend far more widely. Finding the right order for the words in a long sentence can be surprisingly challenging, even for experienced writers. Keeping words, phrases, and clauses grammatically balanced is less difficult where a pairing of two is concerned—though even here it is easy enough to go astray if you're not careful:

needs checking	This holiday we plan on keeping healthy and we'll get lots of rest.
revised	This holiday we plan on keeping healthy and getting lots of rest.
needs checking	The new government aims to reduce conflict with its neighbours and increasing the rate of economic growth.
revised	The new government aims to reduce conflict with its neighbours and to increase the rate of economic growth.
needs checking	The study concludes that Facebook use is associated with declines in subjective measures of well-being, and the more people use Facebook, the worse they tend to feel.
revised	The study concludes that Facebook use is associated with declines in subjective measures of well-being, and that the more people use Facebook, the worse they tend to feel.

> [Repetition of the function word *that* makes clear to the reader how the second part of the sentence is connected to the first; the sentence's second part reports another of the same study's conclusions.]

When it is a matter of keeping three or more elements parallel or in balance, everything becomes more difficult.

needs checking   His accomplishments included a succession of strategic successes during World War II, helping to revive Europe after the war, and he founded an important new international organization.

revised   His accomplishments included a succession of strategic successes during World War II, a plan to revive Europe after the war, and the foundation of an important new international organization.

or   He is remembered for his strategic successes during World War II, for his plan to revive Europe after the war, and for the foundation of an important new international organization.

> [These are only two of many ways in which the sentence might be revised so as to make its three parts grammatically parallel.]

needs checking   A plant-based, whole foods diet is associated with improvements in heart condition, greater life expectancy, diabetes is reduced, lowering of cancer rates, less chance of Alzheimer's, and also there are other health benefits.

revised   A plant-based, whole foods diet is associated with improvements in heart condition, greater life expectancy, lower rates of diabetes, lower incidence of cancer, lower incidence of Alzheimer's, and many other health benefits.

or   A plant-based, whole foods diet typically improves heart condition; increases one's life expectancy; significantly lowers one's chances of being afflicted with diabetes, heart disease, cancer, or Alzheimer's; and is associated with many other health benefits as well.

> [Again, these are only two of many ways in which the problem of the sentence's faulty parallelism may be corrected.]

In the above examples parallelism is a matter of grammatical structure first and foremost. But the importance of balance and parallelism to writing is not only a matter of grammar.

Sentences that are balanced and that include parallel structures tend to be both more comprehensible and more pleasing to the reader. In the following examples the initial sentence is not grammatically incorrect; the revisions are a matter of style rather than of correctness. You may judge for yourself as to how they compare in terms of the reader's experience.

worth checking　Teams with very low payrolls are unlikely to achieve much success, even in the regular season, and very unlikely to be able to win in the postseason against teams who are able to afford the best-paid stars. The Oakland As are often cited as an exception to the rule that low budget teams are unlikely to succeed in baseball, and it's true that they have enjoyed a surprising degree of success in the regular season. Perhaps inevitably, however, they have not enjoyed much success in the postseason.

revised　Teams with very low payrolls are likely to struggle in the regular season, and to struggle even more if they reach the playoffs and face teams who can afford the best-paid stars. If the Oakland As's low payroll makes their regular season success seem surprising, it also makes their postseason failures seem inevitable.

worth checking　What Marianne and her mother conjectured one moment as perhaps being possible, the next moment they believed to be probable. Anything they wished might happen they soon found themselves hoping for, and soon after that the hope would become an expectation.

revised　What Marianne and her mother conjectured one moment, they believed the next; with them, to wish was to hope, and to hope was to expect.

　　　(Jane Austen, *Sense and Sensibility*)

worth checking Our nation is made up of people of all sorts of religious beliefs. Many Americans are Christians but we also have Jews, Muslims, and Hindus among us, and there are also many American nonbelievers. America has also been shaped by many languages and cultures, from all over the world.

revised We are a nation of Christians and Muslims, Jews and Hindus, and nonbelievers. We are shaped by every language and culture, drawn from every end of this earth.

(Barack Obama, First Inaugural Address)

In most cases, revising to strengthen parallel structures in your writing will have the happy byproduct of making it more concise. But that's not always the case; the second sentence from the Obama passage quoted above is longer than it need be, but a pleasing instance of parallelism nonetheless.

Even careful balancing cannot make a steady diet of long sentences palatable; a rich source of rhythm in any well written essay is the short sentence. When revising their work, careful writers look to balance long sentences and short ones—and to notice such things as a preponderance of "there is ..." and "it is ..." sentences.

needs checking It is important to consider the cultural as well as the economic effects of globalization. In the past few years there have been many people who have argued that these would be even more significant, and would inevitably cause the disappearance of many nations as distinct cultural entities.

revised Globalization has cultural as well as economic effects. In the past few years many have argued that these are even more significant, and that they will eventually cause the disappearance of many nations as distinct cultural entities.

Additional Material Online
Exercises on balance and parallelism may be found at
sites.broadviewpress.com/writingcdn.
Click on **Exercises** and go to **P3, "Style."**

CONTEXTS OF WRITING

5. ACADEMIC WRITING: ESSAYS AND ARGUMENTS

5a. From Topic to Thesis Statement

Each writer requires a purpose, one that is more than the mere desire to earn this month's salary or this term's B+ in history.

The stated assignment is an obvious place to begin. "Discuss the rise to power of Francisco Franco." Or "Thoroughly explain the advances in medical imaging since the beginning of this century." Or "Analyze the connections between Maya Angelou's poetry and her memoirs." Very few writers are absolutely free to devise their own purposes.

But it's important for all writers to become engaged with the topic they are writing about. What if (returning to Francisco Franco) a prospective writer is bothered by the whole notion of "power" in the world of Spanish politics and warfare? Ignoring that abstract and difficult word might very well short-circuit her ability to handle the assignment—whereas grappling with its definition might provide sufficient purpose to set her writing in gear. Rather than half-heartedly narrate a string of events from the 1930s or merely list the political parties of that era, she would be motivated to write by the tension and ambiguity surrounding a single word in the assignment. Focusing on the nature of power might lead the writer to a tentative statement of her main assertion or thesis:

- Like most fascists, Franco saw power as an end in itself, not merely as a means to achieving other ends.

Unlike the topic, the **thesis statement** expresses an argumentative purpose and a point of view. It should be meaningful, clear, and concise—typically, according to most authorities, no more than a sentence or two. You'll likely want to put it in the first paragraph of a short essay; for long essays or when complex arguments are being made, it may be helpful to postpone the thesis statement for several paragraphs, and/or to extend it over a full paragraph, setting out a series of claims.

Thesis Statements: Some Examples

needs checking   *In this paper I will examine various reasons for launching the war in Kosovo in 1999.* [This is a statement of topic rather than a thesis.]

revised   *The moral case for Canada and its allies to wage a bombing-only war against Yugoslavia in 1999 was stronger than the strategic one; air attacks alone had never before been enough to win a war.* [This is the same topic, but now a position has been taken.]

needs checking   *Art is important to society in many ways, and I will talk about them in this essay. One of the artists I will focus on is Robert Mapplethorpe.* [This is too general and too vague to have significance.]

revised   *The controversial art of Robert Mapplethorpe deserves to be exhibited—and at public expense—even if most people find it abhorrent.* [This is more limited, more precise, more interesting.]

needs checking   *The purpose of this essay is to explore the interplay between poetry and prose. I will demonstrate that good poets don't usually write good prose and vice versa.* [This might be the subject for a book, not an essay. Also, the generalization would be hard to defend: "What about Thomas Hardy or Boris Pasternak?" the professor will ask.]

revised   *Though Maya Angelou's memoirs are more acclaimed, her best work is her poetry; it has an elliptical quality that allows for more active readerly engagement.* [A narrower but still controversial thesis on a similar topic.]

A thesis statement need not declare anything earth-shattering, but it should not be trivial or self-evident. Effective thesis statements are molded to fit both the length of the essay and the expertise of its writer. There is no logical sense in asserting, at the outset of a 3,000-word history paper, that *every military leader since Attila the Hun has repeated his mistakes.* The vocabulary of absolutes (*every, all, best, only,* etc.) commits a writer to universal coverage—and authoritative knowledge—of the topic. Strength in argumentative writing often comes from a willingness to qualify assertions and to acknowledge that contrary points of view are, if not convincing, at least intelligent and comprehensible. Words such as *often, usually,* and *largely,* and phrases such as *for the most part,* and *to a great extent* are not necessarily signs that the writer lacks the courage of her convictions; more frequently they are indications that she is careful and discerning.

5b. The Nature of Argument

When people use the noun *argument* in everyday speech, of course, they tend to use it in this sense: *a heated exchange of opposing views*—a type of argument that tends to be angry and loud and not very well reasoned. To speak of the argument of an essay, however, or of an argument presented in a debate, is to use the noun *argument* in a different sense: *a reason or set of reasons presented in order to persuade others.*

Here is the beginning of an argument in the first sense:

> "I can't believe that some people still think marijuana should be illegal; how dumb is that?"
>
> "Said the stoner. You just want everyone to be as stupid as you are."
>
> "You're the stupid one if you think marijuana makes you stupid."
>
> "So go ahead, smoke your brains out. See if I care."

Neither person here is advancing arguments in the second sense of that word. They are making assertions, hurling insults, and ascribing motivations for the other person's views. But they are not providing reasons for what they believe—let alone putting a series of reasons together into a coherent whole.

For the argument in a persuasive essay, it is not enough simply to assert what you feel. An argument in this sense may be passionately advanced, or even scathing, but it is not angry; it aims to bring light, not heat. An argument explains; draws distinctions; considers possible exceptions to generalizations; provides evidence; asks questions, suggests answers—and responds to objections. An argument is alert for ambiguities and contradictions. An argument tries to consider a range of different possibilities—often including hypothetical possibilities that may help to clarify the ideas involved. But an argument in this sense is never open-ended: it must always lead to a conclusion.

How does one construct this sort of argument in writing? There are many ways in which that question can be answered; a little further on we will discuss at some length various modes of thought that may be involved in constructing arguments (*cause and effect, classification, generalization,* and so on). But in another sense there is a two-word answer to the question *How does one construct an argument?*—with paragraphs.

5c. Argument Structure and Paragraphing

On what basis is writing divided into paragraphs? We should be careful to note that different principles apply to narrative, descriptive, and persuasive writing (see 2a, above). But most essay writing for undergraduates is persuasive writing—writing that aims to present an argument. As it happens, it's with persuasive writing that the structuring of paragraphs is both most difficult and most important. The paragraph is the structural unit of argument in an essay of this sort. And in such essays paragraphs come in three basic types: body paragraphs, which comprise the bulk of the essay; introductory paragraphs; and concluding paragraphs. In order to keep things clear both in the mind of the writer (as the essay is being composed) and in the mind of the reader (as the essay is being read), each of the paper's significant points should have its own body paragraph. But how many significant points should an essay include? In practice, that depends less on the subject of the essay than on the length of the essay. Let's say you have been asked to write a paper of 1,000 to 1,500 words arguing either for or against the legalization of marijuana. That's a topic on which it's possible to make a concise case in a sentence or two, and just as possible to make an in-depth case in a 500-page book. How many significant points should you try to make in an essay of 1,000 to 1,500 words? The short answer in most cases is four or five body paragraphs, plus introductory and concluding paragraphs. How long should a paragraph be? Extremely short or extremely long paragraphs should generally be avoided in academic essay writing. It's all too easy for writers to lose their focus in writing an extremely long paragraph—and for readers to lose their focus as they try to wade through it. At the other extreme, the one-sentence paragraph is rarely appropriate to academic writing. It is a punchy form that may have the force of an exclamation mark in certain styles of journalistic writing; like the exclamation mark itself, though, it very rarely serves to further the flow of an argument in academic writing.

The *average* length of a paragraph, then, tends to be in the range of 150 to 250 words. Some significant points can be made in a couple of sentences, and some may require a full page or more to elaborate properly, but in most cases 150–250 words will be an appropriate amount of space to devote to introducing and explaining a significant point.

Let's take the marijuana topic as an example. Say you decide to argue in favour of legalization. Here's what a simple outline for your 1,000–1,500-word essay might look like, with topic sentences for each paragraph:

> First paragraph (introduction): Sketch the contemporary context and provide this thesis statement: *In both financial and social terms, the costs to society of enforcing laws against marijuana use far outweigh the benefits.*

> Second paragraph: Laws prohibiting marijuana use encourage more serious crime; organized crime is often financed through the illegal sale of marijuana.

Third paragraph: Enforcing marijuana laws incurs huge unnecessary costs on police resources, the courts, and the correction system.

Fourth paragraph: On the other hand, legalizing marijuana and taxing it provides a public revenue source: Canada's experience.

Fifth paragraph: The harm caused by smoking marijuana is far, far less than that caused by other legal substances— notably alcohol.

Sixth paragraph: The claim that legalizing marijuana leads to greater hard drug use commits the slippery slope fallacy.

Seventh paragraph (conclusion): Summarize and reiterate thesis.

As everyone knows, there is more than one side to every argument. Let's say you'd prefer to argue against legalization. Then your plan might look like this:

First paragraph (introduction): Sketch the contemporary context and provide this thesis statement: *The risks to society of legalizing marijuana far outweigh the benefits.*

Second paragraph: It is often argued that marijuana isn't *very* harmful, but no one suggests that marijuana is not to some degree a harmful drug.

Third paragraph: Smoking marijuana causes harm to the lungs in addition to chemical changes in the brain; eating it creates a severe danger of overdose.

Fourth paragraph: When legalized, this harmful drug becomes more widely used: cite Canada's experience.

Fifth paragraph: There is abundant evidence that many users of marijuana move on to other, more dangerous, "hard" drugs.

Sixth paragraph: Some argue that marijuana is less danger- ous than alcohol, legal since the 1920s. But when we see the harm done by alcohol, shouldn't that make us more reluctant to make another dangerous drug legally available?

Seventh paragraph (conclusion): Summarize and reiterate thesis.

Notice, first, that although these two essays argue two directly opposing viewpoints, they don't deal with exactly the same topics. The first outline emphasizes financial costs and benefits; the second outline focuses on the dangers and harms associated with the drug; each essay uses arguments that best support its thesis. Notice, also, that some topics described in the outline are more closely related than others; different decisions could be made about how to combine and arrange them. Finally, these examples are not meant to suggest that every argument boils down to two opposing views; two people might agree that marijuana should remain legalized, for example, but disagree as to how sales should be regulated, as to the degree to which the government should itself participate in the market, etc.

i) Organizing paragraphs in longer essays

The paragraph structure of longer essays tends to be more complex than in the two examples provided above. It is often helpful to think of such structures in terms of paragraph clusters as well as individual paragraphs and to formulate an outline that includes groups of subordinate paragraphs. It's important to be aware, though, that any paragraph outline you develop during the planning and writing process should be regarded as subject to change as you move forward. Such a document is an important step in the process—but even at later stages you may well find that you need to make structural adjustments. You may decide that a paragraph is really expressing two important ideas instead of one, and should be split in two. You may decide that a couple of paragraphs represent an unnecessary digression, and should simply be cut. Or you may decide that one or more paragraphs would be more effective if they were moved to a different position in the essay. Like so many other things, it's virtually impossible to get all this right in your first draft; paragraphing should be something you pay almost as much attention to in the revision process as you do during the planning process.

As a sample, we include here the outline for a long essay by Robin Lee, "Monumental Problems" (included in full on the companion website to this book, and excerpted as an example of MLA Style on pages 265–75 below). As you'll see, Lee's outline is considerably more elaborate than the paragraph outlines for shorter essays that we looked at above.

Paragraph-by-Paragraph Essay Outline

Introduction

1. Introduction to the topic; thesis statement (thesis: historical and political and ethical all important BUT so too is the aesthetic side)

Arguments Concerning Historical Monuments: The Background

Misconceptions

2. clearing away misconceptions (i) replacing monuments not a practice invented recently
3. clearing away misconceptions (ii): idea of replacing monuments not peculiar to the political left
4. clearing away misconceptions (iii): removing monuments poses no threat to freedom of speech
5. clearing away misconceptions (iv): purpose of monuments is to honour those represented (not to preserve the historical record)
6. clearing away misconceptions (v): removing monuments is *not* "erasing history"

Our values today

7. arguments about monuments are arguments about our values *today*—examples of John A. Macdonald and of Robert E. Lee/Jefferson Davis
8. another aspect of arguments over our values today: ideas about capitalism
9. the historical side: seeing historical figures in the light of the standards of their own time; history's nuances
10. issues of social psychology relevant to the issues: examples from Atlantic Canada and from New Orleans

11. [transition paragraph] Confederate statues in New Orleans

Options

12. options for dealing with controversial monuments (i): leave monuments where they are and level the playing field by erecting new monuments beside them to present other sides of the story

13. options for dealing with controversial monuments (ii): continue to display all controversial monuments, but in a museum context where they can be contextualized. The problem of cost

The Aesthetic Side of Monuments Controversies

14. statues and monuments: introduce topic of the aesthetic side

The Roosevelt monument

15. the Roosevelt monument (i): introduce example of Theodore Roosevelt monument

16. the Roosevelt monument (ii): background—the Roosevelt monument

17. the Roosevelt monument (iii): changing the status of the object (Roosevelt monument becomes statue)

18. the Roosevelt monument (iv): discussion of the aesthetic qualities of the statue

The Lee and Jackson Monument

19. the Baltimore Robert E. Lee and Stonewall Jackson monument (i): background

20. the Baltimore Robert E. Lee and Stonewall Jackson monument (ii): discussion of the aesthetic qualities of the statue

21. the Baltimore Robert E. Lee and Stonewall Jackson monument (iii): short paragraph wrapping up discussion of the Baltimore statue

22. the aesthetic qualities of other, less attractive monuments: a John A. Macdonald statue and two other examples.

Conclusion

23. summary of arguments, including the issue of cost of preservation—cost issue underlines the importance of taking the aesthetic into consideration

24. return to thesis: we need not commit to preservation of all monuments forever. In making choices, we should take the aesthetic as well as the ethical and the political into account

For more on using paragraphs to structure arguments, we recommend Ian Johnston's *Essays and Arguments: A Handbook on Writing* (revised edition 2015); it's a text that has a proven track record of improving students' skills in formulating written arguments.

> **Additional Material Online**
> Exercises on paragraphing may be found at
> **sites.broadviewpress.com/writingcdn**.
> Click on **Exercises** and go to
> **P2.5, "Making Sense: Organization."**

5d. Your Arguments, Others' Arguments

Another way to look at the organization of arguments is in terms of one's own ideas and those of others. When the concepts of plagiarism and of "original work" are discussed, it is rightly emphasized that any essay (or article, or web posting, or full-length book) should present one's own ideas, not simply regurgitate the ideas of others. But does that mean one's own work has to be written without reference to that of others? No—far from it. Nor does "original" in the context of academic writing mean that an essay or academic book has to present ideas no one has thought of before. It simply means that the ideas put forward should be thought through and synthesized by you as an individual—that you should not simply borrow someone else's thinking.

That process of thinking-through, synthesizing, and developing an argument cannot and should not be done in a vacuum. An essay in which you try to think through a topic entirely on your own, without reference to the arguments others have made, tends to be far less interesting than an essay that draws on others' arguments for support, and also that engages directly with opposing arguments. The importance of engaging in this way with the arguments of others is the central point of one of the past generation's most influential books about the nature of academic argument, Gerald Graff and Cathy Birkenstein's *They Say / I Say*. As they point out,

> the underlying structure of effective academic writing—and of responsible public discourse—resides not just in stating your own ideas, but in listening closely to others around us, summarizing their views in a way they will recognize, and responding with our own ideas in kind.... [T]o argue well you need to do more than assert your own ideas. You need to enter a conversation, using what others say (or might say) as a launching pad or sounding board for your own ideas. (3)

Engaging with the arguments of others is important as a means of helping your reader to locate what you are saying in a broader context. But it is also important in helping you to formulate your own arguments for the reader. Obviously it can be helpful to draw on the arguments of others to support the views you are trying to convince your reader to adopt. By citing the arguments others have made—and, where appropriate, by summarizing or quoting from those arguments in support of your own—you can often make the points in your argument more persuasive.

Even more important is to come to grips with what those who oppose the arguments you wish to make have said. Crafting strong arguments often entails pointing out weaknesses in the arguments of those who argue opposing positions—but it also entails seeking out the strongest points that have been made against the position you have adopted. If you're arguing in favour of legalized marijuana, for example, it would not be a good strategy to focus largely on refuting the argument put forward in the 1936 propaganda film *Reefer Madness* (that consumption of marijuana is likely to lead to insanity and suicide). Instead, you should look to refute the most credible arguments against legalization that have been put forward in our own time—the arguments advanced by the American Medical Association, for example—and focus on refuting those.

What if you aren't able to find strong arguments that challenge the points you wish to make? That may be a sign of several things. First of all, you should ask yourself if you have chosen a sufficiently interesting and challenging topic. If you are thinking of writing an essay arguing that men and women should receive equal pay for equal work, or that racism is bad, you're not likely to find strong and interesting opposing views to come to grips with.

But what if you are thinking of writing an essay arguing a particular position about a newly published short story, or about a very recent political development, or about a philosophical position that has recently been advanced for the first time? You may not be able to find strong and interesting opposing views to come to grips with in those sorts of cases either—but that doesn't mean you've chosen a poor topic. So what should you do—just state your own views and not worry about opposing arguments? Here's a better way: invent as strong a set of opposing arguments as you can. You should try to anticipate the strongest possible argument you can imagine might be made by someone taking an opposing position. If you can persuasively counter any such arguments, you will have surmounted an important test—and written a first-rate essay.

In this connection it is worth drawing attention to the phrase in parentheses in the passage from Graff and Birkenstein quoted above: "You need to enter a conversation, using what others say (or might say) as a launching pad or sounding board for your own ideas." There are many ways in which writers introduce what others might say into their arguments. Sometimes these will merely be straw person arguments, but in many cases they represent a genuine effort on the part of the writer to imagine and to counter the strongest possible case that might be made against one's own position. Here are some ways in which ideas of this sort can be introduced:

An opponent might argue that.... But that would be to....

On the other side, it could be suggested that.... But in that case....

> We may well imagine the counter argument to this—
> that.... But this counter argument does not hold up to
> close scrutiny....

The discussions of integrating quotations and using signal phrases (pages 220–21, 287–88) may also be helpful in this connection.

5e. Online, On the Screen, On the Page

Proofreading may check some of the bad cognitive habits that computers breed in many writers who work only on screen; it certainly will not eliminate them all. For some of us, computers can be wonderful facilitators of flow; many people find it easier to get a lot of ideas out of their heads and "on paper" by using a computer than by using a pen and paper. But the same habits of scrolling that can facilitate flow in writing and in reading can distort our ability to arrange ideas in an ordered fashion so as to best present an argument. Though researchers are far from understanding why, they have now assembled a considerable body of evidence suggesting that seeing a succession of printed pages enables one to combine and connect ideas in ways that are not always evident if one restricts oneself to scrolling on the screen. This is why it is helpful for most writers to work with paper as well as on screen. Once you have a complete draft of a piece of writing, we recommend that you print it out and review the hard copy both with an eye for the big picture (Are the ideas presented in the best order? Should an extra paragraph be added anywhere to explain your ideas further?), and with an eye to the details (individual words and phrases, punctuation, typos). It's usually a good idea to treat these operations separately—to deal with matters of organization first, and not to worry about typos or small infelicities of style until the second or third draft.

We offer here several other pieces of advice—recognizing as we do so that a piece of advice which may be quite helpful to some students may seem so obvious to some others as to make them wonder why we would have devoted space to something any fool should know already.

- **Don't be all thumbs.** Many people nowadays do more typing with their thumbs on their smartphones than they do using all their fingers on a full-sized keyboard, and with voice recognition software becoming better and better all the time, it may seem as though touch typing is a skill that will soon be of little use. It is a skill that many high schools no longer teach; is it worth your while to learn it? For the foreseeable future, the answer is certainly yes. For academic writing, touch typing remains an invaluable skill. It can substantially reduce the time you spend compiling notes as you do your research, and it can significantly reduce the time you spend writing.

- **Try turning off your screen.** Many writers have an almost irresistible urge to start editing and revising their work even as they are in the preliminary stages of drafting and working out their ideas. For most of us, trying to edit at this stage doesn't make our writing any better; it simply causes us to lose our train of thought. If you are one of those who sometimes experiences this problem (and if you know how to touch-type!), we recommend that you try turning off your screen as you are generating your ideas—free writing or trying to shape a first draft.

- **Some things are best disabled.** Modern word processing software almost always has a number of built-in features that can turn out to be frustrating time wasters in many writing situations. If, for example, you are creating a numbered list of items, you may well find that the software you are using wants to format your list quite differently from the way you would prefer. If you are copying lines of poetry that all begin with words written in lower case, you are likely to find that your software will automatically insert capital letters. If you learn how to disable the automatic formatting functions in your software, it will save you a great deal of time in your writing career.

- **The art of saving.** Even if you have a reliable automatic saving mechanism that should provide you with a backup of anything you are writing, it is still a good idea to save frequently. But it's important as well to save in ways that will keep to an absolute minimum the chance of confusion arising later. If you are about to cut any significant amount of text from what you are working on, it's a good idea to save first and then save again under a new name, creating a new version. It's a good idea, though, not to leave windows open with more than one version at a time; it's all too easy to take a break and then return and start adding material to what you think is the latest version, discovering only later that you have muddled two versions. Saving different versions in a clear and consecutive fashion by using a simple numbering system, for instance, can help prevent confusion—as can the careful use of folders and subfolders.

- **Searching low and high.** Every program has its own search function, and every computer is also set up with a global search function. If you have misplaced a file, the search function within your word processing program or on your hard drive can be used to help track it down. Learn how to use these search functions, and you should be able to find almost anything you have lost or misplaced, using threads of words that you remember you have used in a document, even if you cannot remember the document's name.

- **Finding and replacing.** The *find* and the *replace* functions in your word processing software are tremendously valuable. The find function should allow you to go to exactly what you are looking for within seconds, so long as you can remember a relevant word, and the *find and replace* function can save you a great deal of time in the revision process. It's usually a good idea, though, to resist any urge you may have to instantly replace a particular word or phrase with what you have decided is a better version; if you take just a little more time to let the computer guide you to each instance where the word or phrase occurs and give your okay to the change in each case, that can save you a good deal of embarrassment.

- **Use track changes.** Some students imagine that the track changes function is used primarily when one is working collaboratively. In fact, it's tremendously useful when you are working independently as well, allowing you to keep a full record of what you have done in previous versions as part of a single document. It's sometimes assumed that the track changes function will always create a cluttered screen if it is activated. In fact, any good software program nowadays allows you to hide the tracked changes even when the function is activated.

- **Cutting and pasting from the Internet.** It can be a real time saver if, for example, you are quoting a long passage from a text that's available online to simply cut and paste rather than retyping. When you do that, though, be sure to "paste special" using "unformatted text," so you do not carry HTML formatting into your paper. Next, check the text you have imported carefully; look, for example, for any vertically straight quotation marks and change them to curved quotation marks, and be sure to put the material you have imported into the same font that you are using for the rest of your essay. (Watch out as well for accidental plagiarism if you are cutting and pasting; all direct quotations must be attributed!)

For more advice on writing in a digital context, we recommend you consult the discussion of email in the "Writing in the Workplace" section of this book.

6. STYLES AND DISCIPLINES

6a. The Language of Academic Writing

Academic writing often depends upon the use of academic jargon; much as the term *jargon* is often used pejoratively, its core meaning is *specialized language used by a particular group* (*whether academic or professional*). Such language may sometimes be used in ways that are overblown or unnecessarily wordy. But it is important to remember that, properly used, academic or professional jargon is a means of communicating more economically than would be possible with less specialized language. Here is an example, drawn from the academic discipline of philosophy:

> When it comes to particular cases, is it possible for a consequentialist to respond in any coherent fashion to deontological arguments? Or for the deontologist to respond in any coherent fashion to consequentialist arguments? Inevitably, the two will talk past each other.

When it comes to particular cases, is it possible for someone who believes that whether an action is right or wrong depends largely on the consequences it produces to respond in any coherent fashion to the arguments of someone who believes that the rightness or wrongness of actions must be based on those actions possessing inherent qualities according to which each action is required, permitted, or forbidden? Or for the latter to respond in any coherent fashion to the arguments of the former? Inevitably, the two will talk past each other.

The first of these, in which the specialized jargon of academic philosophy is used, is obviously far more economical. To be sure, *consequentialist* and *deontologist* are terms to be avoided if you are writing for an audience with no philosophical background. But if you are writing for an audience of philosophers or philosophy students, such terms are essential tools of the trade.

In everyday usage, of course, *jargon* is often used as a synonym for ***unnecessarily*** *technical or difficult language*. Language of that sort is indeed to be avoided:

needs checking   In order to ensure that the new delivery structure for regional renal care will be optimally functional, there must be accessibility for populations throughout the region to interdigitated modalities of care.

revised   If the new system of regional renal care is to work well, hospitals and clinics must be located in or near the main population centers.

needs checking   Our plan is more philosophical than operational in terms of framework.

revised   We are at the idea stage; our plan hasn't been tested yet.

The goal in academic writing, then, is to balance the requirements of the academic discipline with those of communication—to write in a varied and flexible style, using everyday words and expressions when appropriate, and using academic terms when those are the most effective and economical means of expression.

The tone of academic writing is typically one of careful argument. The aim is to persuade the reader through logic and through the marshalling of evidence (rather than, for example, through attempting to exhort or entertain the reader). It is thus always important when writing in an academic context to provide support for whatever claims you make, and to be careful in how you phrase those claims. Almost all academic writers rely heavily on words and on phrases such as *for the most part, mainly, tends to ...*, and so on, in order to ensure that the claims they are making allow for some exceptions. Conversely, they generally avoid words such as *always* and *never*, which would leave their arguments open to being refuted through a single exception. Most academic essays are formal pieces of writing, and should be approached as such. Readers expect a calm and disinterested tone, free of extreme emotion and of slang or conversational usage. That should not be taken to imply that thinking rigorously about a topic precludes feeling strongly about it—or conveying to the reader how the writer feels. But academic writing should foreground the topic, not the personality of the writer; it's for that reason that many instructors advise their students to avoid using first-person pronouns. Such advice may indeed be appropriate in many academic contexts. But even more than most stylistic guidelines, this one should not be regarded as written in stone. The pronouns *I* and *me* appear frequently in many scholarly essays—as they do in acclaimed literary essays by writers such as George Orwell, Susan Sontag, and Rebecca Solnit. The degree to which it is considered appropriate in formal writing to employ the first-person remains a contentious topic, and one on which usage conventions in different disciplines differ considerably. (See below, 6Cii and 6Ciii.)

6b. Writing about Literature / Writing about Texts

One sort of convention in academic writing that can take some getting used to is the way in which verb tenses are used. Many students find writing about literature particularly challenging in this respect; its conventions present fundamental problems for the student at the level of sentence structure.

The past tense is, of course, normally used to name actions which happened in the past. But when one is writing about what happens in a work of literature (or, in some cases, about what is said in other sorts of texts), convention decrees that we use the simple present tense.

needs checking　Romeo fell in love with Juliet as soon as he saw her.
revised　Romeo falls in love with Juliet as soon as he sees her.

needs checking　In her short stories, Alice Munro explored both the outer and the inner worlds of small town life.
revised　In her short stories, Alice Munro explores both the outer and the inner worlds of small town life.

Additional Material Online
For more on the conventions of writing in different academic disciplines, go to
sites.broadviewpress.com/writingcdn.

If literature in its historical context is being discussed, however, the simple past tense is usually the best choice:

needs checking　Shakespeare writes *Romeo and Juliet* when he was about thirty years of age.
revised　Shakespeare wrote *Romeo and Juliet* when he was about thirty years of age.

needs checking　Alice Munro wins the 2013 Nobel Prize in Literature for her mastery of the contemporary short story.

revised   Alice Munro won the 2013 Nobel Prize in Literature for her mastery of the contemporary short story.

In some circumstances either the past or the present tense may be possible in a sentence, depending on the context:

correct   In her early work Munro often explored themes relating to adolescence.

[appropriate if the focus is on historical developments relating to the author]

also correct   In her early work Munro often explores themes relating to adolescence.

[appropriate if the focus is on the work itself]

Often in an essay about literature the context may require shifting back and forth between past and present tenses. In the following passage, for example, the present tense is used except for the sentence that recounts the historical fact of Eliot refusing permission:

T.S. Eliot's most notorious expression of antisemitism is the opinion he expresses in *After Strange Gods* that in "the society that we desire," "any large number of free-thinking Jews" would be "undesirable" (64). Tellingly, Eliot never allowed *After Strange Gods* to be reprinted. But his antisemitism emerges repeatedly in his poetry as well. In "Gerontion," for example, he describes ...

In such cases even experienced writers have to think carefully during the revision process about the most appropriate tense for each verb. Note in the following example the change in verb tense from *was* to *is*.

needs checking   In *The Two Gentleman of Verona* Shakespeare exhibited a degree of technical accomplishment unprecedented in the English drama. He still had much to learn as a dramatist and as a poet; in its wit or its power to move us emotionally *The Two Gentlemen of Verona* was at an enormous remove from the great works of a few years later. But already, in 1592, Shakespeare had mastered all the basic techniques of plot construction that were to sustain the structures of the great plays.

revised   In *The Two Gentleman of Verona* Shakespeare exhibits a degree of technical accomplishment unprecedented in the English drama. He still had much to learn as a dramatist and as a poet; in its wit or its power to move us emotionally *The Two Gentlemen of Verona* is at an enormous remove from the great works of a few years later. But already, in 1592, Shakespeare had mastered all the basic techniques of plot construction that were to sustain the structures of the great plays.

The same principles that are used in writing about literature often apply in certain other disciplines when you are writing about texts. In many other disciplines the present tense is the tense most commonly used in such circumstances, if you are treating the ideas you are discussing as "live" ideas:

needs checking   In an important recent book, Nelly Ferguson surveyed the history of the decline of empires, and predicted that during the course of the twenty-first century China will replace the United States as the world's leading power.

revised   In an important recent book, Nelly Ferguson surveys the history of the decline of empires, and predicts that during the course of the twenty-first century China will replace the United States as the world's leading power.

needs checking   In their 2017 paper Smith and Johnson suggested that parental influence is more important than that of peers, even for adolescents. This essay will examine these claims and assess their validity.

revised   In their 2017 paper Smith and Johnson suggest that parental influence is more important than that of peers, even for adolescents. This essay will examine these claims and assess their validity.

It is important to remember that the use of the present tense in academic writing is not dependent on how recently the ideas being discussed were first put forward; the key thing is whether or not you are discussing them as live ideas today. You may use the present tense when discussing a paper written six months ago—but you may also use the present tense when discussing a text dating from twenty-four centuries ago. Just as you may say when writing about literature that Shakespeare *explores* the potentially corrosive effects of ambition, so too you may say that Aristotle *approaches* ethical questions with a view as much to the virtue of the doer as to the rightness of the deed, and that Marx *values* highly the economic contribution of labour—even though Shakespeare and Aristotle and Marx are themselves long dead. As with the text of a story or poem, the writings of dead thinkers may be discussed as embodying live thoughts—ideas that may retain interest and relevance.

Conversely, if the ideas you are discussing are being considered historically rather than as of current relevance, you should not use the present tense.

needs checking   The renowned astronomer Fred Hoyle advances arguments against the big bang theory of the origin of the universe. Hoyle suggests that the universe perpetually regenerates itself.

[Hoyle's arguments have now been refuted.]

revised   The renowned astronomer Fred Hoyle advanced arguments against the big bang theory of the origin of the universe. Hoyle suggested that the universe perpetually regenerates itself.

As is the case with writing about literature, academic writing in disciplines such as history or philosophy or political science may often look at a text both from a historical perspective and from the perspective of the live ideas that are put forward within it. In such circumstances the writer needs to be prepared to shift verb tenses depending on the context:

needs checking   In *An Introduction to the Principles of Morals and Legislation*, Jeremy Bentham asked what question should be foremost in people's minds as they considered how to treat non-human animals: "The question is not, Can they reason?, nor Can they talk? but, Can they suffer? Why should the law refuse its protection to any sensitive being?" As Bentham saw it, then, sentience—and specifically, a capacity for suffering—was crucial to whether a non-human animal should be granted moral standing.

revised In *An Introduction to the Principles of Morals and Legislation*, Jeremy Bentham asks what question should be foremost in our minds as we consider how to treat non-human animals: "The question is not, Can they reason?, nor Can they talk? but, Can they suffer? Why should the law refuse its protection to any sensitive being?" As Bentham sees it, then, sentience—and specifically, a capacity for suffering—is crucial to whether or not a non-human animal should be granted moral standing.

consistency in verb tense when integrating quotations: If one is writing about literature the writing will usually be in the present tense, but the quotations one wishes to use are likely to be in the past tense. Often it is thus necessary, if you are incorporating a quotation into a sentence, to rephrase and/or adjust the length of the quotation in order to preserve grammatical consistency. If a quotation is set apart from the body of your own writing, on the other hand, you do not need to (and should not) rephrase.

needs checking Emma Bovary lives largely through memory and fantasy. She daydreams frequently, and, as she reads, "the memory of the Vicomte kept her happy" (244).

[The past tense *kept* is inconsistent with the present tense *reads* and *daydreams*.]

revised Emma Bovary lives largely through memory and fantasy. She daydreams frequently, and, as she reads, the "memory of the Vicomte" (244) keeps her happy.

or   Emma Bovary lives largely through memory and fantasy. She daydreams frequently, and blends fact and fiction in her imaginings: "Always, as she read, the memory of the Vicomte kept her happy. She established a connection between him and the characters of her favorite fiction" (244).

For more on integrating quotations, see *Citation and Documentation*, below, pages 219–20.

6c. Writing about Science

The many academic forms of writing about science include the review article (in which a writer surveys and assesses evidence on a particular topic from various sources); the research or experimental report, usually in the form of an article (in which a researcher writes up the results of an experiment of specific scope—lab reports are good practice for articles of this kind); the conference presentation or a poster board (in which scientists report in a limited or abbreviated fashion about specific research); the abstract (in which scientists provide a brief summary of the findings of a report or research paper); and the funding application, generally intended for a national or commercial grant or funding body (which usually includes an abstract and a statement of the importance of the research, along with a costing breakdown for the research).

i) Structure of the research paper

The research article is in many ways the paradigmatic type of scientific writing. Unlike articles in the humanities, research articles in the sciences are generally organized into specific sections that usually appear in a set order: Introduction, Methods, Results, and Discussion. The opening section of the article, the *Introduction*, tells the reader the purpose and nature of the study. How does it fit in with previous research? What has it been designed to show? What was the hypothesis? The norm is to keep the introduction fairly brief; normally, it explains a bit about the background to the paper and indicates why the research was undertaken. The paper's introduction may, in fact, include a background section or be called *Background*. While it is appropriate to position the paper in the larger context of previous research here, extended discussion of that larger picture is not normally included in the introduction.

The *Methods* section is often very detailed. An important principle is that the paper should provide enough information about how the research was set up and conducted that other researchers can replicate the results. The reader also needs enough information to be able to understand the rationale for each step in the process.

The *Methods* section in a scientific research paper is always written in the past tense. When you are conducting your own research, however, it can be helpful to set out the details of the process beforehand in the present and/or future tenses, and then read over your notes with a view to the larger picture. Is the research being set up in the most unbiased way possible? Can the proposed method truly be expected to provide evidence one way or the other as to whether the hypothesis is valid? Are the most useful statistical methods being used to assess the data?

The *Results* section, as its name suggests, details the results at length. It often includes tables, charts, and graphs as a way of visually presenting these results.[1] The *Discussion* section provides an analysis of the meaning of those results, both in terms of the particular experiment and in terms of past experiments in the same area. Do the results confirm or refute the original hypothesis? What questions are left unanswered? What significance does the data have in the context of other research in this area? In what ways is the research subject to drawbacks (e.g., small sample size, indeterminate findings, confounding elements, short timeframe)? Do the results prompt any recommendations for the future?

---

1   *Results* and *Discussion* are usually treated as separate sections of a paper; some journals, however, ask authors to combine them into one section of the paper.

Finally, scientific papers are almost always accompanied by an abstract, which comes before the actual paper. The *Abstract* summarizes the entire paper in no more than one or two paragraphs (usually 250 words or less); it is meant to convey the essence of the research to those who may not have time to read the entire paper, or who may be trying to determine if the entire paper will be of interest to them. Abstracts are often included in searchable databases for this latter purpose.

ii) Scientific tone and stylistic choices

Most contemporary natural sciences writers strive for objectivity of tone, while writers in the humanities and social sciences may foreground their own subject positions and sometimes adopt a less formal tone. Look, for example, at the way in which anthropologist Emily Martin opens her classic article on "The Egg and the Sperm":

> As an anthropologist, I am intrigued by the possibility that culture shapes how biological scientists describe what they discover about the natural world.... In the course of my research I realized that the picture of egg and sperm drawn in popular as well as scientific accounts of reproductive biology relies on stereotypes central to our cultural definitions of male and female. The stereotypes imply not only that female biological processes are less worthy than their male counterparts but also that women are less worthy than men. Part of my goal in writing this article is to shine a bright light on the gender stereotypes hidden within the scientific language of biology. Exposed in such a light, I hope they will lose their power to harm us.

Martin acknowledges at the outset that she occupies a specific position in relation to her research, and she uses the first person frequently ("I am intrigued," "I realized," "my goal"). Moreover, she acknowledges that her motive for conducting and publishing her research is not merely to expand objective knowledge about the world; she aims not only to shine a bright light on gender stereotypes, but also to reduce "their power to harm us." And yet, at its core, Martin's article is an example of careful scientific inquiry: she conducted a thorough survey of relevant scientific literature, her assessment of it follows scientific standards of objectivity, and she makes a strong argument based on clear and well-documented evidence.

Academics writing in natural science disciplines such as biology, chemistry, and physics, as well as those writing in the behavioral sciences (e.g., psychology, anthropology, sociology), all value scientific standards of objectivity and strive to make strong arguments based on strong evidence. However, differences in style and tone can be very noticeable, with the natural science disciplines tending towards a more formal and impersonal style than Martin adopts. But tone varies widely within the behavioural sciences as well; compare Martin's discussion of egg and sperm representations with the following behavioural science abstract for a 2012 scientific article by Ethan Kross and others that received a great deal of attention in general-interest media, "Facebook Use Predicts Declines in Subjective Well-Being in Young Adults":

> Over 500 million people interact daily with Facebook. Yet, whether Facebook use influences subjective well-being over time is unknown. We addressed this issue using experience-sampling, the most reliable method for measuring in-vivo behavior and psychological experience. We text-messaged people five times per day for two-weeks to examine how Facebook use influences the two components of subjective well-being: how people feel moment-to-moment and how satisfied they are with their lives. Our results indicate that Facebook use predicts negative shifts on both of these variables over time. The more people used Facebook at one time point, the worse they felt the next time we text-messaged them; the more they used Facebook over two-weeks, the more their life satisfaction levels declined over time. Interacting with other people "directly" did not predict these negative outcomes. They were also not moderated by the size of people's Facebook networks, their perceived supportiveness, motivation for using Facebook,

gender, loneliness, self-esteem, or depression. On the surface, Facebook provides an invaluable resource for fulfilling the basic human need for social connection. Rather than enhancing well-being, however, these findings suggest that Facebook may undermine it.

There are obvious differences in tone between this passage and that by Martin quoted above. Most obviously, the writers employ terminology specific to the academic discipline in which the authors are writing: "subjective well-being," "predicts," "moderated by," and "negative outcomes." More generally, the abstract is much more impersonal in tone than the first paragraph of Martin's paper; the reader is not told of any moment of realization which led to these researchers' work, or of what effects they hope their research will have. Instead, the passage provides a summary of the reasons for the study, the nature of the study, the main results, and some sense of their significance—all in reasonably direct and specific prose.

Notice the relative brevity of the sentences used as the abstract opens—the first is only eight words long. Long sentences are certainly sometimes appropriate (and indeed necessary)—but in scientific writing as in other sorts, varying sentence lengths is a good way to help maintain reader interest.

Expressing ideas concisely and varying sentence length are two ways of making your writing clear and readable. Using parallel or balanced sentence structures is another. Notice how the parallel grammatical structures in the following sentence (*the more ... the worse ...; the more ..., the more ...*) emphasize the study's findings: "The more people used Facebook at one time point, the worse they felt the next time we text-messaged them; the more they used Facebook over two weeks, the more their life satisfaction levels declined over time."

It is often imagined that complex and difficult-to-read sentence structures strike an appropriately academic tone—that direct sentences and rhetorical balance are for journalists or novelists, not students and scholars. If scientific research is important, however, then surely it's worthwhile to communicate that research in clear and readable prose.

iii) The first person and the active voice

Students writing in disciplines such as biology, physics, psychology, or engineering are often advised to avoid grammatical structures associated with what might seem a subjective approach—most notably, the first person (*I* or *we*). Such advice is often also given to students writing English or history papers, and the reason is much the same: instructors want to discourage students from thinking of the writing of an academic paper as an exercise in expressing one's likes or dislikes. Unsubstantiated opinions are not appreciated in any of the academic disciplines. But how well one has supported one's argument bears no necessary relation to whether or not one has used the first person. In the Emily Martin example quoted above, Martin uses the first person extensively, but she doesn't just express an opinion; her study is supported using a lot of evidence, and the discussion itself is objective in nature.

Similarly, the abstract of the paper about Facebook by Kross et al. does not achieve its more formal and impersonal tone by avoiding the first person. Quite the contrary: Kross et al. use the first person twice in the first three sentences of the abstract: "We addressed," "We text-messaged."[1] Scientific objectivity, then, is not a matter of avoiding the first person; it is rather a matter of avoiding bias when framing one's research questions, of designing research projects intelligently and fairly, and of interpreting the results ethically.

Discussions of impersonality and objectivity in scientific writing have also often been framed in terms of the question of whether to use the active or the passive voice. For most of the twentieth century, many instructors in the natural sciences tried to train students to use the passive voice[2]—to write things like "It *was decided* that the experiment *would be conducted* in three stages" and "These results *will be dis-*

---

1   In the case of group authorship, which is very common in the sciences, the plural must, of course, be used.

2   As Randy Moore and others have pointed out, nineteenth-century scientists used the active voice and the first person freely. The active voice and "first-person pronouns such as *I* and *we* began to disappear from scientific writing in the United States in the 1920s."

cussed *from several perspectives"* in order to convey a more impersonal and objective tone. In the late twentieth century, however, the scientific community began to swing around to the view that, much as the passive might sometimes have its place, the active voice should be the default writing choice. Here is Randy Moore, writing in *The American Biology Teacher* in 1991:

> The notion that passive voice ensures objectivity is ridiculous[; ...] objectivity has nothing to do with one's writing style or with personal pronouns. Objectivity in science results from the choice of subjects, facts that you choose to include or omit, sampling techniques, and how you state your conclusions. Scientific objectivity is a personal trait unrelated to writing.

The 1990s saw heated debates in the pages of certain scientific journals on the matter of whether the active or the passive should be the default. But in the end the decision was clear: the active voice was the best choice. Nearly every major scientific journal now recommends that its authors use the active voice in most situations—and that they use the first person where appropriate as well.

The various *Nature* journals, the American Chemical Society Style Guide, and the American Society of Civil Engineers Style Guide are representative. The following instructions are from their respective websites:

> *Nature* journals prefer authors to write in the active voice ("we performed the experiment ...") as experience has shown that readers find concepts and results to be conveyed more clearly if written directly.

> Use the active voice when it is less wordy and more direct than the passive.... Use first person when it helps to keep your meaning clear and to express a purpose or a decision.

> Wherever possible, use active verbs that demonstrate what is being done and who is doing it....

Instead of: Six possible causes of failure were identified in the forensic investigation.

Use: The forensic investigation identified six possible causes of failure.

Though the active voice is better as a default choice, the passive voice can be useful in many ways, including as a way of shifting attention away from the researcher to the experiment itself. The following statements, for example, all make effective use of the passive:

- The cooling process was completed in approximately two hours.

- This compound is made up of three elements.

- Phenomena of this sort may be seen only during an eclipse.

6d. Writing in the Workplace

Tone may be the most important aspect of business and professional writing. The adjective *businesslike* conjures up images of efficiency and professional distance, and certainly it is appropriate to convey those qualities in most business reports, memos, and correspondence. In a great deal of business and professional writing, however, it is also desirable to convey a warm, personal tone; striking the right balance between the personal and the professional is at the heart of the art of business writing. Here are some guidelines.

- Consult your colleagues. Circulate a draft of any important document to others and ask their opinion. Is the tone too cold and formal? Is it too gushy and enthusiastic? Is it too direct? Or not direct enough?

- Be careful about suggesting you are speaking for your entire organization. Unless you are sure, you are well advised to qualify any extreme statements.

needs checking Our organization underprices every competitor.
revised Our prices are typically lower than those of major competitors.

needs checking	There is no way we would ever cut back on research and development.
revised	As an organization we have a strong commitment to research and development.

Given that most business and professional communication operates within a hierarchical power structure, it is particularly important to foreground consideration in memos, letters, and emails. Avoid direct commands wherever possible; give credit to others when things go right; and take responsibility and apologize when things go wrong.

needs checking	Here is the material we spoke of. Send the report in by the end of the month to my attention.
revised	I enclose the material we spoke of. If you could send in the report by the end of the month to my attention, I'd be very grateful.

needs checking	I am writing in response to your complaint. We carry a large number of products with similar titles, and sometimes errors in shipping occur. Please in future specify the ISBN of the item you are ordering, as that will help keep errors to a minimum.
revised	Thank you for your letter—and my sincere apologies on behalf of our company for our mistake. As you may know, we carry a large number of products with similar titles, and (particularly in cases where our customer service department is not able to double check against an ISBN) errors do sometimes occur. But that is an explanation rather than an excuse; I do apologize, and I have asked that the correct item be shipped to you immediately. Thank you for drawing this matter to my attention.

Email

Email has for many years now been the dominant form of communication in the workplace. While there is general agreement that email is a relatively informal medium of communication, there is little consensus as to *how* informal it should be. In the workplace, it is always better to err on the side of being more rather than less formal in your emails whenever you are uncertain. As a general principle to follow, we would suggest that you always try to put yourself in the shoes of whoever will be receiving your email. That's a very different thing from acting according to the maxim *do unto others as you would have them do unto you.* You may well prefer to receive messages with only "Hey!" as a salutation (or with no salutation at all), but you will be well advised not to presume that others in the workplace feel the same. Try to think not only of the position but also of the temperament of the person you are emailing. If it's someone high up in the organization who you know to be always very busy and very formal in style, write your message accordingly. If it's an email to a young colleague who you know prefers that things be kept informal, then you can bring down the level of formality a bit. Even in this latter context, though, you should write in a style appropriate to your organization—a style that would not seem in any way embarrassing to you if your supervisor were to read what you had written.

These principles apply equally within your own workplace and when you are writing to people outside of your organization.

needs checking Hey, Barbara Lewis. My name is Harry Phelps and I am writing from Broadview Press. I'd really like to tell you about some new books that I'm hoping you'll choose as textbooks for your courses.

revised Dear Professor Smith

I gather you are scheduled to teach the Philosophy 200 "Knowledge and Reality" course next term. It's in that connection that I'm writing now; we at Broadview have just published a new anthology in this area that I thought might be of interest.

proofreading: It's too often assumed that, as an informal means of communication, emails don't require proofreading. That may well be the case if you are dashing off a message of no more than a few words to a trusted colleague who is also a close friend. For anything beyond that, however, it's very important to read over your messages carefully before you send them—not only in order to catch and correct typos, but also to be sure that you are saying what you want to say clearly (and that you have not made any mistakes that might be embarrassing!).

salutations: Opinions differ widely as to whether or not one should always include a salutation in an email. As a general rule, you should—though with internal workplace communications you may omit the salutation if you are confident your recipient is comfortable with that level of informality.

In writing someone outside your organization (or someone high up in your organization's hierarchy who you do not know well), it's advisable to use the same sort of formal salutation you would in a formal letter: Dear Ms. Jenkins; Dear Professor Ahmed; etc. In responding to an email you have received, it's good practice to follow the style of salutation that the writer has followed. If she has written *Hello Christine* and signed off as *Julia*, it is appropriate to respond *Hello Julia* and sign your message *Christine*.

the dangers of *Forward* and *Reply All*: It's all too easy to make embarrassing mistakes with email by hitting *Reply All* when you meant to hit *Reply*, or by forwarding a message and forgetting that the thread you are forwarding may include confidential information which one or more recipients should not be privy to—or may include uncomplimentary remarks about one or more of the individuals involved. In order to avoid these sorts of embarrassments (and also in the interests of fostering a workplace environment of respect and goodwill) a good habit to cultivate is not to commit to writing anything you would be embarrassed to have a colleague or a client discover that you have said.

subject line: It may seem an obvious point that one should include a subject line appropriate to what you are writing in an email, but many organizational communications are derailed because people forget the obvious. If a new subject is introduced at the end of an email thread, and you want to communicate with the same people about this subject, take the extra ten seconds to change the subject line; if you don't, there's a real possibility that a busy recipient, seeing yet another email apparently concerning a matter that has already been decided, may not even open the email.

Using an appropriate subject line is also a real help to everyone concerned when it comes to trying to locate the email weeks or months later; everyone relies from time to time on searches for a keyword relating to a subject dealt with in email correspondence.

emails about scheduling: Much as people often complain about time wasted in meetings, almost as much time can sometimes be wasted in setting up meetings. Here are some suggestions as to how to cut down on that wasted time.

If you are emailing several people to try to set up a meeting, suggest more than one possible time. And check people's schedules on your organization's e-calendar to make sure you suggest times when others are likely to be free.

If you are one of, say, eight recipients of a message asking what time(s) would work for a meeting, use *Reply*—not *Reply All*. There is no need for all the recipients to know that you can make it on the Tuesday but not the Wednesday; let the organizer of the meeting sort all that out, and you can reduce needless proliferation of emails.

6e. Slang and Informal English

Many words and expressions often used in conversation are considered inappropriate in academic, business, or professional writing. Here is a short list of words and expressions to avoid in formal writing:

AVOID •	REPLACE WITH
anyways	anyway
awfully	very, extremely
boss	manager, supervisor
bunch	group
(except for grapes, bananas etc.)	
buy	bargain
(as a noun—"a good buy")	
go (to mean "say")	say
have got	have, own
kid	child, girl, boy
kind of, sort of	rather, in some respects
lots of	a great deal of
mad	angry
(unless to mean "insane")	

All contractions (it's, he's, there's, we're, etc.) should generally be avoided in formal writing, as should conversational markers such as *like* and *well*.

needs checking   Let's say for example unemployment got much worse, the government would need to act.

revised   If, for example, unemployment became much worse, the government would need to act.

7. THE SOCIAL CONTEXT

7a. Gender

The healthy revolution in attitudes towards gender roles in recent generations has created some awkwardness in English usage—though not nearly so much as some have claimed. *Chair* is a simple non-sexist replacement for *chairman*, as is *business people* for *businessmen*. Nor is one forced into *garbageperson* or *policeperson*; *police officer* and *garbage collector* are entirely unobjectionable even to the linguistic purist. Nor can the purist complain if *fisher* replaces *fisherman*; far from being a new or artificial coinage, *fisher* was linguistic currency when the King James version of the Bible was written in the early seventeenth century. Here again, there is no need for the *-person* suffix.

The use of *mankind* to mean *humanity*, and of *man* to mean *human being*, have for some years been rightly frowned upon. (Ironically enough, *man* originally had *human being* as its **only** meaning; in Old English a *werman* was a male adult human being, a *wifman* a female.) A remarkable number of adults still cling to sexist usages, however, and even still try to convince themselves that it is possible to use *man* in a gender-neutral fashion.

Well, why **can't** *man* be gender neutral? To start with, because of the historical baggage such usage carries with it. Here, for example, is what the best-selling novelist Grant Allen had to say on the topic in a magazine called *Forum* in 1889:

> In man, I would confidently assert, as biological fact, the males are the race; the females are merely the sex told off to recruit and reproduce it. All that is distinctly human is man—the field, the ship, the mine, the workshop; all that is truly woman is merely reproductive—the home, the nursery, the schoolroom.

But the baggage is not merely historical; much of the problem remains embedded in the language today. A useful litmus test is how sex and gender differences are approached. Look, for example, at this sentence from an issue of *The Economist*:

> One of the most basic distinctions in human experience—that between men and women—is getting blurrier and blurrier.

Now let's try the same sentence using *man's* instead of *human*:

> One of the most basic distinctions in man's experience—that between men and women—is getting blurrier and blurrier.

In this sort of context we are all forced to sense that something is amiss. We have to realize when we see such examples that *man* and *he* and even *mankind* inevitably carry with them some whiff of maleness; they can never fully and fairly represent all of humanity. (If they didn't carry with them some scent of maleness it wouldn't be possible to make a joke about the difficulty of turning *men* into *human beings*.) Most contexts are of course more subtle than this, and it is thus often easy for humans—but especially for men—not to notice that the male terms always carry with them connotations that are not gender-neutral. *Humanity, humans, people*—these words are not in any way awkward or jargon-ridden; let's use them.

pronouns: To replace *man* with *humanity* is not inherently awkward to even a slight degree. But the pronouns are more difficult. Clearly the consistent use of *he* to represent both sexes is unacceptable. Yet *he/she, s/he,* or *he or she* are undeniably awkward, primarily because they are not inclusive—they leave out nonbinary people. The use of *they* as a singular pronoun has long been commonplace in spoken language, and it is now widely accepted in formal writing as well, both as a pronoun for a nonbinary individual and as a gender-neutral replacement for *he/she*. Some instructors may still prefer students to adhere to older grammatical rules that insist pronouns should match their subjects in number (i.e., that a singular subject cannot use *they* as a singular pronoun). If that is the case for some of your instructors, you can still avoid biased language by revising your sentences to make pronouns such as *he/she* unnecessary. The following examples illustrate various ways to avoid using discriminatory gendered pronouns: using *they* instead of *he/she*, removing the pronoun entirely, and revising the sentence so that both the subject and the pronoun are plural. All of these methods are good ways to ensure your writing remains grammatical while avoiding discriminatory language.

needs checking	Every gardener should wait until the frost risk has passed to plant her seeds outdoors.
revised	Every gardener should wait until the frost risk has passed to plant their seeds outdoors.

or   Every gardener should wait until the frost risk has passed to plant seeds outdoors.

or   Gardeners should wait until the frost risk has passed to plant their seeds outdoors.

Many nonbinary or otherwise gender-nonconforming people use pronouns other than, or in addition to, *he* or *she*. The most common of these is the singular *they*, but many other pronouns exist, and some people use more than one set of pronouns (e.g., one person might be accurately described by *he* or *they*, while another might be accurately described by *she* or *he*). Regardless of the specifics, whenever someone tells you what pronouns should be used to refer to them, it is important to respect their wishes and use these pronouns. The pronouns *she* and *he* are fine to use if you know that the person you are discussing in your writing identifies as a man or a woman; if you don't know, you are better off using the singular *they*. Because trans people often need to specify their pronouns in social and professional situations, it is a best practice for everyone to do so (e.g., by specifying your pronouns in your email signature, including them when you write your name on a name tag, or, in some contexts, stating them when you introduce yourself).

Questions relating to pronouns and to gender issues extend also to group pronouns such as *we* and *us* or *they* and *them*. It is always good to think about the first or third person pronouns one is using, and who they may include or exclude. In some cases it may be better to repeat a noun than to replace it with a pronoun.

worth checking   The twentieth century brought a revolution in the roles that women play in North American society; in 1900 they still were not allowed to vote in any North American jurisdiction.

[If the writer is male and addressing an audience of both women and men, it is more inclusive to avoid using the third person "they."]

revised   The twentieth century brought a revolution in the roles that women play in North American society; in 1900 women still were not allowed to vote in any North American jurisdiction.

or   The twentieth century brought a revolution in gender roles in North American society; in 1900 women still were not allowed to vote in any North American jurisdiction.

Of course issues of gender are not confined to the right word choice. Consider the following descriptions of political candidates with essentially the same backgrounds:

- Carla Jenkins, a lawyer and a school board trustee, is also the mother of three lovely daughters.
- George Kaplan, a lawyer and a school board trustee, has a long record of public service in the region.
- George Kaplan, a lawyer and a school board trustee, is also the father of three lovely daughters.
- Carla Jenkins, a lawyer and a school board trustee, has a long record of public service in the region.

The impression left in many minds by such phrasings is that the person described as having a long record of public service is well suited to public office, while the person whose parenting is emphasized may be better suited to staying at home.

Some may feel that parenthood is relevant in such cases; if you do, be sure to mention it both for women and for men. The general rule should be that, when describing a person, you should mention only the qualities you feel are relevant. And be sure to describe women and men with the same lens: if you feel it necessary to refer to relationship status or physical appearance, be sure to do so for men as well as women; if you mention degree qualifications or career achievements, be sure to do so for women as well as men.

7b. Race and Ethnicity, Class, Religion, Sexual Orientation, Disability, etc.

The issues discussed above regarding when to use *we* and *us* or *they* and *them* apply just as much where matters of race or religion or sexual orientation are concerned as they do to matters of gender:

worth checking   Indigenous Canadians represent approximately 5% of the total Canadian population. Our political party believes strongly that they should be represented in our parliament.

revised   Indigenous Canadians represent approximately 5% of the total Canadian population; our political party believes strongly that Indigenous Canadians should be represented in Canada's parliament.

or   Our political party believes strongly that Indigenous Canadians—who represent approximately 5% of the total Canadian population—should be represented in Canada's parliament.

worth checking   I would like to conclude my remarks with a prayer that has meant a great deal to me. We all know how God can bring light into our lives; certainly He has done so for me.

> [appropriate if the speaker is addressing a crowd that she knows is entirely made up of fellow believers—but inappropriate if the speaker is addressing a mixed crowd of believers, agnostics, and atheists]

revised   I would like to conclude my remarks with a prayer that has meant a great deal to me. Many of you may have experienced the feeling of God bringing light into your life; certainly He has done that for me.

> [appropriate if the speaker is addressing a mixed crowd of believers, agnostics, and atheists]

Another important principle is to avoid the use of unnecessary racial or religious identifiers. As with gender, mentioning a person's race, religion, or sexual orientation in connection with occupation is a common habit, but one that reinforces stereotypes as to what sort of person one would naturally expect to be a lawyer or a doctor or a nurse. Unless race or gender or religion is in some way relevant to the conversation, it is inappropriate to refer to someone as a male nurse, or a Jewish doctor, or a Native lawyer. Nor is it generally appropriate to stereotype members of particular groups even in ways that one considers positive; by doing so one may fail to give credit for individual achievement, while leaving the harmful impression of the group possessing qualities that are essential to it.

needs checking	Of course she gets straight As in all her subjects; she's from Hong Kong.
revised	It's no wonder she gets straight As in all her subjects; her parents have given her a great deal of encouragement, and she works very hard.

Many other issues of bias in language are specific to particular categories; the discussion below is of course far from comprehensive.

race: As with gender or disability or sexual orientation, one should not foreground racial or cultural background unless it is clearly relevant to what is being discussed. The more we foreground a person's race or gender when it is *not* a characteristic relevant to the discussion, the more we encourage people to emphasize race or gender rather than focusing on other human attributes.

worth checking	I was given a ticket for speeding last week; a black police officer pulled me over just after I'd crossed the Port Mann bridge. So I had to pay the bridge toll *and* an eighty dollar fine!
revised	I was given a ticket for speeding last week; a police officer pulled me over just after I'd crossed the Port Mann bridge. So I had to pay the bridge toll *and* an eighty dollar fine!

worth checking I've heard that Professor Andover's course in American literature is very interesting. She's of Asian background from the look of her; she just joined the department this year. Apparently she's an expert on Bob Dylan and the connections between literature and music.

[It may not be immediately apparent to some readers that there is anything odd or problematic about this example. Substitute "She's white—of Caucasian racial background from the look of her" and the point may become more clear; the racial or cultural background of Professor Andover is not relevant here.]

revised I've heard that Professor Andover's course in American literature is very interesting. She just joined the department this year; apparently she's an expert on Bob Dylan and the connections between literature and music.

It's one thing to acknowledge this principle; it's quite another to put it into practice, since in many cases doing so goes against the habits of a lifetime. For most North Americans, the only thing that might be thought of as objectionable in the following passage from David Sedaris's highly amusing autobiographical essay "Guy Walks into a Bar Car" is the loud man's off-colour joke:

When a couple of seats opened up, Johnny and I took them. Across the narrow carriage, a black man with a bushy mustache pounded on the Formica tabletop. "So a nun goes into town," he said, "and sees a sign reading, 'Quickies—Twenty-five Dollars.' Not sure what it means, she walks back to the convent and pulls aside the mother superior. 'Excuse me,' she asks, 'but what's a quickie?'

"And the old lady goes, 'Twenty-five dollars. Just like in town.'"

As the car filled with laughter, Johnny lit a fresh cigarette. "Some comedian," he said.

Sedaris's account of the train journey unfolds over several pages. The man with the mustache continues to tell crude jokes—and Sedaris continues to identify him not as as *the man with the bushy mustache* or *the loud man*—but as *the black man*—even as other (presumably white) people are identified in other ways:

> "All right," called the black man on the other side of the carriage. "I've got another one." … A red-nosed woman in a decorative sweatshirt started to talk, but the black fellow told her that he wasn't done yet … As the black man settled down, …
>
> "Here's a clean one," the black man said….

But why should it matter, you may ask. Maybe his blackness is what the writer has noticed first about the man. Isn't that harmless enough? The short answer is no. If writers identify people first and foremost by their race and not by other, more individualized characteristics, they subtly colour perceptions—both their readers' and their own. And that is of course particularly harmful when the characterization is a negative one. Sedaris is a wonderful writer, but in this instance he would have been a better writer had he referred repeatedly to *the mustachioed man* (or *the loudmouth*) and not to *the black man*. If North American history included the mass enslavement of mustachioed men or loudmouthed men, the point might be argued rather differently. But it doesn't.

• **Aboriginal/First Nations/Indian/Indigenous:** In Canada the word *Indian* has become tainted by centuries of history in which those who had taken the land from the Indigenous peoples used the word *Indian* to denigrate those peoples. It's not uncommon for some First Nations people to refer to one another informally or ironically as Indians. If you hear an Indigenous person calling another Indigenous person "Indian," does that mean it's all right for every Canadian to do that? Emphatically not: given that many First Nations people consider the term offensive, other Canadians should avoid using it. (One exception is discussions of individuals or groups who embrace the term because of the political rights it connotes; the word Indian is still used by the Canadian government to indicate Indian status.) The most widely accepted terms used to refer to Indigenous Canadians are *Indigenous people* and, less often, *First Peoples*. Canada's Indigenous peoples can be divided into three large groups—*First Nations, Inuit,* and *Métis*—and these terms should be used when you are referring to one group specifically, but be careful not to make the common mistake of using "First Nations" when you really mean Indigenous people more generally:

needs checking	In the past decade, government policies have reflected a change in attitude toward First Nations rights in Canada, from the Far North to the Great Lakes.
revised	In the past decade, government policies have reflected a change in attitude toward Indigenous rights in Canada, from the Far North to the Great Lakes.

Whenever you can, the best thing to do is refer to a specific tribe[1] or nation:

worth checking	Jeannette Armstrong is a First Nations writer, professor, and activist.
revised	Jeannette Armstrong is a Syilx Okanagan writer, professor, and activist.

It is also important to avoid talking about Indigenous cultures as if they exist only in the past. To do so takes part in a centuries-old practice of romanticizing Indigenous cultures as tragically doomed by colonization and falsely declaring them to be dying or extinct. This practice contributes to the ongoing erasure of Indigenous lives and helps to conceal the ongoing impacts of colonization on Indigenous people.

---

1   In Canada the term "band" remains a commonly used term in, for example, government documents, but "tribe" is now preferred by most Indigenous groups.

needs checking   The Teme-Augama Anishnabai lived in the Temagami area for thousands of years.

revised   The Teme-Augama Anishnabai have lived in the
Temagami area for thousands of years.

• **African American/African Canadian/Black/black:** For
the past two or three generations *Black* (or *black*) and (in the
United States) *African American* have been widely considered
appropriate terms. The latter, of course, is only appropriate if
one is referring to an American:

needs checking   Nelson Mandela is widely considered to have been
the greatest leader of his generation—not just the
greatest African American leader, but the greatest
leader, period.

revised   Nelson Mandela is widely considered to have been
the greatest leader of his generation—not just the
greatest Black leader, or the greatest African leader,
but the greatest leader, period.

In Canada *Black Canadians* is a much more widely used term
than is *African Canadians*.

We know that it is correct to capitalize words that describe
ethnicity or national origin, such as *Hispanic American*, *African American*, *Irish Canadian*, and so on. But what about
white or *black*? According to some style guides, these should
not be capitalized because they describe skin colour rather
than nationality or ethnicity. According to this argument, a
white or black person might be from anywhere, and a given
person's ethnicity would not be accurately described as *white*
or *black* but as, say, *Somali* or *Danish*.

Many, however, argue that a large number of North
Americans do in fact use *Black* as a term of ethnic identification—and for a very good reason. Whereas North Americans
of, say, Italian or Irish background can readily explore their
"pre-American" ethnic background, Black North Americans
whose ancestors were enslaved find it more difficult to do so:
they have fewer ways of knowing if their ancestors came from
(to pick only three of many examples, each with cultures at

least as different one from another as are those of France and Spain and Italy) the Khassonke-speaking Khasso Empire in what is now Mali, the Yoruba-speaking Oyo Empire in what is now Nigeria, or the Asante-speaking Ashanti Kingdom in what is now Ghana.

Given that the history of slavery has deprived most Black North Americans of the connection to specific national roots that most other North Americans have, many people choose the identifier *Black* as a primary descriptor of ethnicity. When *Black* is being used in this way, capitalization recognizes its legitimacy as an ethnicity—whereas not capitalizing it, some argue, may be taken to implicitly disparage Black people and culture.[1]

Should we capitalize *Black* at all times? Some argue that consistently capitalizing *Black* is a pragmatic approach, since it can sometimes be difficult to distinguish in practice between its use as a descriptor of skin colour and its use as the proper name of an ethnic group. Of writers who use this approach, a few capitalize *White* as well, for the sake of symmetry. But *white* is often capitalized in the writings of white suprema-cists, and most writers rightly want to avoid any association with that ideology. Moreover, *white* simply doesn't serve as a primary ethnic identifier for any large group in the way that *Black* does in North America—or indeed in any area where a history of slavery stripped large numbers of people of their original ethnic identity. (Conversely, in many parts of the world *black* is not capitalized because it implies nothing what-soever as to culture or ethnicity; in Zambia virtually everyone has black skin, but the Bemba, Tonga, Kaonde, etc. all have different linguistic and cultural traditions.)

---

1   These issues of usage, it should be noted, remain controversial. The *New York Times*, for example, mandates use of capitalized "Black," but black *New York Times* language issues columnist John McWhorter prefers not to capitalize (see "Capitalizing 'Black' Isn't Wrong, But It Isn't That Helpful, Either," 4 March 2022).

class: Another example of a widely used expression that is strongly coloured with bias is the expression *white trash*. The implications of the expression are brought forward in the following passage:

> The [Jerry Lee] Lewis and [Jimmy] Swaggart clans were, in the harsh modern parlance, white trash. They lived in the black part of town, and had close relations with blacks. Mr. Swaggart's preaching and Mr. Lewis's music were strongly influenced by black culture. "Jimmy Swaggart was as black as a white man can be," said black elders in Ferriday. (*The Economist*, 15 April 2000)

This passage brings out the implication of the expression; the 'trashiness' that is the exception for white people is implicitly regarded as the norm for black people.

The inappropriateness of expressions such as "white trash" is starting to be widely acknowledged. Less widely understood is the degree to which various expressions that are often used to describe wealthy people carry class baggage. Think, for example, of expressions such as these:

- She comes from a good family.
- He's making a good income now.
- By some definitions the couple may not be rich, but they are certainly well-off.

A centuries-old tradition among the rich and the middle class in North American and European culture holds that it is vulgar to refer to oneself or to friends and acquaintances as rich. For generations it has been accepted among the wealthy (and among many who aspire to wealth) that in most situations one should use euphemisms when referring to wealth and income. Many euphemisms do no harm, of course. But when one uses phrases such as *good family* to mean *rich family*, one is subtly colouring the financial with the moral. By implication, such phrasings further disadvantage those already disadvantaged by poverty, lending it a taint of a moral as well as a financial shortfall.

worth checking	The novel focuses on a woman who comes from a good family in New York; when the family falls on hard times, she faces difficult choices.
revised	The novel focuses on a woman who has moved in high society in New York; when her family falls on hard times, she faces difficult choices.

Even when you are using accepted terminology to discuss class, it is good to keep in mind the effects your word choice might have. *Lower class*, for example, is a widely used term that suggests a negative value judgement; descriptors such as *working class* (where appropriate) and *low-income* may be preferable.

religion: Given the generally high level of awareness in Western society of the evils of antisemitism it is extraordinary that *jew* is still sometimes used in casual conversation as a verb in the same way that *gyp* is used—and that *Jewish* can still sometimes be encountered as a synonym for *stingy*. These are usages that have their roots in a long tradition of anti-Jewish prejudice—in the many centuries during which most Christian societies prohibited Jews from entering most respectable occupations, leaving Jews little choice but to provide services such as moneylending that Christians needed but for various reasons did not want to provide themselves. Moneylending then became part of the vicious stereotyping that surrounded Jews. Like other extremely offensive terms discussed in this book, terms that preserve old antisemitic prejudices should never be allowed to go unchallenged. When they are challenged, speakers will often realize they have been unthinkingly using a coinage learnt in childhood—and will change.

A difficult issue is how to refer to extremists affiliated with a particular religion. Should those who profess faith in Islam but believe it is acceptable to kill and maim vast numbers of civilians who are associated with organizations they despise (Osama bin Laden's followers killing 2,996 people on September 11, 2001, followers of the Islamic State movement killing thousands in Iraq and Syria) be called Islamic fundamentalists, or Islamists, or jihadis, or terrorists, or simply mass killers? If someone claims to be following the Islamic faith and commits extreme acts of horrendous violence against unarmed civilians in the name of his faith, many argue that it's entirely fair to describe that person as an Islamic extremist. But fair to whom? When the two words are brought together, inevitably something of the one rubs off on the other, leaving some suggestion in the minds of those reading or hearing the term that extremism comes naturally to Muslims. Many North Americans may appreciate this point more clearly if we think of the phrase *Christian extremist*. Would it seem appropriate to use that term to describe one of the murderers of a dozen or more workers in abortion clinics in North America in the 1980s and 1990s (most of whom professed to be inspired by their Christian faith)? Probably not: a strong argument can be made that no religion deserves to be identified through the actions of its most violent and unprincipled adherents.

The best way to approach such questions may be to be as specific as possible—and to try to use language that cannot be taken to equate the beliefs of an entire religion with those of extremists on the fringes of that religion.

worth checking   Hindu terrorists killed over a thousand Muslims in the violence in India's Gujarat state in 2002.

revised   Extremists believed to be associated with the Vishva Hindu Parishadm (VHP) killed over a thousand Muslims in the violence in India's Gujarat state in 2002.

sexual orientation: There remains a great deal of confusion in North America over what constitutes acceptable language regarding sexual orientation. We can start with those very words—*sexual orientation*. That term has for the most part now replaced *sexual preference* when it comes to describing gay, lesbian, bisexual, heterosexual, and other sexualities—and for a good reason. The word "preference" carries with it a connotation of choice—the notion that one *chooses* whether or not to be gay. It was on that sort of presumption that past generations tried to "cure" people of same-sex desires. It's on that presumption too that some still refer to a "gay lifestyle," as if sexual orientation were akin to deciding either to settle down in a quiet, leafy suburb or to travel round the world as a backpacker. In fact, of course, gay, lesbian, and bisexual people choose from among just as many lifestyles as do heterosexual people. And, as a great many scientific studies have shown, most people—whether they are gay, lesbian, heterosexual, bisexual, asexual, or anything else—do not "choose" the genders they are or are not attracted to.

gay/homosexual: The term *gay* is now preferred to the term *homosexual*; why is that? Because of its history, is the short answer. The term *homosexual* was for so many generations used as a term of abuse—and, in the medical profession, as a term naming a form of mental illness—that it has now become tainted. That said, there are still a variety of contexts in which the word may (and should) still be used.

needs checking Wilde was said to have had a gay relationship with Lord Douglas.

    [A term such as "gay relationship" is anachronistic when applied to events in other historical eras—such as the famous trial of Oscar Wilde in the 1890s—and "homosexual" may better reflect the terminology and cultural categories of the time.]

revised Wilde was said to have had a homosexual affair with Lord Douglas.

    [However, in some contexts, it may be possible or even preferable to avoid using *homosexual* while still reflecting historical realities:]

or Following his romantic affair with Lord Douglas, Wilde was charged with the crime of "gross indecency."

"That's so gay": Soon after the word *gay* came to be recommended in the late twentieth century as the preferred non-pejorative term for same-sex sexual orientation, the expres-

sion "that's so gay" began to be widely used in conversation by young people. Its meaning? "That's really stupid," or "That's weak and ineffectual." Inevitably such usages connect at some level with other meanings; it's impossible if you use such a term to avoid a broader association of what is gay with what is stupid, weak, and ineffectual. (Imagine if people started to use the expression "that's so white" or "that's so black" or "that's so Christian" to mean "that's really stupid.") Much as many have protested that "that's so gay" is an "innocent expression," it's not. The cumulative repetition of this and similar colloquial expressions does a great deal to reinforce human prejudice against gays, lesbians, and bisexuals, and to make it more difficult for those who are gay to be open about it, and proud of it.

ability, disability, and neurodivergence: The language we use when we talk about disability, health conditions, and neurodivergence has a profound impact on the individuals and communities of people who identify as disabled, autistic, blind, or Deaf (and many other designations). Confusingly, this language isn't always clearly agreed upon by all, and it is evolving quickly. While professionals and policy makers have historically been taught to use "person first" language (e.g., *girl with autism* or *woman with vision impairment*), many disabled self-advocates now express a preference for "disability first" language (e.g., *autistic girl* or *blind woman*). These preferences, they say, relate to individuals' perceptions of their state of being; autism or blindness aren't add-ons to their personality but intrinsic parts of who they are.

We recommend that you defer to an individual or community's preferred terms of reference where possible (in much the same way that we honour an individual's gender pronouns or ethnic self-identification terms). If that preference is unknown, try to employ specific terms for the physical, mental, or cognitive impairment and use them respectfully and with consideration for your audience or reader (who may well identify as disabled themselves).

As with gender and race or cultural background, there is no need to mention a disability unless it is relevant to the topic of discussion.

needs checking   Professor Caswell joined the History Department in 2019. A distinguished scholar, he is the author of several books on early American society. He's confined to a wheelchair, though.

> [If you are outlining Professor Caswell's credentials and accomplishments, his physical disability is not something you need to mention.]

revised   Professor Caswell joined the History Department in 2019. A distinguished scholar, he is the author of several books on early American society.

Notice also how the reference to the wheelchair is worded in the above example. Phrases such as "confined to a wheelchair" can subtly colour people's judgements as to whether or not someone will be an asset to a community, or a burden on it.

needs checking   The members of the interviewing committee noticed that Professor Caswell is confined to a wheelchair.

revised   The members of the interviewing committee noticed that Professor Caswell uses a wheelchair.

The term *neurodivergence*, an umbrella category that includes autism, ADHD, and many other traits, is used to describe nonstandard ways of thinking and learning as normal variations in human brain function; the term does not necessarily imply any form of impairment. An individual may identify as *neurodivergent*, if they possess any of the traits considered part of this category, or *neurotypical*, if they do not.

humans and other animals: In recent decades the ways in which humans treat other animals have become the subject of widespread discussion. But there has been scant attention paid to how changing attitudes should be reflected in English usage. In particular, the issue of what pronouns to use has until recently been little discussed.

• *he/she/it—pronoun issues:* No one nowadays thinks it odd to refer to a pet as *he* or *she*, but beyond that there is a great deal of inconsistency. At issue is not only *it* versus *he* or *she* (or *they*), but also *who* and *whom* versus *that* and *which*. Should we say *the dog that lives next door* or *the dog who lives next door*? Should we say *the pig that plays a central role in* Charlotte's Web? Or *the pig who plays a central role in* Charlotte's Web? Should we say *the pig that they ate for dinner* or *the pig who they ate for dinner*?

In contexts where non-human animals are portrayed as pets or as friendly and lovable, "who" seems to be quite accepted. "The cat who ..." and "The dog who ..." are commonly used, as are "the pig who ..." and "the cow who" in contexts such as children's stories. Wild animals too we seem comfortable referring to as living creatures rather than things. In the case of the non-human animals many humans make a practice of eating, though, *it*, *that*, and *which* are used far more frequently. Should they be? Is a cow any more a thing than is a tail-wagging Labrador? Is a calf or a piglet any more a thing than is a kitten or a puppy? For many people there may be no easy answers to such questions, but they are surely worth asking; as has often been the case in human history, debates over appropriate linguistic usage provide some of the most interesting windows into large ethical, political, and epistemological issues.

What should you do if you are writing of non-human animals? Treat them grammatically as things? Or treat them in the way we do fellow beings? Is there any good reason to refer to any animal as *it* rather than *he* or *she* (or *they*)? Or to say *that* rather than *who*? Try as we might, we can't see any.

worth checking   The cow that's pictured on that carton of milk looks a lot happier than a real cow looks when its children have been taken away from it so that humans can drink the milk it produces.

revised   The cow who's pictured on that carton of milk looks a lot happier than a real cow looks when her children have been taken away from her so that humans can drink the milk she produces.

Much as it may seem forced or odd to refer to non-human animals in this way, English usage of this sort in fact represents a return to linguistic practice that was once well established. In 1865, for example, one Dr. Kidd recounted in the *Times* of London how he had saved a cow during the cattle plague of that year: "The men thought her dying …," "Determined not to give her up …" "little by little she revived." With "intensive" farming practices having become near universal in North America, most of us now have little or no contact with living cows and pigs and sheep and hens; no doubt it is not by coincidence that the growth of factory farming has been accompanied by a shift in the English language towards usages that encourage us to think of non-human animals as things rather than as living creatures.

> **Additional Material Online**
> Exercises on bias-free language may be found at
> **sites.broadviewpress.com/writingcdn**.
> Click on **Exercises** and go to
> **P3, "Style: How to Be Good with Words."**

7c. Bias-free Vocabulary: A Short List

actress	actor
alderman	councillor
anchorman	anchor/news anchor
Anglo-Saxon	early medieval, pre-conquest

(Note: The term "Anglo-Saxon" has come to be commonly used by white supremacist groups as a synonym for "white.")

Asiatic	Asian
bad guy	villain
bogeyman	bogey monster
brotherhood	fellowship, community

(when not speaking of all-male situations)

businessman	businessperson, entrepreneur
caveman	cave-dweller
chairman	chair
cleaning lady	cleaner
clergyman	minister, clergy member
common man	common person, average person, ordinary person
congressman	representative, congressperson
con-man	con-artist
draftsman	drafter
Eskimo	Inuit

(Note: Some Alaskan groups still prefer *Eskimo*. Note also that *Inuk* is the singular form of *Inuit*; because *Inuit* translates as *the people*, there is no need to refer to the group as the *Inuit people*.)

farmer's wife	farmer
fireman	firefighter
fisherman	fisher
forefathers	ancestors
foreman	manager, supervisor
freshman	first-year student

frontman	figurehead, front
garbageman	garbage collector
grandfather	grandparent
	(Note: As in "Under this clause of the contract, transactions that occurred on or before 31 December will be grandparented.")
gunman	shooter
guys	you all, everyone, folks
gyp	cheat, con
Gypsies	Roma
	(Note: *Gypsy* may still be a useful term of self-description for some of Roma background.)
handyman	handyperson
hearing impaired	deaf, Deaf
	(Note: This depends on context; in limited contexts, *hearing impaired* may be appropriate.)
homosexual	gay
	(unless *homosexual* is being used in historical contexts)
homosexual couple	couple, gay couple
	(if sexual orientation is relevant)
Indians	Indigenous people, First Peoples
	(Note: *First Nations*, *Inuit*, and/or *Métis* may also be used. Wherever possible it is best to specify the relevant nation [e.g., Mississauga, Cayuga, Seneca]. The above references current Canadian usage; in the United States, *American Indian* and *Native American* remain commonly used.)
infantryman	footsoldier
insurance man	insurance agent
layman	layperson
longshoreman	shiploader, stevedore
maid	housekeeper

mailman	letter carrier, mail carrier
male nurse	nurse
man	humanity
man (an exhibit)	staff
man (a ship)	crew
man enough	strong enough
manhandle	rough-up, attack
manhole	sewer hole, access hole
manhole cover	sewer cover, access hole cover, utility cover
man hours	staff time, work time, person hours
mankind	humankind, people, humanity, humans
manly	self-confident, courageous, straightforward
manmade	handmade, human-made, constructed
man of letters	intellectual
middleman	intermediary, go-between
midget	little person, dwarf, person of short stature
minority group	marginalized group, underrepresented group
mothering	parenting
mother tongue	native language, first language
Negro	Black, African American
niggardly	stingy
	(Note: The word *niggardly* has no etymological connection with the n-word. Since the one suggests the other to many minds, however, it is safer to avoid using it.)
Oriental	Asian, Middle Eastern
penmanship	handwriting
policeman	police officer
postman	letter carrier, mail carrier
preferred pronouns	pronouns (avoid use of "preferred")
Renaissance man	Renaissance person, polymath
salesman, saleslady	salesperson, sales clerk, sales representative
seaman	sailor, mariner
sex change surgery	gender confirmation surgery
slave	enslaved person
slaveowner	enslaver
Siamese twins	conjoined twins

snowman	snowbody (rhymes with *nobody*), snow person
spokesman	representative, spokesperson, agent
sportsman	sportsperson
sportsmanship	sportship
statesman	politician, political figure
stewardess	flight attendant
unsportsmanlike	unsporting
waitress	server
weatherman	weather forecaster
widower	widow
womanly	warm, tender, nurturing, sympathetic (or other more specific adjective suited to the circumstance)
workman	worker, labourer, wage earner

GRAMMAR

8. BASIC GRAMMAR: AN OUTLINE

8a. Parts of Speech

● Nouns

Nouns are words that name people, things, places, or qualities. Some examples follow:

- names of people: *boy*, *John*, *parent*
- names of things: *hat*, *spaghetti*, *fish*
- names of places: *Springfield*, *Zambia*, *New York*
- names of qualities: *silence*, *intelligence*, *anger*

  Nouns can be used to fill the gaps in sentences like these:

- I saw _____ at the market yesterday.
- He dropped the _____ into the gutter.
- Has learning Italian taken a lot of _____?
- Hamilton is a _____ with several hundred thousand people living in it.
- _____ is my favourite ski resort.

  Some nouns (e.g., *sugar*, *milk*, *confusion*) are uncountable—that is, we cannot say *a milk*, *two milks*, or *three milks*.

● Pronouns

Pronouns replace or stand for nouns. For example, instead of saying, *The man slipped on a banana peel* or *George slipped on a banana peel*, we can replace the noun *man* (or the noun *George*) with the pronoun *he* and say *He slipped on a banana peel*.

personal and indefinite pronouns: Whereas a personal pronoun such as *he* or *she* refers to a definite person, the words *each*, *every*, *either*, *neither*, *one*, *another*, and *much* are indefinite. They may be used as pronouns or as adjectives; in either case, a singular verb is generally needed. (See section 7a above for a discussion of exceptions.)

- Each player wants to do her best.
  > (Here the word *each* is an adjective, describing the noun *player*.)
- Each wants to do her best.
  > (Here the word *each* is a pronoun, acting as the subject of the sentence.)
- Each of the players wants to do her best.
  > (The word *each* is still a pronoun, this time followed by the phrase *of the players*. But it is the pronoun *each* that is the subject of the sentence; the verb must be the singular *wants*.)

possessive pronouns and adjectives: See under "Adjectives" below.

relative pronouns: These pronouns relate back to a noun that has been used earlier in the same sentence. Consider how repetitious these sentences sound:

- I talked to the man. The man wore a red hat.

We could of course replace the second *man* with *he*. Even better, though, is to relate or connect the second idea to the first by using a relative pronoun:

- I talked to the man who wore a red hat.
- I found the pencil. I had lost the pencil.
- I found the pencil that I had lost.

The following are all relative pronouns:

who	whose (has other uses too)
which	that (has other uses too)
whom	

Try replacing the second noun in the pairs of sentences below with a relative pronoun, so as to make only one sentence out of each pair:

- I polished the table. I had built the table.
- Senator Collins is vacationing this week in Maine's Acadia National Park. The senator cancelled a planned holiday last fall.

- The word *other* has often been used by literary theorists when speaking of a sense of strangeness in the presence of cultural difference. *Other* is usually preceded by the definite article when so used.

pronouns acting as subject and as object: We use different forms of some pronouns depending on whether we are using them as subjects or objects and whether they are singular or plural.

	singular	*plural*
Subject	I	we
Pronouns	you	you
	he/she/it	they
	who, what, which	who, what, which

	singular	*plural*
Object	me	us
Pronouns	you	you
	him/her/it	them
	whom, what, which	whom, what, which

- She loves Frankie.

     (Here the pronoun *she* is the subject of the sentence.)
- Frankie loves her.

     (Here the word *her* is the object; *Frankie* is the subject.)
- That's the woman who loves Frankie.

     (Here the pronoun *who* is the subject of the clause *who loves Frankie.*)
- That's the woman whom Frankie loves.

     (Here the pronoun *whom* is the object of the verb *love*; *Frankie* is the subject of the clause *whom Frankie loves.*)

The distinctions between *I* and *me* and between *who* and *whom* are treated more fully under "Subject and Object Pronouns," pages 130–31.

● Articles

Articles (determiners often classed as a form of adjective) are words used to introduce nouns. There are only three of them: *a*, *an*, and *the*. Articles show whether or not one is drawing attention to a particular person or thing.

For example, we would say *I stood beside a house* if we did not want to draw attention to that particular house, but *I stood beside the house that the Taylors used to live in* if we did want to draw attention to the particular house. *A* (or *an* if the noun following begins with a vowel sound) is an indefinite article—used when you do not wish to be definite or specific about which thing or person you are referring to. *The* is a definite article, used when you do wish to call attention to the particular thing or person, and when a noun is followed by a specifying phrase or clause (such as *used to live in*, which follows the noun *Taylors*). Remember that if you use *the*, you are suggesting that there can be only one or one group of what you are referring to.

Choose the appropriate article (*a*, *an*, or *the*):

- _____ moon shone brightly last night.
- She had _____ long conversation with _____ friend.
- Have you ever driven _____ car?
- Have you driven _____ car that your wife bought on Monday?

● Adjectives

Adjectives are words used to tell us more about (describe or modify) nouns or pronouns. Here are some examples of adjectives:

big	good	heavy
small	bad	expensive
pretty	careful	healthy
quick	slow	unexpected

- The small boy lifted the heavy table.
    > (Here the adjective *small* describes or tells us more about the noun *boy*, and the adjective *heavy* describes the noun *table*.)
- The fast runner finished ahead of the slow one.
    > (*Fast* describes *runner* and *slow* describes *one*.)

Notice that adjectives usually come before the nouns that they describe. This is not always the case, however; when the verb *to be* is used, adjectives often come after the noun or pronoun, and after the verb:

- That woman is particularly careful about her finances.
    > (*Careful* describes *woman*.)
- It is too difficult for me to do.
    > (*Difficult* describes *it*.)

Adjectives can be used to fill the gaps in sentences like these:

- This _____ sweater was knitted by hand.
- As soon as we entered the _____ house we heard a clap of _____ thunder.
- Those shoes are very _____.
- Derrida's argument could fairly be described as _____.

Some words can be either adjectives or pronouns, depending on how they are used. That is the case with the indefinite pronouns (see above), and also with certain possessives (words that show possession):

	singular	*plural*
Possessive	my	our
Adjectives	your	your
	his/her	their
	whose	whose
Possessive	mine	ours
Pronouns	yours	yours
	his/hers	theirs
	whose	whose

- I have my cup, and he has his.

    (Here the word *his* is a pronoun, used in place of the noun *cup*.)
- He has his cup.

    (Here the word *his* is an adjective, describing the noun *cup*.)
- Whose book is this?

    (Here the word *whose* is an adjective, describing the noun *book*.)
- Whose is this?

    (Here the word *whose* is a pronoun, acting as the subject of the sentence.)

● Verbs

Verbs are words that express actions or states of affairs. Most verbs can be conveniently thought of as "doing" words (e.g., *open, feel, do, carry, see, think, combine, send*), but several verbs do not fit into this category. Indeed, the most common verb of all—*be*—expresses a state of affairs, not a particular action that is done. Verbs are used to fill gaps in sentences like these:

- I _____ very quickly, but I _____ not _____ up with my brother.
- She usually _____ to sleep at 9:30.
- Stephen _____ his breakfast very quickly.
- They _____ a large farm near Chicago.
- There _____ many different languages that people _____ in India.

One thing that makes verbs different from other parts of speech is that verbs have tenses; in other words, they change their form depending on the time you are talking about. For example, some present tense forms of the verb *to be* are as follows: *I am, you are, he is*, etc.; these are some past tense forms: *I was, you were, he was*, etc. If you are unsure whether or not a particular word is a verb, one way to check is to ask if it has different tenses. For example, if you thought that perhaps the word *football* might be a verb, you need only ask yourself if it would be correct to say, *I footballed, I am footballing, I will football*, and so on. Obviously it would not be, so you know that *football* is the noun that names the game, not a verb that expresses an action. See chapter 9 below for a discussion of verb tenses.

● Adverbs

These words are usually used to tell us more about (describe or modify) verbs, although they can also be used to tell us more about adjectives or about other adverbs. They answer questions such as *How ...?, When ...?,* and *To what extent ...?,* and often they end with the letters *ly*. Here are a few examples, with some adjectives also listed for comparison:

Adjective	Adverb
careful	carefully
beautiful	beautifully
thorough	thoroughly
sudden	suddenly
slow	slowly
easy	easily
good	well

- He walked carefully.
  > (The adverb *carefully* tells us how he walked; it describes the verb *walked*.)
- He is a careful boy.
  > (The adjective *careful* describes the noun *boy*.)
- My grandfather died suddenly last week.
  > (The adverb *suddenly* tells how he died; it describes the verb *died*.)
- We were upset by the sudden death of my grandfather.
  > (The adjective *sudden* describes the noun *death*.)
- She plays the game very well.
  > (The adverb *well* tells us how she plays; it describes the verb *plays*. The adverb *very* describes the adverb *well*.)
- She played a good game this afternoon.
  > (The adjective *good* describes the noun *game*.)

- She played a very good game.
> (The adverb *very* describes the adjective *good*, telling us how good it was.)
- Our friends will meet the new baby soon.
> (The adverb *soon* describes the verb *will meet*, telling when the action will happen.)

Choose adverbs to fill the gaps in these sentences:

- Ralph writes very _____.
- The judge spoke _____ to her after she had been convicted on six counts of stock manipulation and fraud.
- They were _____ late for the meeting this morning.

● Prepositions

Prepositions are joining words, normally used before nouns or pronouns. Some of the most common prepositions are as follows:

about	across	after	at
before	for	from	in
into	of	off	on
over	to	until	with

Choose prepositions to fill the gaps in these sentences:

- I will tell you _____ it _____ the morning.
- Please try to arrive _____ eight o'clock.
- He did not come back _____ Seattle _____ yesterday.
- I received a letter _____ my sister.

● Conjunctions and Conjunctive Adverbs

Conjunctions and conjunctive adverbs are normally used to join groups of words together, and in particular to join clauses together. Conjunctions can be divided into three types: coordinating, subordinating, and correlative.

coordinating conjunctions: Coordinating conjunctions join parallel groupings of words. Since there are only seven such conjunctions in English, they can be memorized easily. Some people use the acronym *FANBOYS* as a memory aid:

> **F**or
> **A**nd
> **N**or
> **B**ut
> **O**r
> **Y**et
> **S**o

- Carmen thought the movie was silly, but we really liked it.

  > (The coordinating conjunction *but* joins the main clauses *Carmen thought the movie was silly* and *we really liked it.* Note that a comma precedes a coordinating conjunction used in this way.)

- His anxiety about public performance made him uncomfortable yet improved his playing.

  > (The coordinating conjunction *yet* joins the verb phrases *made him uncomfortable* and *improved his playing.*)

- The novel was short, dense, and gripping.

  > (The coordinating conjunction *and* joins the adjectives *short*, *dense*, and *gripping*. When joining more than two words or phrases, a coordinating conjunction may be preceded either by a comma or not, as long as the choice is consistent in a single piece of writing.)

subordinating conjunctions: Subordinating conjunctions join subordinate clauses to main clauses. Any clause beginning with a subordinating conjunction is a subordinate clause. English has many subordinating conjunctions; here is a partial list of commonly used ones (note that some are groups of words):

after	although	as	as long as
as though	because	before	even though
if	in order that	since	so that
unless	until	whereas	while

- They stopped playing because they were tired.

(The subordinating conjunction *because* joins the clauses *They stopped playing* and *they were tired*, making the second of these subordinate.)

- I will give her your message if I see her.

(The subordinating conjunction *if* joins the clauses *I will give her your message* and *I see her*, making the second of these subordinate.)

conjunctive adverbs: Conjunctive adverbs, as their name suggests, are adverbs that join word groups as well as modifying them. Conjunctive adverbs can join main clauses together or join a stand-alone main clause to a previous sentence; either way, and unlike other types of conjunctions, conjunctive adverbs need not appear exactly at the beginning of the word groups they join. Wherever it appears, a conjunctive adverb must be set off with commas or preceded by a semi-colon if (and only if) it joins two clauses in one sentence. Here are some common conjunctive adverbs (note that some of them are phrases):

alternatively	certainly	furthermore
however	indeed	in fact
in other words	likewise	meanwhile
moreover	nonetheless	on the other hand
otherwise	similarly	that is
therefore	thus	unfortunately

- Miss Polly was busy hiding the silverware. Meanwhile, the Foley brothers arrived at the ranch.

(*Meanwhile* links the two sentences by indicating the time relationship between them.)

- That new tablet is fantastic. No one, however, will want to pay such a high price for it.

(*However* signals a contrast between the points made in the two sentences. Because it is embedded in its sentence, *however* is set apart with commas.)

- I have excellent reasons for abandoning this project; unfortunately, the others on my team disagree with me.

(*Unfortunately* here links two independent clauses, and so is preceded by a semi-colon and followed by a comma.)

correlative conjunctions: Correlative conjunctions come in pairs and can join single words or word groups. Here are some examples:

both ... and	either ... or	neither ... nor
not only ... but also	so ... that	such ... as

Whatever is joined by correlative conjunctions must have the same grammatical structure, as in the examples below:

• That dishcloth is both smelly and unsanitary.

> (*Both* and *and* join the adjectives *smelly* and *unsanitary*.)

• Neither the dollar nor the economy will fare well if oil prices drop any lower.

> (*Neither* and *nor* join the noun phrases *the dollar* and *the economy*.)

• Not only is our candidate well educated but she is also personable.

> (*Not only* and *but also* join the clauses *our candidate is well educated* and *she is personable*. Note that when joining clauses, *not only* requires that the usual order of subject and verb in the following clause be reversed. Note as well that *but also* is here split by the following clause's subject and verb.)

Many conjunctions can also act as other parts of speech, depending on how they are used. Notice the difference in each of these pairs of sentences:

• He will not do anything about it until the morning.

> (Here *until* is a preposition joining the noun *morning* to the rest of the sentence.)

• He will not do anything about it until he has discussed it with his wife.

> (Here *until* is a subordinating conjunction introducing the clause *he has discussed it with his wife*.)

- I slept for half an hour after dinner.
    > (Here *after* is a preposition joining the noun *dinner* to the rest of the sentence.)
- I slept for half an hour after they had gone home.
    > (Here *after* is a subordinating conjunction introducing the clause *they had gone home*.)
- She wants to buy that dress.
    > (Here *that* is an adjective describing the noun *dress*: "*Which dress?*" "*That dress!*")
- George said that he was unhappy.
    > (Here *that* is a subordinating conjunction introducing the clause *he was unhappy*.)

Choose conjunctions to fill the gaps in the following sentences:

- We believed _____ we would win.
- They sat down in the shade _____ it was hot.
- My father did not speak to me _____ he left.

8b. Parts of Sentences

● Subject

The subject is the thing, person, or quality about which something is said in a clause. The subject is usually a noun or pronoun.

- The man went to town.
    > (The sentence is about the man, not about the town; thus, the noun *man* is the subject.)
- Groundnuts are an important crop in Nigeria.
    > (The sentence is about groundnuts, not about crops or about Nigeria; thus, the noun *groundnuts* is the subject.)
- Nigeria is the most populous country in Africa.
    > (The sentence is about Nigeria, not about countries or about Africa; thus, the noun *Nigeria* is the subject.)
- He followed me up the stairs.
    > (The pronoun *He* is the subject.)

core subject: The core subject is the single noun or pronoun that forms the subject.

complete subject: The complete subject is the subject together with any adjectives or adjectival phrases modifying it:

- The woman in the huge hat went to the market to buy groceries.

    (The core subject is the noun *woman* and the complete subject is *the woman in the huge hat*.)

● Object

An object is something or someone towards which an action or feeling is directed. In grammar an object is the thing, person, or quality affected by the action of the verb. (To put it another way, it receives the action of the verb.) Like a subject, an object normally is made up of a noun or pronoun.

direct object: The direct object is the thing, person, or quality directly affected by the action of the verb. A direct object usually answers the question *What?* or *Who?* Notice that direct objects are not introduced by prepositions.

indirect object: The indirect object is the thing, person, or quality that is indirectly affected by the action of the verb. All indirect objects could be expressed differently by making them the objects of the prepositions *to* or *for*. English often allows these prepositions to be omitted. Indirect objects answer the questions *To whom?* and *For whom?*

- Stanton hit the ball a long way.

    (What did he hit? The ball. *The ball* is the direct object of the verb *hit*.)
- She threw me her hat.

    (What did she throw? Her hat. *Her hat* is the direct object. To whom did she throw it? To me. *Me* is the indirect object. Note that the sentence could be rephrased: *She threw her hat to me*.)
- They gave their father a watch for Christmas.

    (The direct object is *watch*, and the indirect object is *father*.)

● Predicate

The predicate is everything that is said about the subject. In the example under "Subject," *The woman in the huge hat went to the market to buy groceries*, the group of words *went to the market to buy groceries* is the predicate. A predicate always includes a verb.

● Clauses and Phrases

A clause is a distinct group of words that includes both a subject and a predicate. Thus a clause always includes a verb.

A phrase is a distinct group of words that does *not* include both a subject and a verb. Examples:

Clauses	*Phrases*
because he is strong	because of his strength (no verb)
before she comes home	before the meeting (no verb)
the professor likes me	from Halifax
a tree fell down	at lunch
who came to dinner	in the evening

Types of clauses

main clause (or **independent clause**): A main clause is a group of words that is, or could be, a sentence on its own.

subordinate clause (or **dependent clause**): A subordinate clause is a clause that could not form a complete sentence on its own.

Except for the coordinating conjunctions (*and, but, or, nor, for, yet,* and *so*), conjunctions do not introduce main clauses, so if a clause begins with a word such as *because, although,* or *if,* you can be confident it is a subordinate clause. Similarly, relative pronouns introduce subordinate clauses—never main clauses.

- She lives near Victoria.

    (One main clause here forms a complete sentence. The pronoun *She* is the subject, *lives* is the verb, and the preposition *near* and the noun *Victoria* together form a phrase.)

- He danced in the street because he was feeling happy.
  - main clause: He danced in the street
  - subject: _____
  - predicate: _____
  - subordinate clause: because he was feeling happy
  - subject: _____
  - predicate: _____
- Mavis has a cat who likes to drink from the kitchen faucet.
  - main clause: Mavis has a cat
  - subject: _____
  - predicate: _____
  - subordinate clause: who likes to drink from the kitchen faucet
  - subject: _____
  - predicate: _____

Subordinate clauses may be further subdivided as follows:

adjectival subordinate clause: a subordinate clause that tells us more about a noun or pronoun. Adjectival clauses begin with relative pronouns such as *who, whom, whose, which,* and *that.*

adverbial subordinate clause: a subordinate clause that tells us more about the action of the verb—telling *how, when, why,* or *where* the action occurred.

noun subordinate clause: a clause that acts like a noun to form the subject or object of a sentence.

Examples:

- He talked at length to his cousin, who quickly became bored.
  - (*Who quickly became bored* is an adjectival subordinate clause, telling us more about the noun *cousin.*)
  - subject of subordinate clause: the pronoun *who*
  - verb in subordinate clause: _____
  - subject of main clause: the pronoun *He*
  - verb in main clause: _____
- My husband did not like the gift that I gave him.
  - (*That I gave him* is an adjectival subordinate clause telling us more about the noun *gift.*)

       subject of subordinate clause: the pronoun *I*
       verb in subordinate clause: _____
       subject of main clause: _____
       verb in main clause: _____

- The boy whom she wants to marry is very poor.

  (*Whom she wants to marry* is an adjectival subordinate clause telling us more about the noun *boy*. Notice that here the subordinate clause appears in the middle of the main clause, *The boy is very poor.*)

  subject of subordinate clause: _____
  verb in subordinate clause: _____
  subject of main clause: _____
  verb in main clause: _____

- I felt worse after I had been to the doctor.

  (*After I had been to the doctor* is an adverbial subordinate clause telling us when I felt worse.)

- He could not attend because he had broken his leg.

  (*Because he had broken his leg* is an adverbial subordinate clause telling us why he could not attend.)

- She jumped as if an alarm had sounded.

  (*As if an alarm had sounded* is an adverbial subordinate clause telling us how she jumped.)

- What he said was very interesting.

  (*What he said* is a noun clause acting as the subject of the sentence, in the same way that the noun *conversation* acts as the subject in *The conversation was very interesting.*)

- Sue-Ellen told me that she wanted to become a lawyer.

  (*That she wanted to become a lawyer* is a noun clause acting as the object, in the same way that the noun *plans* acts as the object in *Sue-Ellen told me her plans.*)

Types of phrases

adjectival phrase: a phrase that tells us more about a noun or pronoun.

adverbial phrase: a phrase that tells us more about the action of a verb, answering questions such as *When ...?*, *Where ...?*, *How ...?*, and *Why ...?*

- The boy in the new jacket got into the car.

  (*In the new jacket* is an adjectival phrase telling us more about the noun *boy*.)

- I drank from the cup with a broken handle.

  (*With a broken handle* is a phrase telling us more about the noun *cup*.)

- We went to the park.

  (*To the park* is an adverbial phrase telling where we went.)

- They arrived after breakfast.

  (*After breakfast* is an adverbial phrase telling when they arrived.)

Distinguishing phrases and clauses

- They were late because of the weather.

  (*Because of the weather* is an adverbial phrase telling us why they were late. It has no verb.)

- They were late because the weather was bad.

  (*Because the weather was bad* is an adverbial clause telling us why they were late.)

  subject: _____

  verb: _____

- The man at the corner appeared to be upset.

  (*At the corner* is an adjectival phrase telling us more about the noun *man*.)

- The man who stood at the corner appeared to be upset.

  (*Who stood at the corner* is an adjectival clause telling us more about the noun *man*.)

  subject: _____

  verb: _____

● Parts of Speech and Parts of the Sentence

- After the generous man with the big ears has bought presents, he will quickly give them to his friends.

  Parts of speech:

  after: *conjunction* the: *article*

generous: _____ man: _____

with: _____ the: _____

big: _____ ears: _____

has bought: _____ presents: _____

he: _____ will give: _____

quickly: _____ them: _____

to: _____ his: _____

friends: _____

Parts of the sentence:

main clause: He will quickly give them to his friends.

subject: _____

predicate: _____

verb: _____

direct object: _____

indirect object: _____

subordinate clause: After the generous man with the big ears has bought presents,

Is this an adjectival or an adverbial subordinate clause?

core subject: the noun _____

complete subject: _____

adjectival phrase: with the big ears

this phrase tells us more about the noun: _____

predicate: _____

direct object: _____

Additional Material

A discussion of run-on sentences and sentence fragments ("incomplete sentences") may be found on **pages 135–48**.
For exercises on grammar go to
sites.broadviewpress.com/writingcdn.
Click on **Exercises**.

9. VERBS AND VERB TENSE DIFFICULTIES

9a. The Infinitive

The infinitive is the starting point for building a knowledge of verb tenses; it is the most basic form of the verb. Some examples of infinitives are *to go, to be, to do, to begin, to come, to investigate*. The infinitive form remains the same whether the action referred to happens in the past, the present, or the future.

The most commonly made mistake involving infinitives is the colloquial substitution of *and* for *to*, especially in the expression *try and do it* for *try to do it*. The great issue in this area among grammarians, however, is the **split infinitive**—the infinitive which has another word or words inserted between to and the verb: *to quickly go; to forcefully speak out; to thoroughly investigate*. Some authorities argue that it is always grammatically incorrect to break up the infinitive in this way. Most, however, see the matter as one of awkwardness rather than incorrectness. In most cases a sentence with a split infinitive will sound more awkward than one without—but this is not a firm and fast rule.

9b. The Simple Present Tense

	SINGULAR	PLURAL
1st person	I say	we say
2nd person	you say	you say
3rd person	he, she, it says	they say

9c. Subject–Verb Agreement

Almost all of us occasionally have problems in writing the third person of the simple present tense correctly. All too often the letter *s* at the end of the third person singular is left out. The simple rule here is that whenever you use a verb in the third person singular of the simple present tense, it *must* end in *s*.

needs checking	The compound change shape when heated.
revised	The compound changes shape when heated.
	[*Compound*, which is the subject, is an *it* and therefore third person singular.]

It is not particularly difficult to make the subject agree with the verb in the above example, but even professional writers often have trouble with more complex sentences. Two common categories of subject–verb agreement errors are discussed below.

i) The subject and verb are separated by a long phrase or clause.

needs checking	The recent history of these African nations illustrate a variety of points.
revised	The recent history of these African nations illustrates a variety of points.

Here the writer has made the mental error of thinking of *nations* as the subject of the verb *illustrate*, whereas in fact the subject is the singular noun *history*. "The history illustrate ..." would immediately strike most people as wrong, but the intervening words have in this case caused grammatical confusion.

needs checking	As the statement by Belgium's Prime Minister about his country's deficit and unemployment problems indicate, many nations are in the same shape, or worse.
revised	As the statement by Belgium's Prime Minister about his country's deficit and unemployment problems indicates, many nations are in the same shape, or worse.
	[The subject is the singular noun *statement*, so the verb must be *indicates* rather than *indicate*.]

needs checking	Courses offered range from the history of the Greek and Roman world to the twenty-first century, and covers Britain, Europe, North America, Africa, and the Far East. (History Dept. Prospectus, Birkbeck College, University of London)
revised	Courses offered range from the history of the Greek and Roman world to the twenty-first century, and cover Britain, Europe, North America, Africa, and the Far East.

Sometimes a long sentence can in itself throw off a writer's sense of subject–verb agreement, even if subject and verb are close together. In the following example the close proximity of the subject *simplifications* to the verb has not prevented error:

needs checking	The decline in the quality of leadership is mirrored in the crude simplifications which characterizes the average person's view of the world.
revised	The decline in the quality of leadership is mirrored in the crude simplifications which characterize the average person's view of the world.

ii) The error of using *there is* instead of *there are* when the subject is plural has become more and more frequent in writing as well as in speech.

When these two expressions are used, remember that the subject comes after the verb; use *is* or *are* depending on whether the subject is singular or plural:

needs checking	There's many more opportunities of that sort than there used to be.
revised	There are many more opportunities of that sort than there used to be.

9d. Historical Present

To use the "historical present" is to use the present tense in a narrative set in the past. In many medieval histories the narrative alternates frequently between the present tense and the past tense, but from the sixteenth century until the late twentieth century most narratives of past action were recounted using the past tense. The historical present was used on a very selective basis by some historians and journalists (and by a few writers of fiction), the purpose being to lend a sense of immediacy to particular scenes that the writer wanted to express with memorable vividness.

In the twenty-first century the historical present has become much more commonly used in a wide variety of contexts. Many works of fiction are now written entirely in the present tense. Many works of history shift back and forth continually between the past tense and the historical present. Even newscasts now use the historical present frequently. As in earlier eras, the aim is presumably to impart a greater sense of immediacy and interest to what is being recounted. It is all too easy in such circumstances, however, to create a sense of confusion rather than a sense of immediacy in the reader's mind—particularly given that the present tense is often also used idiomatically to refer to future events (e.g., *We arrive at 9:00 in the morning* rather than *We will arrive at 9:00 in the morning*). It is essential, then, to pay careful attention to what tenses are being used.

needs checking　Throughout the day, shells fall on the city. Dozens are killed. The President, however, refused to authorize a ceasefire. The Cabinet holds an emergency meeting tonight.

[The passage begins in the historical present, but then switches to the past tense. The fourth sentence shifts back to present tense— but it is not clear what time is being referred to. Is the emergency meeting also in the past (and the report being filed late at night)? If so, what was the outcome of the meeting? Or is the report being filed before "tonight"—in which case the emergency meeting is still in the future.]

revised　Throughout the day, shells fell on the city. Dozens were killed. The President, however, refused to authorize a ceasefire. The Cabinet will hold an emergency meeting tonight.

or Throughout the day, shells fall on the city. Dozens are killed. The President, however, refuses to authorize a ceasefire. The Cabinet will hold an emergency meeting tonight.

Additional Material Online

Exercises on subject–verb agreement may be found at **sites.broadviewpress.com/writingcdn**. Click on **Exercises** and go to **M2.1, "Verbs and Verb Issues."**

9e. Survey of Verb Tenses

1st PERSON:

the present progressive (or continuous) tense	I am finishing
the simple past tense	I finished
the past progressive (or continuous) tense	I was finishing
the simple future tense	I will finish
the future progressive (or continuous) tense	I will be finishing
the present perfect tense	I have finished
the past perfect tense	I had finished
the future perfect tense	I will have finished
the conditional	I would finish
the past conditional	I would have finished
the present perfect continuous	I have been finishing
the past perfect continuous	I had been finishing
the future perfect continuous	I will have been finishing
the conditional continuous	I would be finishing
the past conditional continuous	I would have been finishing

9f. Voice

Most verbs have both an **active** and a **passive** voice. The active is used when the subject of the verb is doing the action, whereas the passive is used when the subject of the verb is receiving the action or being acted on.

Some examples:

ACTIVE	PASSIVE
I did it.	It was done.
She hit him.	He was hit.
They will give a speech.	The speech will be given.

(See also 1e and 6c.)

9g. Mood

Most sentences in English are in the *indicative mood*, which is used when we are expressing facts and opinions or asking questions. We use the *imperative mood* when giving orders or advice, and we use the *subjunctive mood* to denote actions that are wished for or imagined, or would happen if certain conditions were met. Some examples:

> If I were you, I would do what she says.

> The doctor advises that he stop smoking immediately.
> (not *that he stops*)

needs checking	If a bank was willing to lend money without proper guarantees, it would go bankrupt very quickly.
revised	If a bank were willing to lend money without proper guarantees, it would go bankrupt very quickly.

For more on conditions see pages 156–58.

COMBINING VERB TENSES: SOME CHALLENGES

9h. The Past Perfect Tense

The chief use of the past perfect tense is to show that one action in the past was completed before another action in the past began:

> I told my parents what <u>had happened</u>.
> 			[The happening occurred before the telling.]

> She thought very seriously about what he <u>had said</u>.
>
> [The saying occurred before the thinking.]

The past perfect is particularly useful when the writer wishes to flashback, or move backwards in time:

needs checking The tail was still moving, but the snake itself was quite dead. It crawled out from under a rock and slowly moved towards me as I was lowering the canoe at the end of the portage.

revised The tail was still moving, but the snake itself was quite dead. It had crawled out from under a rock and had moved slowly towards me as I had been lowering the canoe at the end of the portage.

The past perfect is frequently used when we are reporting speech indirectly:

> She said that she had finished the work.

9i. Combining Tenses—Quoted Material

It is often difficult to achieve grammatical consistency when incorporating quoted material in a sentence:

needs checking Prime Minister Wilson admitted at the time that "such a policy is not without its drawbacks."

[The past tense *admitted* and the present tense *is* do not agree.]

There are two ways of dealing with a difficulty such as this:

(a) Change the sentence so as to set off the quotation without using the connecting word *that*. Usually this can be done with a colon.

(b) Use only that part of the quotation that can be used in such a way as to agree with the tense of the main verb.

revised Prime Minister Wilson did not claim perfection: "such a policy is not without its drawbacks," he admitted.

or Prime Minister Wilson admitted at the time that such a policy was "not without its drawbacks."

9j. Irregular Verbs

The majority of verbs in English follow a regular pattern—I *open* in the simple present tense, I *opened* in the simple past tense, I *have opened* in the present perfect tense, and so forth. Most of the more frequently used verbs, however, follow different patterns. For example, we say *I went* instead of *I goed*. Here is a list of irregular verbs in English:

BASE FORM	SIMPLE PAST	PAST PARTICIPLE
arise	arose	arisen
awake	awoke/awaked	awoken/awaked/woken
be	was/were	been
bear	bore	borne
beat	beat	beaten
become	became	become
begin	began	begun
bend	bent	bent
bite	bit	bitten
bleed	bled	bled
blow	blew	blown
break	broke	broken
bring	brought	brought
build	built	built
burn	burned/burnt	burned/burnt
burst	burst	burst
buy	bought	bought
can	could	been able
catch	caught	caught
choose	chose	chosen
cling	clung	clung
come	came	come
dig	dug	dug
dive	dived/dove	dived
do	did	done
drag	dragged	dragged
draw	drew	drawn

dream	dreamed/dreamt	dreamed/dreamt
drink	drank	drunk
drive	drove	driven
eat	ate	eaten
fall	fell	fallen
feel	felt	felt
fight	fought	fought
find	found	found
fit	fit	fitted
flee	fled	fled
fling	flung	flung
fly	flew	flown
forbid	forbade	forbidden
forecast	forecast	forecast
forget	forgot	forgotten
forgive	forgave	forgiven
freeze	froze	frozen
get	got	got
give	gave	given
go	went	gone
grind	ground	ground
grow	grew	grown
hang	hanged/hung	hanged/hung
have	had	had
hear	heard	heard
hide	hid	hidden
hold	held	held
hurt	hurt	hurt
keep	kept	kept
kneel	knelt	knelt
know	knew	known
lay	laid	laid
lead	led	led
lean	leaned/leant	leaned/leant
leap	leaped/leapt	leaped/leapt
learn	learned/learnt	learned/learnt
leave	left	left
lend	lent	lent

let	let	let
lie	lay	lain
light	lighted/lit	lighted/lit
lose	lost	lost
make	made	made
may	might	
mean	meant	meant
meet	met	met
must	had to	had to
pay	paid	paid
prove	proved	proven/proved
put	put	put
read	read	read
ride	rode	ridden
ring	rang	rung
rise	rose	risen
run	ran	run
saw	sawed	sawed/sawn
say	said	said
see	saw	seen
seek	sought	sought
sell	sold	sold
sew	sewed	sewed/sewn
shake	shook	shaken
shall	should	
shine	shone	shone
shoot	shot	shot
show	showed	showed/shown
shrink	shrank	shrunk
shut	shut	shut
sing	sang	sung
sink	sank	sunk
sit	sat	sat
sleep	slept	slept
smell	smelled/smelt	smelled/smelt
sow	sowed	sowed/sown
speak	spoke	spoken
speed	speeded/sped	speeded/sped

spell	spelled/spelt	spelled/spelt
spend	spent	spent
spill	spilled/spilt	spilled/spilt
spin	spun	spun
spit	spat	spat
split	split	split
spread	spread	spread
spring	sprang	sprung
stand	stood	stood
steal	stole	stolen
stick	stuck	stuck
sting	stung	stung
strike	struck	struck
swear	swore	sworn
sweep	swept	swept
swim	swam	swum
swing	swung	swung
teach	taught	taught
tear	tore	torn
tell	told	told
think	thought	thought
throw	threw	thrown
tread	trod	trodden/trod
understand	understood	understood
wake	waked/woke	waked/woken
wear	wore	worn
weep	wept	wept
win	won	won
wind	wound	wound
wring	wrung	wrung
write	wrote	written

needs checking A problem had arose even before the discussion began.

revised A problem had arisen even before the discussion began.

needs checking In 1948 Newfoundlanders choose to join Canada.

revised In 1948 Newfoundlanders chose to join Canada.

needs checking	Thucydides analyzed the events that lead to the Peloponnesian war.
revised	Thucydides analyzed the events that led to the Peloponnesian war.
needs checking	The report laid on her desk until Thursday afternoon.
revised	The report lay on her desk until Thursday afternoon.
needs checking	The government's majority shrunk in the election.
revised	The government's majority shrank in the election.
needs checking	Pictures were taken while the royal couple swum in what they had thought was a private cove.
revised	Pictures were taken while the royal couple swam in what they had thought was a private cove.

10. DANGLING CONSTRUCTIONS

An error made with remarkable frequency by writers at all levels of ability—including holders of graduate degrees in English—is that of allowing large chunks of their sentences to "dangle," unrelated grammatically to the core of the sentence. For that reason several pages are devoted here to the problem of dangling grammatical constructions (also known as dangling modifiers).

Participles, gerunds, and infinitives may all be used to introduce phrases that modify a noun that forms the subject of an independent clause. In these pages we will focus on participles, which are involved in most dangling modifier errors.

A present participle is an *-ing* word (*going, thinking,* etc.). When combined with a form of the verb *to be,* participles form part of a finite verb. They can also be used in a number of ways on their own (as non-finite verbs), however:

• The president felt that visiting China would be unwise at that time.

> [Here *visiting China* acts as a noun phrase.]

- Having taken into account the various reports, the committee decided to delay the project for a year.

> [Here *having taken into account the various reports* acts as an adjectival phrase modifying the noun *committee*.]

The danger of dangling occurs with sentences such as the second example above. If the writer does not take care that the participial phrase refers to the subject of the main clause, the first chunk of the sentence will be left to dangle, unrelated grammatically to the rest of the sentence. That's what happens in this sentence:

- Having taken into account the various reports, the decision was made to delay the project for a year.

> [Here the noun *decision* is the subject of the main clause—but since the decision didn't do the taking into account, the adjectival phrase *having taken into account the various reports* dangles, with no noun to modify.]

This sort of problem is much more easily recognized in simpler sentences:

needs checking   Waiting for a bus, a brick fell on my head.
                   [Bricks do not normally wait for buses.]
revised   While I was waiting for a bus, a brick fell on my head.

needs checking   Leaving the room, the lights must be turned off.
                   [Lights do not normally leave the room.]
revised   When you leave the room you must turn off the lights.

needs checking   Walking around Whistler recently, help-wanted signs were everywhere
                   [Signs do not normally walk around the town.]
revised   When I was walking around Whistler recently, I saw help-wanted signs everywhere.

or   Help-wanted signs are visible everywhere these days in Whistler.

In sentences such as this one the absurdity is easy to notice; again, it is much more difficult to do so with longer and more complex sentences.

needs checking   Considering all the above-mentioned studies, the evidence shows conclusively that smoking can cause cancer.

revised   Considering all the above-mentioned studies, we conclude that smoking causes cancer.

better   These studies show conclusively that smoking can cause cancer.

needs checking   Turning for a moment to the thorny question of Joyce's style, the stream of consciousness technique realistically depicts the workings of the human mind.

[The stream should not be doing the turning.]

revised   Turning for a moment to the thorny question of Joyce's style, we may observe that his stream of consciousness technique realistically depicts the workings of the human mind.

better   Joyce's style does not make *Ulysses* easy to read, but his stream of consciousness technique realistically depicts the workings of the human mind.

needs checking   Considered from a cost point of view, Combo Capital Corporation could not really afford to purchase Skinflint Securities.

[Combo is not being considered; the purchase is.]

revised   Considered from the point of view of cost, the purchase of Skinflint Securities was not a wise move by Combo Capital Corporation.

better   Combo Capital Corporation could not really afford to buy Skinflint Securities.

needs checking Once regarded as daringly modern in its portrayal of fashionable *fin de siècle* decadence, Wilde draws on traditional patterns to create a powerful Gothic tale.

[The novel is an "it"; Oscar Wilde was a "he."]

revised *The Picture of Dorian Gray* was once regarded as daringly modern in its portrayal of fashionable *fin de siècle* decadence. In the novel Wilde draws on traditional patterns to create a powerful Gothic tale.

needs checking To conclude this essay, the French Revolution was a product of many interacting causes.

[The French Revolution concluded no essays.]

poor To conclude this essay, let me say that the French Revolution was a product of many causes.

better The explanations given for the French Revolution, then, are not mutually exclusive; it was a product of many interacting causes.

needs checking In reviewing the evidence, one point stands out plainly.

[A point cannot review evidence.]

poor In reviewing the evidence, we can see one point standing out plainly.

better One point stands out plainly from this evidence.

Notice that the best way to eliminate the problem of dangling constructions is often to dispense with the original phrase entirely.

Additional Material Online
Exercises on dangling constructions and on nouns and pronouns may be found at
sites.broadviewpress.com/writingcdn.
Click on **Exercises** and go to **M2.1** and **M2.3.**

11. NOUN AND PRONOUN DIFFICULTIES

(See also pages 94–96, 152–54.)

Nouns are words that name people, things, places, or qualities. The following words are all nouns: *boy*, *John*, *spaghetti*, *Zambia*, *silence*, *anger*.

Pronouns replace or stand for nouns. For example, instead of saying "The man slipped on a banana peel" or "George slipped on a banana peel," we can replace the noun *man* (or the noun *George*) with the pronoun *he* and say "He slipped on a banana peel." A discussion of some problems commonly experienced with nouns and pronouns follows.

11a. Singular and Plural Nouns

Some nouns are unusual in the way that a plural is formed. Here is a list of some that frequently cause mistakes:

appendix	appendixes or appendices
attorney general	attorneys general
bacterium	bacteria
basis	bases
court martial	courts martial
crisis	crises
criterion	criteria
curriculum	curricula
datum	data
ellipsis	ellipses
emphasis	emphases
erratum	errata
father-in-law	fathers-in-law
focus	focuses or foci
index	indexes or indices
matrix	matrixes or matrices
medium	media
millennium	millennia
nucleus	nuclei
parenthesis	parentheses

phenomenon	phenomena
referendum	referenda or referendums
runner-up	runners-up
stratum	strata
symposium	symposia
synthesis	syntheses
thesis	theses

needs checking The chief criteria on which an essay should be judged is whether or not it communicates clearly.

revised The chief criterion on which an essay should be judged is whether or not it communicates clearly.

needs checking This data proves conclusively that the lake is badly polluted.

revised These data prove conclusively that the lake is badly polluted.

needs checking The media usually assumes that the audience has a very short attention span.

revised The media usually assume that the audience has a very short attention span.

needs checking The great popularity of disco music was a short-lived phenomena.

revised The great popularity of disco music was a short-lived phenomenon.

11b. Singular Pronouns

The pronouns *anybody, anyone, each, each other, either, every, neither, nobody, no one, one another* are all singular. In order to be grammatically correct, they should therefore take singular verbs.

needs checking According to a poll of the electorate and the party, neither seem satisfied with the leader's performance.

revised According to a poll of the electorate and the party, neither seems satisfied with the leader's performance.

The particular case of balancing grammatical agreements, syntactical awkwardness, and issues of gender is discussed in Section 7a.

Following is a list of common indefinite pronouns:

> always plural: *both, many*
>
> always singular: *another, anybody, anyone, anything, each, either, every, everybody, everyone, everything, neither, nobody, no one, nothing, one, somebody, someone, something*
>
> singular or plural, depending on the context: *all, any, more, most, none, some*

- Some of the house is painted blue.
- Some of the houses on this street are painted blue.

11c. Unreferenced or Wrongly Referenced Pronouns

Normally a pronoun must refer to a noun in the previous sentence or clause.

needs checking	A herbalist knows a lot about the properties of plants. They can often cure you by giving you medicine.
revised	A herbalist knows a lot about the properties of plants. He can often cure you by giving you medicine.
better	Herbalists know a lot about the properties of plants. They can often cure you by giving you medicine.

Confusion can result if there is more than one possible referent for a pronoun.

needs checking	My father and my brother visited me early this morning. He told me that something important had happened.
revised	My father and my brother visited me early this morning. My father told me that something important had happened.

needs checking   The deficit was forecast to be $20 billion, but turned out to be over $200 billion. This reflected the government's failure to predict the increase in interest rates and the onset of a recession.
[This *what*?]

revised   The deficit was forecast to be $20 billion, but turned out to be over $200 billion. This vast discrepancy reflected the government's failure to predict the increase in interest rates and the onset of a recession.

11d. Subject and Object Pronouns

Different forms of certain pronouns are used depending on whether we are using them as a subject or an object. *I, we, he/she/it, they,* and *who* are subject pronouns, whereas *me, us, him/her/it, them,* and *whom* are object pronouns.

He shot the sheriff.
[Here the pronoun *he* is the subject of the sentence.]

The sheriff shot him.
[Here the word *him* is the object; the *sheriff* is the subject.]

That is the man who shot the sheriff.
[Here the pronoun *who* is the subject of the clause *who shot the sheriff.*]

That is the man whom the sheriff shot.
[Here the pronoun *whom* is the object; the *sheriff* is the subject.]

Perhaps as a result of the slang use of *me* as a subject pronoun ("Me and him got together for a few beer last night"), the impression seems to have lodged in many minds that the distinction between **I** and **me** is one of degree of politeness or formality rather than one of subject and object.

needs checking   There is no disagreement between you and I.

revised   There is no disagreement between you and me.

[Both *you* and *I* are here objects of the preposition *between*. "Between you and I" is no more correct than is "I threw the ball at he."]

Though the grammatical distinction between **who** and **whom** is in theory just as clear as the distinction between *I* and *me* or the distinction between *she* and *her*, in common usage it is much more blurred. The subject–object distinction in this case has largely broken down; the grammatically correct form often sounds awkward, and many authorities no longer insist on the distinction always being maintained. For example, even grammatical purists sometimes find themselves saying "I didn't know who I was talking to," even though the rules say it should be *whom* (subject—*I*; object—to *whom*).

12. ADJECTIVE AND ADVERB DIFFICULTIES

Adjectives are words used to tell us more about (*describe* or *modify*) nouns or pronouns. *Big, small, good, careful,* and *expensive* are all examples of adjectives. Adverbs are usually used to tell us more about (*describe* or *modify*) verbs, although they can also be used to modify adjectives or other adverbs. *Carefully, expensively, suddenly,* and *slowly* are all examples of adverbs. In conversation adjectives are often substituted for certain adverbs, but this should not be done in formal writing.

needs checking   She did good on the test.
revised   She did well on the test.

needs checking   He asked them not to talk so loud.
revised   He asked them not to talk so loudly.

needs checking   The governors thought it should be worded different.
revised   The governors thought it should be worded differently.

needs checking	They promised to do the job cheaper, easier, and quicker.
revised	They promised to do the job more cheaply, more easily, and more quickly.

12a. Comparatives and Superlatives

Most adjectives and adverbs have comparative and superlative forms; the comparative is used when comparing two things, the superlative when comparing three or more.

needs checking	Smith was the most accomplished of the two.
revised	Smith was the more accomplished of the two.

Always be careful not to construct double comparisons:

needs checking	Gandalf is much more wiser than Frodo.
revised	Gandalf is much wiser than Frodo.

13. COMPLETE AND INCOMPLETE SENTENCES

What constitutes a complete or incomplete sentence? What constitutes a run-on sentence, or a sentence fragment?

An incomplete sentence (or sentence fragment) is a group of words that has been written as if it were a complete sentence, but that, as a matter of grammatical correctness, needs something else to make it complete. If you write "And in the morning" and put a period after what you have written, the sentence has been left incomplete. It's a sentence fragment, not a complete sentence. Your reader will be left wondering "And in the morning, what?" Similarly, the group of words "When the meeting ends" cannot form a complete sentence on its own; grammatically, it is structured as a dependent (or subordinate) clause. Like independent clauses, dependent clauses include both a subject and a verb. Unlike independent clauses, though, they begin with a subordinating word. Subordinating conjunctions such as *because*, *although*, and *when* may be used in this way, as can relative pronouns such as *that*, *which*, and *whose*. To turn a dependent clause into a complete sentence, one can either transform it into an independent clause ("The meeting will end tomorrow") or attach it to a separate, independent clause ("When the meeting ends tomorrow, we should have a comprehensive agreement").

Focusing on the word "fragment," some people imagine incomplete sentences to be always very short. That's not the case. The idea of a sentence fragment is a grammatical concept, unrelated to how many words there may be in a phrase or clause; whether a sentence is complete or not is a matter of grammatical correctness, not a matter of sentence length. The first (quite short) group of words below forms a complete sentence, while the much longer group of words that follows is a sentence fragment:

> Marina walked to the sea.

> While Marina was walking to the sea and thinking of her father.

To correct the mistake here, one can either remove the subordinating conjunction *while*—

> Marina was walking to the sea and thinking of her father.

Or add an independent clause—

> While Marina was walking to the sea and thinking of her father, she heard the sound of a wood thrush.

In similar fashion, the grammatical concept of a run-on sentence is just that—a grammatical concept. A run-on sentence need not be long. Here is a very short example of a comma splice (one form of run-on sentence):

> Night fell, the moon rose.

To correct it, one can divide it into two sentences—

> Night fell. The moon rose.

or connect the two parts with a coordinating conjunction—

Night fell, and the moon rose.

or use a semi-colon rather than a comma to separate the independent clauses—

Night fell; the moon rose.

Let's look at four more examples:

Protests were widespread, but the authorities refused to back down.
[complete sentence—two independent clauses, joined by a coordinating conjunction (*but*)]

Although protests were widespread, the authorities refused to back down.
[complete sentence—subordinate clause (introduced by the subordinating conjunction *although*), followed by a main (or independent) clause]

Protests were widespread, however the authorities refused to back down.
[comma splice (a form of run-on sentence). *However* is a conjunctive adverb; if it is used to join independent clauses, it must be preceded by a semi-colon rather than a comma.]

The authorities refused to back down. Although protests were widespread.
[The second is an incomplete sentence—as a subordinating conjunction, *although* cannot introduce a clause that can stand independently as a complete sentence.]

Students often experience considerable frustration when faced with examples such as these. In all four cases the meaning is plain, yet—according to the conventional rules of English grammar and usage—only two of the four are correct. The distinctions among categories such as coordinating conjunctions, subordinating conjunctions, and coordinating adverbs—confusing enough in themselves—become understandably more confusing when the words involved mean more or less the same thing. It may seem hard not to feel that the definitions of *complete sentence* and *incomplete sentence* are, to the extent that they rely on such distinctions, purely arbitrary. Such feelings are not unreasonable. Yet those distinctions matter in the academic world and in the world of work; if you are able to understand and follow the conventions of English grammar and usage in your writing, it is sure to be noted and appreciated by many of your instructors and co-workers.

The question of what constitutes a complete sentence, then, is a highly complicated one. It involves the structures of English grammar (94–111) and the conventions governing the use of various joining words (19–20, 101–02), as well as the rules governing the use of periods, commas, and semi-colons (162, 163, 166). For a full understanding, we recommend you read all these sections, in addition to the material below. We recommend as well that you complete all of the interactive exercises that are included in the M1.3 section of the companion website for this book.

14. RUN-ON SENTENCES AND SENTENCE FRAGMENTS

14a. Run-on Sentences

A run-on sentence is a sentence that continues running on when, as a matter of grammatical correctness, it should be broken up into two or more sentences. Sometimes people use the expression *run-on sentence* loosely to refer to a sentence that is simply very long, regardless of whether or not it is grammatically correct. A well-constructed long sentence, though, can be an excellent means of expressing complex ideas; for the sake of clarity, then, it's important not to confuse the idea of a long sentence with the idea of a run-on sentence. The term *run-on sentence* should be used only when issues of grammatical correctness are involved.

One variety of run-on sentence (a **fused sentence**) occurs when independent clauses are not separated by any punctuation.

needs checking Early last Thursday we were walking in the woods it was a lovely morning.

revised Early last Thursday we were walking in the woods. It was a lovely morning.

A second (and more common) variety of run-on sentence occurs when a comma (rather than a period or a semi-colon) is used between independent clauses, without the addition of any coordinating conjunction. This type of run-on sentence is called a **comma splice**.

needs checking It was a lovely morning, we were walking in the woods.

revised It was a lovely morning. We were walking in the woods.

or It was a lovely morning, and we were walking in the woods.

In simple examples such as those above, the matter may seem straightforward. Sometimes, though, it is not so simple. The conventions of English dictate that only certain words may be used to join two independent clauses into one sentence. The seven coordinating conjunctions (*and, but, or, for, nor, so,* and *yet*) may be used to join independent clauses; other classes of joining words—notably, conjunctive adverbs—may not be used in the same way. Some of the words most commonly used as conjunctive adverbs are *also, besides, consequently, finally, hence, however, indeed, likewise, meanwhile, moreover, nevertheless, next, otherwise, still, then,* and *therefore.*[1]

---

1   A cautionary note: Categorizing words by their part-of-speech function is not always easy, since some words can function in more than one way. Notably, several of the words listed here that can function as conjunctive adverbs can also act as ordinary adverbs or as adjectives. In the sentence *Finally, we must consider taking concrete action* the word "finally" functions as a conjunctive adverb, whereas in the sentence *He was finally ready* the word "finally" functions as

When a coordinating conjunction is used to connect two independent clauses, then, you may combine them into a single sentence, with a comma separating the two clauses. But when a conjunctive adverb is used to indicate how the ideas of two independent clauses are connected to each other, you must use a period (or semi-colon) to separate the ideas from each other. They should not be "spliced" together with a comma:

needs checking   The temperature stayed below freezing, therefore the ice did not melt.

revised   The temperature stayed below freezing. Therefore, the ice did not melt.

or   The temperature stayed below freezing, so the ice did not melt.

> [The word *therefore* is a conjunctive adverb, not a coordinating conjunction; it thus may not be used to join independent clauses. The word *so* is a coordinating conjunction, and may thus be used to join independent clauses—provided that a comma is used as well.]

needs checking   You had better leave now, otherwise we'll call the police.

revised   You had better leave now. Otherwise, we'll call the police.

or   You had better leave now; otherwise, we'll call the police.

> [The word *otherwise* is a conjunctive adverb, not a coordinating conjunction, and thus may not be used to join independent clauses.]

---

an ordinary adverb modifying the adjective "ready." Similarly, in the sentence *Otherwise, thousands will die of starvation* the word "otherwise" functions as a conjunctive adverb, whereas in the sentence *She will respond quickly if she is not otherwise occupied* the word "otherwise" acts as an ordinary adverb modifying the adjective "occupied." Additional information on this topic (together with an interactive exercise) is included on the companion website.

needs checking With the exception of identical twins no two people have exactly the same genetic makeup, hence
it is impossible for two people to look exactly the
same.

revised With the exception of identical twins no two people have exactly the same genetic makeup. Hence,
it is impossible for two people to look exactly the
same.

or With the exception of identical twins no two people have exactly the same genetic makeup; hence,
it is impossible for two people to look exactly the
same.

needs checking During the rainy season more water flows over
Victoria Falls than over any other falls in the
world, however several other falls are higher than
Victoria.

revised During the rainy season more water flows over
Victoria Falls than over any other falls in the
world. However, several other falls are higher than
Victoria.

or During the rainy season more water flows over
Victoria Falls than over any other falls in the
world; several other falls, however, are higher than
Victoria.

needs checking Money was tight and jobs were scarce, therefore
she decided to stay in a job she did not like.

revised Money was tight and jobs were scarce; therefore,
she decided to stay in a job she did not like.

Notice in the above cases that one way to correct a comma
splice is often to use a semi-colon. Unlike a comma, a semi-
colon may be used as a connector between clauses. (The discussion of the semi-colon below may be helpful in this connection.)

The most common culprit when it comes to run-on sentences may well be the word *then*. The word *then* may act as an
ordinary adverb or as a conjunctive adverb, but it can never act
as a coordinating conjunction, and thus should not be used to

join two clauses together into one sentence. *And then* may be used, or a semi-colon, or a new sentence may be begun.

needs checking   We applied the solution to the surface of the leaves then we made observations at half-hour intervals.

revised   We applied the solution to the surface of the leaves. Then we made observations at half-hour intervals.

or   We applied the solution to the surface of the leaves; then we made observations at half-hour intervals.

or   We applied the solution to the surface of the leaves, and then we made observations at half-hour intervals.

needs checking   Yugoslav troops began withdrawing, then the NATO bombing was suspended and the war in Kosovo ended.

revised   Yugoslav troops began withdrawing. Then the NATO bombing was suspended and the war in Kosovo ended.

needs checking   The pilot checked the speedometer and the altimeter, then she knew what to do.

revised   The pilot checked the speedometer and the altimeter. Then she knew what to do.

or   The pilot checked the speedometer and the altimeter; then she knew what to do.

or   The pilot checked the speedometer and the altimeter, and then she knew what to do.

needs checking   The Montreal Canadiens produced vital goals early in the game, then they wrapped their iron defence around the Calgary Flames.

revised   The Montreal Canadiens produced vital goals early in the game, and then they wrapped their iron defence around the Calgary Flames.

or   The Montreal Canadiens produced vital goals early in the game; then they wrapped their iron defence around the Calgary Flames.

and and *but*: Almost every schoolchild is advised at some point that one should not begin a sentence with *and* or *but*. Many are taught to follow a more general rule—that one should not begin a sentence with any of the seven coordinating conjunctions (*and*, *but*, *for*, *nor*, *or*, *so*, *yet*). As we noted above in discussing coordinating conjunctions (pages 136 to 138), that advice is wrong, and that rule does not exist. It is perfectly correct to begin a sentence with *and* or *but* (or another of the coordinating conjunctions) so long as all the needed components of a complete sentence are present. Coordinating conjunctions may be used to join two independent clauses so as to make one sentence; they may also be used, however, as a pointer to the way in which the idea of one sentence connects to the idea of the previous one:

> Smith has written that Buckner's error led directly to Boston's World Series loss. **But that is not the way it happened.** Buckner's error was only one of several developments leading to Boston's loss in Game 6 of that series; the Red Sox still had to lose Game 7 to lose the series.

> Jones points out that the fact of the riot having broken out following the speech does not prove the speech caused the riot. **And he makes a fair point.** The order of events tells us nothing in itself; we have to look carefully at the content of the speech to understand the ways in which it was incendiary.

Notice that the bolded sentences above include both a subject ("that" in the "But" sentence, "he" in the "And" sentence) and a verb ("is" in the "But" sentence, "makes" in the "And" sentence). By way of contrast, consider the groups of words bolded below:

> Buckner's error occurred in the eighth inning. There was still the ninth inning to come. **And Game 7 the next day.**

> Ellis has said that he was willing to give Trump the benefit of the doubt before the assault on the Capitol. **But not now.**

The first group of bolded words does not include a verb; it cannot be a complete sentence. And the second group of bolded words includes neither a subject nor a verb; clearly it cannot be a complete sentence either. Whether or not a group of words forms a complete sentence, once again, depends simply on whether or not the elements needed to make a complete sentence are present; the fact that the group of words begins with *and* or *but* is not relevant.

The same is true of the other five coordinating conjunctions. Coordinating conjunctions can join independent clauses within a sentence—or they can start a new sentence:

> Real Madrid might certainly win the cup, as might Barcelona**, or** it might be won by a team that no one is now expecting to have a serious chance. [correct—the coordinating conjunction *or* has been used to join two independent clauses]

> Real Madrid might certainly win the cup, as might Barcelona. **Or** it might be won by a team that no one is now expecting to have a serious chance. [correct—the coordinating conjunction *or* has been used to begin a new sentence]

> In the 2019 Canadian election, the Conservatives won more votes than any of the other parties, **yet** the Liberals won the most seats. [correct—the coordinating conjunction *yet* has been used to join two independent clauses]

> In the 2019 Canadian election, the Conservatives won more votes than any of the other parties. **Yet** the Liberals won the most seats. [correct—the coordinating conjunction *yet* has been used to begin a new sentence]

If there is no prohibition on beginning a sentence with coordinating conjunctions such as *and* or *but*, neither is there any prohibition, as a matter of grammatical correctness, on including *and* or *but* several times within a single sentence. As a matter of style, however, the appearance of more than one *and* or more than one *but* in a single sentence is often a signal that the ideas might better be rephrased.

needs checking   Beaverbrook mobilized the resources of the country to serve the war effort overseas, and he later was
knighted, and he is also well-known for creating a
media empire.

> [So far as the rules of grammar are concerned,
> this cannot be classed as a run-on sentence;
> it is perfectly correct grammatically. But as a
> matter of style, the repetitive structure leaves
> much to be desired.]

revised   Beaverbrook mobilized the resources of the country to serve the war effort—an accomplishment
for which he later was knighted. He is also well-
known for creating a media empire.

or   Beaverbrook, who had created a vast media empire
before the war, then distinguished himself by
mobilizing the resources of the country to serve
the war effort. It was in recognition of this service
that he was knighted.

or   Beaverbrook, who had created a vast media empire
before the war, then distinguished himself by
mobilizing the resources of the country to serve
the war effort; it was in recognition of this service
that he was knighted.

14b. Sentence Fragments (Incomplete Sentences)

As we have seen, a grammatically complete sentence must
include both a subject and a verb. A group of words such as *in
a minute* or *from Toronto to Montreal* includes neither subject
nor verb; such groups of words are simply phrases. But nor can
groups of words such as *which I find very useful* or *if we finish in
time* be complete sentences; such groups of words do include
both a subject and a verb, but they are subordinate (or *dependent*) clauses—see pages 106–09. A grammatically complete
sentence must always include at least one independent clause.

Some sorts of sentence fragments might be classed as
"afterthought fragments"; the writer completes a sentence, and
then adds an afterthought:

needs checking Unemployment was a serious problem in Britain in the early 1990s. In fact, throughout the world.

revised Unemployment was a serious problem in Britain in the early 1990s. In fact, it was a serious problem throughout the world.

or Unemployment was a serious problem in the early 1990s—not just in Britain but throughout the world.

needs checking In Nathaniel Hawthorne's story "Young Goodman Brown," the main character chooses not to trust the members of his own community but instead to presume them to be corrupted by sin. Although he has no way of knowing if they are truly corrupted or not.

revised In Nathaniel Hawthorne's story "Young Goodman Brown," the main character chooses not to trust the members of his own community but instead to presume them to be corrupted by sin, although he has no way of knowing if they are truly corrupted or not.

or In Nathaniel Hawthorne's story "Young Goodman Brown," the main character chooses not to trust the members of his own community. Instead, he presumes them to be corrupted by sin, although he has no way of knowing if they are truly corrupted or not.

needs checking When asked to propose an appropriate punishment after having been convicted by an Athenian jury for having committed impious acts, Socrates suggests that he be provided with free meals at public expense. An award that was typically given to Olympic champions.

revised When asked to propose an appropriate punishment after having been convicted by an Athenian jury of having committed impious acts, Socrates suggests that he be provided with free meals at public expense, an award that was typically given to Olympic champions.

or   When asked to propose an appropriate punishment after having been convicted by an Athenian jury of having committed impious acts, Socrates suggests that he be provided with free meals at public expense—an award that was typically given to Olympic champions.

or   Socrates is asked to propose an appropriate punishment after he has been convicted by an Athenian jury of having committed impious acts. He suggests that he be provided with free meals at public expense—an award that was typically given to Olympic champions.

Notice that in the last two cases, the "afterthought fragment" is preceded by quite a long sentence. It's easy to imagine the writer of such sentences thinking "I've made this sentence pretty long already; I had better stop, and start a new sentence with my next thought." As a matter of style, it's certainly a good thing to pay attention to sentence length—and to vary the lengths of your sentences. But as the last example in each group above illustrates, there are many ways to vary sentence length while still writing entirely in grammatically correct sentences.

We have seen that a sentence fragment need not be short. Indeed, writers can often be led into writing grammatically incomplete sentences by becoming tangled in their thoughts when attempting to write a long sentence. While "afterthought fragments" tend to be short follow-ups after a long sentence, "tangle-thought fragments" are typically themselves quite long:

needs checking   In the event that interest rates remain low and the exchange rate remains favourable, Canadian companies that are contemplating export markets, so long as those markets are stable and the distribution channels are relatively efficient.

    [For all its length, this sentence lacks an independent clause.]

revised   In the event that interest rates remain low and the exchange rate remains favourable, Canadian companies can contemplate export markets with confidence, so long as those markets are stable and the distribution channels are relatively efficient.

or   Interest rates may well remain low and the exchange rate favourable. In that case, Canadian companies can contemplate export markets with confidence— so long as those markets are stable and the distribution channels are relatively efficient.

needs checking   While it is important to acknowledge the important role that Indigenous peoples have played within Canada, no less important, as a matter of historical accuracy as well as of fairness, acknowledging that national borders such as those separating Canada and the United States are, particularly in the case of Indigenous peoples, artificial borders.

revised   While it is important to acknowledge the important role that Indigenous peoples have played within Canada, it is no less important, as a matter of historical accuracy as well as of fairness, to acknowledge that national borders such as those separating Canada and the United States are, particularly in the case of Indigenous peoples, artificial borders.

or   While it is important to acknowledge the important role that Indigenous peoples have played within Canada, it is no less important to acknowledge that national borders such as those separating Canada and the United States are artificial borders. To recognize such artificiality is vitally important where Indigenous peoples are concerned; it's a matter of historical accuracy, and also a matter of fairness.

Here again we may notice that one can vary the length of one's sentences—and the order in which one's thoughts are presented—while being careful to write entirely in grammatically correct sentences.

because: As discussed above, many schoolchildren are given the erroneous impression that one should never begin a sentence with *and* or with *so*. So too with *because*—and the impression is erroneous here, too. The case of *because* is different from that of *and* and *so*, however. Whereas *and* and *so* are both coordinating conjunctions (see above, pages 101–02), *because* is a subordinating conjunction (see above, pages 102–03). A subordinating conjunction cannot be used to introduce an independent clause; subordinating conjunctions introduce dependent clauses. And as we have seen, a sentence with a dependent clause must also include an independent clause if the sentence is to be complete.

needs checking   The government decided to shut down virtually everything. Because of the pandemic.

> [*Because of the pandemic* is a phrase; it lacks both a subject and a verb.]

revised   The government decided to shut down virtually everything because of the pandemic.

or   Because of the pandemic, the government decided to shut down virtually everything.

needs checking   In the early 1980s, Sandinista leaders told their people to be ready for war. Because the United States had been trying to destabilize Nicaragua.

> [*Because the United States had been trying to destabilize Nicaragua* is a dependent clause.]

revised   In the early 1980s, Sandinista leaders told their people to be ready for war, because the United States had been trying to destabilize Nicaragua.

or   In the early 1980s, Sandinista leaders told their people to be ready for war; the United States had been trying to destabilize Nicaragua.

needs checking   Because of the cold and wet weather, which affected the whole area. Many people were desperately trying to find more firewood.

revised   Because of the cold and wet weather, which affected the whole area, many people were desperately trying to find more firewood.

or   The cold and wet weather affected the whole area; many people were desperately trying to find more firewood.

Notice in the above examples that it does not matter whether the word *because* comes at the beginning or in the middle of the sentence; what is important is that the sentence has two parts. And notice too that using a semi-colon to link two clauses where the meaning of the one follows from the meaning of the other can be an attractive alternative. (See also pages 102–03 and 107–09 regarding subordinate clauses and subordinating conjunctions, and pages 137–38 regarding use of the semi-colon.)

14c. Acceptable Sentence Fragments

Writing may be perfectly correct so far as the conventions of English grammar and usage are concerned, and nevertheless be in serious need of improvement: correctness is only one aspect of good writing. And sometimes, good writing may even include sentences that are grammatically incorrect. That is obviously the case with some works of fiction, in which an author may use stream-of-consciousness or other techniques in order to convey characters' thought processes to the reader. But it can also be true of essays and other forms of non-fiction. For skilled writers, the brevity of certain sorts of incomplete sentence may make for an effective means of emphasizing a point or of indicating a change of direction:

In baseball, a lead of four runs going into the ninth inning is a safe lead. **Not this time.**

Is the original film better than the re-make? **In every respect.**

Ellis has said that he was willing to give Trump the benefit of the doubt before the assault on the Capitol. **But not now.**

She wanted it to be a surprise. **A big surprise.**

A tumble on the basepaths by the Rays' best hitter, and two fielding errors by the Dodgers. That was how Game 4 of the 2020 World Series ended.

At the end of every day she felt tired. **Bone tired.**

Popular policies. A strong leader. An experienced staff. All the ingredients for an election victory seemed to be in place.

Contexts in which such writing may be considered appropriate occur far more frequently in informal writing than in formal writing—and instructors at the post-secondary level often disagree as to when it is acceptable to deviate in this sort of way from grammatical conventions. For those reasons, students are well advised to consult their instructors before making a habit of intentionally writing sentence fragments in formal academic writing.

15. EAL: FOR THOSE WHOSE NATIVE LANGUAGE IS NOT ENGLISH

Because of the differences in the ways that the structure of a student's own language may compare with English, students from different linguistic backgrounds are likely to want to focus on different aspects of English; what is particularly challenging for someone whose first language is Vietnamese may seem straightforward to someone whose first language is Spanish, and vice versa. For that reason the following information may be helpful:

- Many speakers of languages such as Chinese (in its various forms), Japanese, and Vietnamese are likely, as a result of the ways in which those languages differ structurally from English, to have particular difficulty with topics treated under the following headings in this chapter (and elsewhere in the book): articles (97, 150–53); infinitives (112); plurals (127–28, 150–53); word order (27–32, 158–59); conjugation of verbs, especially in the simple present tense (99–100, 112–16, 119–23).

- Many speakers of languages such as Russian, Polish, and Bulgarian are likely, as a result of the ways in which those languages differ structurally from English, to have particular difficulty with topics treated under the following headings in this chapter (and elsewhere in the book): articles (97, 150–53); omission of the predicate (107, 132–42); double negatives; the present perfect tense (116); word order (27–32, 158–59); possessives (98–99, 170–71); relative pronouns such as *who* and *which* (95–96); countable and uncountable nouns and words such as *much*, *many*, *little*, and *few* (152–53).

- Many speakers of languages such as French, Spanish, and Italian are likely, as a result of the ways in which those languages differ structurally from English, to have particular difficulty with topics treated under the following headings in this chapter (and elsewhere in the book): relative pronouns such as *who* and *which* (95–96); double negatives; comparatives and superlatives (132);

progressive (or continuous) verb tenses (155); word order (27–32, 158–59).

It is a measure of the degree to which English-speaking North Americans are unaccustomed to learning other languages that "ESL" (English as a Second Language) and "For Multilingual Writers" are the headings most often used when material of this sort is being covered. We prefer the term "EAL" (English as an Additional Language)—a term that that does not presume all native English speakers to be unilingual, and also a term that allows for the possibility that someone learning English may already know several other languages.

Given that there are so many rules in English—and so very many exceptions to many of these "rules," the best that can be done within the confines of a concise handbook is to focus on just a few areas that are particularly likely to cause problems for university-level EAL students. Beyond that, we strongly recommend to all such students that they keep a good EAL reference textbook and a good EAL dictionary handy—and that they read and write as much English of all sorts as possible. It's through reading and writing and speaking and listening that English is best learned—not by trying to memorize all the rules to which there are so very many exceptions.

15a. Articles (and Other Determiners)

Articles belong to a larger group of words known as *determiners*, or *markers*. Determiners are used with nouns; they help the reader or listener to determine which thing, person, place or idea is being referred to, and how many or how much is being referred to. Words such as *this, that, these,* and *those* can act as determiners, for example, as can *any, some, every, each, much, more, enough, a lot of*—and as can any number.

In English, articles (*a, an, the*) are the most frequently used determiners. Unlike many other languages, English often requires the use of articles.

needs checking	Remember to leave back door locked.
revised	Remember to leave the back door locked.

needs checking	Mount Everest is tallest mountain in world.
revised	Mount Everest is the tallest mountain in the world.

needs checking	We are interested in buying house with garage.
revised	We are interested in buying a house with a garage.

There are only three articles—*a*, *an*, and *the*. Articles show whether or not one is drawing attention to a particular person or thing. For example, we would say *I stood beside a house* if we did not want to draw attention to that particular house, but *I stood beside the house that the Taylors used to live in* if we wanted to draw attention to the specific house.

A (or *an* if the noun following begins with a vowel sound) is an indefinite article—used with singular nouns when you do not want to be definite or specific about which thing or person you are referring to. *The* is a definite article, used with singular or plural nouns when you do want to be definite or specific. Remember that, if you use *the*, you are suggesting that there can be only one or one group of what you are referring to.

needs checking	The magnolias are trees that have beautiful blossoms.
revised	Magnolias are trees that have beautiful blossoms.
	[The sentence refers to magnolias in general; no article is required for a plural of this sort.]

needs checking	Magnolias in Washington DC are often admired.
revised	The magnolias in Washington DC are often admired.
	[The sentence refers to a specific group of magnolias—those located in Washington, DC; the definite article is needed.]

Once something has been mentioned once, it can then become specific if it is mentioned subsequently.

needs checking	I drive red Kia; I bought car as soon as I moved here.
revised	I drive a red Kia; I bought the car as soon as I moved here.
	[The first time the car is mentioned it is an unspecified red Kia; the second time the definite article is used to indicate that the specific car already mentioned is the one being referred to.]

ARTICLES AND COUNT/NON-COUNT NOUNS

In order to understand the use of articles in English, it is important to understand the distinction English makes between nouns naming things that are countable (*houses, books, trees,* etc.) and nouns naming things that are not countable (*milk, confusion,* etc.). (A list of frequently-used non-count nouns appears below.) The indefinite article (*a, an*) can be used with singular count nouns (*a radio, an orange*). (Note that the indefinite article is not used with plural nouns.) The definite article *the* can be used both with singular and with plural count nouns (*the carpet, the horses*).

needs checking	She usually wears black hat at the funerals.
revised	She usually wears a black hat at funerals.

needs checking	Hat she is wearing now is same hat she wore at funeral last Thursday.
revised	The hat she is wearing now is the same hat she wore at the funeral last Thursday.

It is often not necessary to use an article before a non-count noun.

needs checking	Everyone needs the water to survive.
revised	Everyone needs water to survive.

needs checking	They were fighting for the justice.
revised	They were fighting for justice.

needs checking	He did not find the happiness until he stopped looking for it.
revised	He did not find happiness until he stopped looking for it.

But when a non-count noun is followed by a specifying phrase or clause (*the furniture in my house, the idea that she had*), the definite article (*the*) should be used.

needs checking	Water in that lake has evaporated; nothing but mud is left.
revised	The water in that lake has evaporated; nothing but mud is left.

needs checking	He did not find happiness that he had sought until he stopped looking for it.
revised	He did not find the happiness that he had sought until he stopped looking for it.

Some non-count nouns name things that it does seem possible to count (sugar, grass, furniture, etc.). In such cases counting must in English be done indirectly: *a grain of sugar, two grains of sugar, three blades of grass, four pieces of furniture*, and so on.

Distinguishing between count and non-count nouns is inevitably a challenge for those whose first language is not English. A dictionary such as *The Oxford Advanced Learner's Dictionary* can be very helpful; unlike most dictionaries it indicates whether or not each noun is a count noun.

needs checking	They bought a nice furniture.
revised	They bought a nice piece of furniture.

15b. Frequently Used Non-count Nouns

abstractions: advice, anger, beauty, confidence, courage, employment, equality, freedom*, fun, happiness, hate, health, honesty, ignorance, information, intelligence, justice, knowledge, love*, peace, poverty, satisfaction, truth*, violence, wealth, wisdom.

intellectual and artistic categories: art*, biology, computer science, literature*, music, painting (as an activity)*, philosophy*, physics, poetry, political science, research, science, sociology.

languages: Cantonese, Chinese, English, French, German, Italian, Japanese, Mandarin, Navajo, Portuguese, Russian, Shona, Swahili, etc.

food and drink: beef, beer, bread, broccoli, butter, cabbage, candy, cauliflower, celery, cereal, cheese, chicken, chocolate, coffee, corn, cream, fish, flour, fruit, ice, ice cream, lettuce, margarine, meat, milk, oil, pasta, pepper, quinoa, rice, salt, spinach, sugar, tea, tofu, water, wine, yogurt.

gases, liquids, etc.: air, blood, gas, gasoline, helium, lava, nitrogen, oxygen, petroleum, rain, smog, smoke*, snow, steam.

materials: aluminum, cement, cloth, clothing, coal, cotton, dirt, gold, grass, ice, lumber, metal, money, paper, plastic, steel, timber, wood, wool.

some others: equipment, furniture, homework, jewellery, luggage, machinery, mail, pollution, scenery, soap, traffic, transportation, weather, work.

Note that a number of words that are non-count nouns in most contexts may in some other contexts be used as count nouns; some of these are marked with an asterisk (*) in the above lists.

- Above all, they yearned for **freedom**.
- That country's constitution enshrines various **freedoms**, including freedom of speech and freedom of assembly.
- She discovered in her second year of university that her first love was **literature**.
- She became familiar with the **literatures** of each South American nation.

Note as well that the plural of many of these non-count nouns may be employed when you want to denote more than one type of the substance. Breads, for example, refers to different sorts of bread; coffees refers to different types of coffee; grasses to different types of grass, and so on.

15c. Continuous Verb Tenses

In English the continuous (or *progressive*) tenses are not normally used with many verbs having to do with feelings, emotions, or senses. Some of these verbs are *to see, to hear, to understand, to believe, to hope, to know, to think* (meaning *believe*), *to trust, to comprehend, to mean, to doubt, to suppose, to wish, to want, to love, to desire, to prefer, to dislike, to hate.*

needs checking	He is not understanding what I mean.
revised	He does not understand what I mean.

needs checking	At that time he was believing that everything on Earth was created within one week.
revised	At that time he believed that everything on Earth was created within one week.

15d. Omission or Repetition of the Subject

With the exception of imperatives (e.g., *Come here! Don't stop!*), where *you* is understood to be the subject, English requires that the subject of the sentence be stated. Some other languages permit the omission of the subject in various circumstances where the subject may be inferred. English does not.

needs checking	The protesters demonstrated peacefully; stood quietly outside the gates of the Prime Minister's residence.
revised	The protesters demonstrated peacefully; they stood quietly outside the gates of the Prime Minister's residence.

If the subject appears after the verb, a frequent requirement in English is for *there* or *it* to be added as an expletive before the verb *to be.*

needs checking	Is not possible to finish the job this week.
revised	It is not possible to finish the job this week.

needs checking	By the end of the twentieth century, were almost 700,000 more people in Vancouver than there had been in 1980.
revised	By the end of the twentieth century, there were almost 700,000 more people in Vancouver than there had been in 1980.

Within a single clause English does not permit the repetition of either the subject or the object.

needs checking	The line that is longest it is called the hypotenuse.
revised	The line that is longest is called the hypotenuse.

needs checking	The members of the cast loved the play that they were acting in it.
revised	The members of the cast loved the play that they were acting in.

15e. The Conditional

Particular rules apply in English when we are speaking of actions which *would happen if* certain conditions were fulfilled. Here are some examples.

If I *went* to Australia, I *would have* to fly.

If I *drank* a lot of gin, I *would be* very sick.

I *would lend* Joe the money he wants if I *trusted* him.

Each of these sentences is made up of a main clause in which the conditional *would have*, *would be*, etc. is used, and a subordinate clause beginning with *if*, with a verb in the simple past tense (*went, drank, trusted*). In all cases the action named in the *if* clause is considered by the speaker to be unlikely to happen, or quite impossible. The first speaker does not really think that she will go to Australia; she is just speculating about what would be necessary if she did go. Similarly, the second speaker does not expect to drink a lot of gin, and the third speaker does not trust Joe. Situations like these, which are not happening and which we do not expect to happen are called *hypothetical situations*; we speculate on what *would* happen *if* but we do not expect the *if* to come true.

If we think the *if* is indeed likely to come true, then we use the future tense instead of the conditional in the main clause, and the present tense in the subordinate *if* clause, as in these examples:

> If I drink a lot of gin I will be very sick.
>> [The speaker thinks it quite possible that he will drink a lot of gin.]

> If I go to Australia, I will have to fly.
>> [The speaker thinks that she may really go.]

Some writers mistakenly use the conditional or the present tense (instead of the past tense form) in the *if* clause when they are using the conditional in the main clause:

needs checking   If I want to buy a car, I would look carefully at all the models available.

revised   If I wanted to buy a car, I would look carefully at all the models available.
>> [The speaker does not want to buy a car.]

or   If I want to buy a car, I will look carefully at all the models available.
>> [The speaker may really want to buy a car.]

needs checking   If the authorities would find out what happened, both boys would be in serious trouble.

revised   If the authorities found out what happened, both boys would be in serious trouble.

or   If the authorities were to find out what happened, both boys would be in serious trouble.

Similar problems occur with the past conditional:

needs checking   If the Titanic would have carried more lifeboats, hundreds of lives would have been saved.

revised   If the Titanic had carried more lifeboats, hundreds of lives would have been saved.

> **Additional Material Online**
> Exercises on the conditional may be found at
> **sites.broadviewpress.com/writingcdn**.
> Click on **Exercises** and go to **M2.1**,
> **"Verbs and Verb Issues."**

15f. Word Order

WORD ORDER (SUBJECT/VERB/OBJECT)

The rules governing word order in English are much more rigid than those of many other languages. For one thing, the subject, verb, and object normally appear in that order. Many other languages permit far more freedom in the ordering of subject, object, and verb, and for that reason this basic structural element of English can be difficult to grasp.

needs checking   Yoshiki opportunities always welcomes.
revised   Yoshiki always welcomes opportunities.
      [Note: Speakers of languages such as Japanese and Korean, in which the verb must always come last in a sentence, are particularly likely to experience this sort of difficulty with English.]

needs checking   Opportunities welcomes Yevgeny always.
revised   Yevgeny always welcomes opportunities.
      [Note: Speakers of languages such as Russian, in which the object may appear before the subject, are particularly likely to experience this sort of difficulty with English.]

In most Romance languages object pronouns come before the verb. This often creates difficulties for native speakers of those languages with the word order required in English, where object pronouns normally follow the verb.

needs checking   When we these give him, he will be very grateful.
revised   When we give him these, he will be very grateful.

WORD ORDER OF QUESTIONS

The word order of questions in English presents several difficulties for most EAL students, primarily because different sorts of questions require different changes to the standard word order of English statements. Questions can be divided into two main categories: yes-no questions and interrogative-word questions. These two main categories can be further subdivided into three categories each (with a one-word form of the verb *to be*; with any other one-word verb; with a multi-word verb).

yes-no questions
Yes-no questions are those that invite a *yes* or *no* answer. Again, they can feature a one-word form of the verb *to be*, any other one-word verb, or a multi-word verb. In each of these cases, word order is handled differently.

> In questions involving one-word forms of *to be*, the usual order of subject-verb is reversed. The statement *The movie is worth watching* puts the subject (*The movie*) first, whereas the question *Is the movie worth watching?* puts the verb (*is*) before the subject.
>
> If a question has a multi-word verb, only the first part of the verb is put before the subject; in the question *Is that car going over the speed limit?* the first part (*Is*) of the verb (*Is going*) is put before the subject (*that car*).
>
> A stranger case occurs if a question uses a one-word form of any verb other than *to be*. In such questions, a form of the auxiliary verb *to do* is added to the verb, and it is this form of *to do* that is put before the subject: *Did she turn left?* (the verb *turn* becomes *did turn*, and *did* is moved to the front of the sentence); *Does he always wear green?* (the verb *wear* becomes *does wear*, and *does* is moved to the front of the sentence).

Notice with multi-word verbs that, regardless of whether they include the auxiliary to do or not, it is only the first part of the verb that carries the tense. The second part takes either the base infinitive or a participial form, depending on the type of verb.

| *needs checking* | Did she went outside? |
| *revised* | Did she go outside? |

| *needs checking* | Are you sit comfortably? |
| *revised* | Are you sitting comfortably? |

interrogative-word questions

Questions that use interrogative words (what, where, when, why, which, who, how) begin with the interrogative and then follow the word order specified above for the three categories of verbs: When were you here? (the verb *were* goes before the subject *you*); Why has he turned around? (the first part of the verb *has turned* goes before the subject *he*); Which flavour do you want? (the auxiliary *do* is added to the verb *want*, and *do* is then put before the subject *you*).

| *needs checking* | What you are doing? |
| *revised* | What are you doing? |

PUNCTUATION

16. THE PERIOD

The period (or full stop) is used to close sentences that make statements. Common difficulties with run-on sentences and incomplete sentences are discussed above in the section on grammar.

Notice that when a question is reported in indirect speech it has the form of a statement, and the sentence should therefore be closed with a period:

needs checking   He asked what time it was?
revised   He asked what time it was.

The period is also used to form abbreviations (*Mr.*, *Ms.*, *Hon.*, *Ph.D.*, *A.M.*, *P.M.*, *Inc.*, etc.). If you are in any doubt about whether or not to use a period in an abbreviation, or where to put it, think of the full form of what is being abbreviated.

needs checking   Jones, Smithers, et. al. will be there in person.
                   [*et al.* is short for the Latin *et alia*, "and others."]
revised   Jones, Smithers, et al. will be there in person.

17. THE COMMA

The comma is used to indicate pauses, and to give the reader cues as to how the parts of the sentence relate to one another.

needs checking   Because of the work that we had done before we were ready to hand in the assignment.
revised   Because of the work that we had done before, we were ready to hand in the assignment.

The omission or addition of a comma can completely alter the meaning of a sentence—as it did in the Queen's University Alumni letter that spoke of the warm emotions still felt by alumni for "our friends, who are dead."

17a. Commas and Non-restrictive Elements

There is a significant difference of meaning between the following two sentences:

> The dancers who wore black looked very elegant.

> The dancers, who wore black, looked very elegant.

In the first sentence, the words *who wore black* restrict the meaning of the noun *dancers*; the implication is that also present were dancers not wearing black, and perhaps looking rather less elegant. In the second sentence the words *who wore black* are set off in commas. This signifies that they do not act to restrict the meaning of the noun *dancers*. Instead, they add information that must be assumed to apply to the entire group; we infer that all the dancers wore black.

One important use of commas, then, is to set off non-restrictive elements of sentences:

restrictive	A company that pays no attention to its customers is unlikely to survive.
non-restrictive	The local grocery, which is always attentive to its customers, has been a fixture for generations.
restrictive	The man with abdominal pains was treated before any of the others.
non-restrictive	Mr. Smith, who suffered from abdominal pains, was treated before the others.
restrictive	The film *Chinatown* is in many ways reminiscent of films of the 1950s.
non-restrictive	Polanski's seventh film in English, *Chinatown*, is regarded by many as the finest film ever made.

Notice that the commas here come in pairs. If a non-restrictive element is being set off in the middle of a sentence, it must be set off on both sides.

needs checking	My sister Caroline, has done very well this year in her studies.
revised	My sister, Caroline, has done very well this year in her studies.

needs checking	The snake which had been killed the day before, was already half-eaten by ants.
revised	The snake, which had been killed the day before, was already half-eaten by ants.

17b. That and Which

It is correct to use *that* in restrictive clauses and *which* in non-restrictive clauses.

needs checking	The only store which sells this brand is now closed.
revised	The only store that sells this brand is now closed.

needs checking	The position which Marx adopted owed much to the philosophy of Hegel.
revised	The position that Marx adopted owed much to the philosophy of Hegel.

Although the use of the word *which* in any restrictive clause provokes a violent reaction among some English instructors, there are some instances in which one may be justified in using *which* in this way. Such is the case, for example, when the writer is already using at least one *that* in the sentence:

needs checking	He told me that the radio that he had bought was defective.
revised	He told me that the radio which he had bought was defective.

17c. Extra Comma

Commas should follow the grammatical structure of a sentence; you should not throw in a comma simply because a sentence is getting long.

needs checking	The ever increasing gravitational pull of the global economy, is drawing almost every area of the Earth into its orbit.
revised	The ever increasing gravitational pull of the global economy is drawing almost every area of the Earth into its orbit.

17d. Commas and Lists

An important use of commas is to separate the entries in lists. Some authorities feel that a comma need not appear between the last and second last entries in a list, since these are usually separated already by the word *and*. Omitting the last comma in a series, however, will occasionally lead to ambiguity. When in doubt, it is generally best to include the serial comma.

needs checking	The book is dedicated to my parents, Ayn Rand and God.
revised	The book is dedicated to my parents, Ayn Rand, and God.

When a list includes items that have commas within them, use a semi-colon to separate the items in the list.

needs checking	The three firms involved were McCarthy and Walters, Harris, Jones, and Engelby, and Cassells and Wirtz.
revised	The three firms involved were McCarthy and Walters; Harris, Jones, and Engelby; and Cassells and Wirtz.

18. THE QUESTION MARK

Any direct question should be followed by a question mark.

needs checking	Would Britain benefit from close ties with Europe. As Brexit recedes further into the past, the question continues to bedevil British political life.

revised   Would Britain benefit from close ties with Europe? As Brexit recedes further into the past, the question continues to bedevil British political life.

If a polite request is couched as a question, a question mark is appropriate.

needs checking   Would you please make sure the pages are in proper order.

revised   Would you please make sure the pages are in proper order?

Sometimes, though, polite inquiries are expressed grammatically in the form of statements rather than questions—in which case the punctuation should follow suit:

needs checking   I wondered if you might have fifteen minutes available later today to discuss Carson's proposal?

revised   I wondered if you might have fifteen minutes available later today to discuss Carson's proposal.

or   Might you have fifteen minutes available later today to discuss Carson's proposal?

19. THE EXCLAMATION MARK

This mark is used to give extremely strong emphasis to a statement or a command. It is often used in personal or business correspondence, but it should be used very sparingly, if at all, in formal written work.

20. THE SEMI-COLON

The chief use of the semi-colon is to separate independent clauses whose ideas are closely related to each other. In most such cases a period could be used instead; the semi-colon simply signals to the reader the close relationship between the two ideas.

correct   The team is not as good as it used to be. It has lost
             four of its five last games.

also correct   The team is not as good as it used to be; it has lost
             four of its five last games.

As discussed elsewhere in this book (pages 137–38) the semi-colon may often be used to correct a comma splice. The semi-colon is also used to divide items in a series that includes other punctuation:

> The following were told to report to the coach after practice: Jackson, Form 2B; Marshall, Form 3A; Jones, Form 1B.

21. THE COLON

This mark is often believed to be virtually the same as the semi-colon in the way it is used. In fact, there are some important differences. The most common uses of the colon are as follows:

- in headings or titles to announce that more is to follow, or that the writer is about to list a series of things
- after an independent clause to introduce a quotation
- after an independent clause to indicate that what follows provides an explanation[1]

Here are some examples:

> *Unquiet Union: A Study of the Federation of Rhodesia and Nyasaland.*

> In the last four weeks he has visited five different countries: Mexico, Venezuela, Panama, Haiti, and Belize.

> The theory of the Communists may be summed up in the single phrase: abolition of private property.

---

1   This use is very similar to the main use of the semi-colon. The subtle differences are that the semi-colon can be used in such situations when the ideas are not quite so closely related, and the colon asks the reader to pause for a slightly longer period.

Be sure to use a colon to introduce a list.

needs checking   The dealership has supplied Mr. Bomersbach with four luxury cars, two Cadillacs, a Mercedes, and a Jaguar.

revised   The dealership has supplied Mr. Bomersbach with four luxury cars: two Cadillacs, a Mercedes, and a Jaguar.

22. THE HYPHEN

This mark may be used to separate two parts of a compound word (e.g., *tax-free*, *hand-operated*). Notice that many such combinations are only hyphenated when they are acting as an adjective:

No change is planned for the short term.

> [*Term* here acts as a noun, with the adjective *short* modifying it.]

This is only a short-term plan.

> [Here the compound *short-term* acts as a single adjective, modifying the noun *plan.*]

The course will cover the full range of nineteenth-century literature.

> [Here the compound *nineteenth-century* acts as a single adjective, modifying the noun *literature.*]

The course will cover the full scope of literature in the nineteenth century.

> [*Century* acts here as a noun, with the adjective *nineteenth* modifying it.]

Hyphens are also used to break up words at the end of a line. When they are used in this way, hyphens should always be placed between syllables. Proper nouns (i.e., nouns beginning with a capital letter) should not be broken up by hyphens.

23. THE DASH

Dashes are often used in much the same way as parentheses, to set off an idea within a sentence. Dashes, however, call attention to the set-off idea in a way that parentheses do not:

> Taipei 101 (then the tallest building in the world) was completed in 2005.

> Taipei 101—then the tallest building in the world—was completed in 2005.

A dash may also be used in place of a colon to set off a word or phrase at the end of a sentence:

> He fainted when he heard how much he had won: one million dollars.
> He fainted when he heard how much he had won—one million dollars.

When typing, you may in most programs use two hyphens (with no space before or after them) to form an "em dash." Some programs also allow you to create an em dash with other keys.

More sophisticated word processing programs (and all typesetting programs) have a separate function for creating an "en dash." That is a dash used in giving a span of numbers—especially dates or ages (e.g., 1924–2009). It is somewhat shorter than an em dash, but somewhat longer than a hyphen. As with the em dash, there should be no extra space before or after an en dash.

24. PARENTHESES

Parentheses are used to set off an interruption in the middle of a sentence, or to make a point which is not part of the main flow of the sentence. They are frequently used to give examples, or to express something in other words. Example:

Several world leaders of the 1980s (Deng in China, Reagan in the US, etc.) were very old men.

25. SQUARE BRACKETS

Square brackets are used for parentheses within parentheses, or to show that the words within the parentheses are added to a quotation by another person.

Lentricchia claims that "in reading James' Preface [to *What Maisie Knew*] one is struck as much by what is omitted as by what is revealed."

26. THE APOSTROPHE

The two main uses of the apostrophe are to show possession (e.g., "Peter's book") and to shorten certain common word combinations (e.g., *can't, shouldn't, he's*).

26a. Contractions

Contractions should be avoided in formal written work. Use *cannot*, not *can't*; *did not*, not *didn't*; and so on.

informal	The experiment wasn't a success, because we'd heated the solution to too high a temperature.
more formal	The experiment was not a success, because we had heated the solution to too high a temperature.

26b. Possession
(See also **its/it's**, page 351.)

The correct placing of the apostrophe to show possession can be a tricky matter. When the noun is singular, the apostrophe must come before the s (e.g., *Peter's, George's, Canada's*), whereas when the noun is plural and ends in an *s* already, the apostrophe comes after the *s*.

worth checking	His parent's house is filled with antiques.
revised	His parents' house is filled with antiques.
	[Note that no apostrophe is needed when a plural is not possessive.]

needs checking	His parent's were away for the weekend.
revised	His parents were away for the weekend.

When a singular noun already ends in *s*, authorities differ as to whether or not a second *s* should be added after the apostrophe:

correct	Ray Charles' music has been very influential.
correct	Ray Charles's music has been very influential.

Whichever convention a writer chooses, he should be consistent. And be sure in such cases not to put the apostrophe before the first *s*.

needs checking	Shield's novel is finely, yet delicately constructed.
	[concerning novelist Carol Shields]
revised	Shields' novel is finely, yet delicately constructed.
	[or "Shields's novel"]

27. QUOTATION MARKS

The main use of quotation marks is to show that the exact words that a person has spoken or written are being repeated:

> "I don't know anyone called Capone," she told the court.

> "I will not make age an issue of this campaign," Ronald Reagan famously remarked when running for president at the age of 73. "I am not going to exploit, for political purposes, my opponent's youth and inexperience," he added.

While the principle of using quotation marks in these ways is straightforward, in practice it is often easy to go wrong. For a discussion of some of the details, see "Direct and Indirect Speech" below (pages 174–78); for a discussion of how to integrate quotations into written work, see the sections on MLA Style and APA Style (pages 224–31 and 278–86).

27a. Other Uses of Quotation Marks

According to different conventions, words that are being mentioned rather than used may be set off by quotation marks, single quotation marks, or italics:

> The words "except" and "accept" are sometimes confused.

> The words 'except' and 'accept' are sometimes confused.

> The words *except* and *accept* are sometimes confused.

Quotation marks (or single quotation marks) are sometimes also used to indicate that the writer does not endorse the quoted statement, claim, or description. Quotation marks are usually used in this way only with a word or brief phrase. When so used they have the connotation of *supposed* or *so-called*; they suggest that the quoted word or phrase is either euphemistic or downright false:

> After a workout the weightlifters would each consume a "snack" of a steak sandwich, half a dozen eggs, several pieces of bread and butter, and a quart of tomato juice.

In the following two versions of the same report the more sparing use of quotation marks in the second version signals clearly to the reader the writer's scepticism as to the honesty of the quoted claim.

> President Charez appeared to stagger as he left the plane. "The President is feeling tired and emotional," his Press Secretary later reported.

> A "tired and emotional" President Charez appeared to stagger as he left the plane.

27b. Misuse of Quotation Marks to Indicate Emphasis

Quotation marks (unlike italics, bold letters, capital letters, or underlining) should never be used to try to lend emphasis to a particular word or phrase. Because quotation marks may be used to convey the sense *supposed* or *so-called* (see above), the common misuse of quotation marks to try to lend emphasis often creates ludicrous effects.

needs checking	All our bagels are served "fresh" daily.
	[The unintended suggestion here is that the claim of freshness is a dubious one.]
revised	All our bagels are served fresh daily.
or	All our bagels are served **fresh** daily.
	[if emphasis is required in an advertisement]

27c. Single Quotation Marks

In North America the main use of single quotation marks is to mark quotations within quotations:

> According to the Press Secretary, "When the Minister said, 'I never inhaled,' he meant it."

Depending on convention, single quotation marks may also be used to show that a word or phrase is being mentioned rather than used (see 27a above).

In the United Kingdom and some other countries, quotation marks and single quotation marks are used for direct speech in precisely the opposite way that North Americans use them; single quotation marks (or inverted commas, as they are sometimes called) are used for direct speech, and double marks are used for quotations within quotations. Here is the correct British version of the above sentence:[1]

> According to the Press Secretary, 'When the Minister said, "I never inhaled", he meant it'.

---

1   Note that it is also conventional in British usage to place closing punctuation *outside* closing quotation marks—though this convention is no longer universally followed.

27d. Direct and Indirect Speech

i) Direct speech

The main rules for writing direct speech in English are as follows:

- The exact words spoken—and no other words—must be surrounded by quotation marks.
- A comma should precede a quotation, but according to North American convention other punctuation should be placed inside the quotation marks. Examples:

    - He said, "I think I can help you."
        (The period after *you* comes before the quotation marks.)
    - "Drive slowly," she said, "and be very careful."
        (The comma after *slowly* and period after *careful* both come inside the quotation marks.)

With each change in speaker a new paragraph should begin. Example:

"Let's go fishing this weekend," Mary suggested. "It should be nice and cool by the water."

"Good idea," agreed Faith. "I'll meet you by the store early Saturday morning."

Canadian usage demands that *all* punctuation go inside the quotation marks in quotations that are stand-alone sentences:

- "An iron curtain is descending across Europe," declared Winston Churchill in 1946.

At the same time, Canadian usage allows writers either to follow the American convention or to make an exception when the punctuation clearly pertains only to the structure of the surrounding sentence, not to the quoted word or phrase:

- Was it Churchill who described the post-war divide between newly Communist Eastern Europe and the West as "an iron curtain"?

The most common difficulties experienced when recording direct speech are as follows:

omission of quotation marks: This happens particularly frequently at the end of a quotation.

needs checking	She said, "I will try to come to see you tomorrow. Then she left.
revised	She said, "I will try to come to see you tomorrow." Then she left.

placing punctuation outside the quotation marks:

needs checking	He shouted, "The house is on fire"!
revised	He shouted, "The house is on fire!"

including the word *that* before direct speech: *That* is used before passages of indirect speech, not before passages of direct speech.

needs checking	My brother said that, "I think I have acted stupidly."
revised	My brother said, "I think I have acted stupidly."
or	My brother said that he thought he had acted stupidly.

needs checking	The official indicated that, "we are not prepared to allow galloping inflation."
revised	The official said, "We are not prepared to allow galloping inflation."
or	The official indicated that his government was not prepared to allow galloping inflation.

when to indent: In a formal essay, any quotation longer than four lines[1] should normally be single-spaced and indented to set it off from the body of the text. Any quotation of more than three lines from a poem should also be single-spaced and indented. Quotations set off from the body of the text in this way should not be preceded or followed by quotation marks.

---

1   This is what the MLA recommends; the APA specifies up to forty words, and *The Chicago Manual of Style* up to one hundred words.

needs checking Larkin's "Days" opens with childlike simplicity: "What are days for? / Days are where we live. / They come, they wake us / Time and time over." But with Larkin, the shadow of mortality is never far distant.

revised Larkin's "Days" opens with childlike simplicity:

>What are days for?
>
>Days are where we live.
>
>They come, they wake us
>
>Time and time over.

But with Larkin, the shadow of mortality is never far distant.

ii) Indirect speech

Indirect speech reports what was said without using the same words that were used by the speaker. The rules for writing indirect speech are as follows:

• Do not use quotation marks.

• Introduce statements with the word *that*, and do not put a comma after *that*. Questions should be introduced with the appropriate question word (*what, why, whether, if, how, when*, etc.).

• First-person pronouns and adjectives (e.g., *I, me, we, us, my, our*) must often be changed to third person (*he, she, they, him, her, them*, etc.) if the subject of the main clause is in third person.

correct "I am not happy with our team's performance," said Paul.

also correct Paul said that he was not happy with his team's performance.

correct I said, "I want my money back."

also correct I said that I wanted my money back.

[Here the subject, *I*, is first person.]

• Second-person pronouns must also sometimes be changed.

• Change the tenses of the verbs to agree with the main verb of the sentence. Usually this involves moving the verbs one step back into the past from the tenses used by the speaker in direct speech. Notice in the first example above, for instance, that the present tense *am* has been changed to the past tense *was* in indirect speech. Here are other examples:

correct	"We will do everything we can," he assured me.
correct	He assured me that they would do everything they could.
	[*Will* and *can* change to *would* and *could*.]
correct	"You went to school near Brandon, didn't you?" he asked me.
correct	He asked me if I had gone to school near Brandon.
	[*Went* changes to *had gone*. Note that questions reported in indirect speech are not punctuated with a question mark.]

- Change expressions having to do with time. This is made necessary by the changes in verbs discussed above. For example, *today* in direct speech normally becomes *on that day* in indirect speech, *yesterday* becomes *on the day before*, and so on.

The most common problems experienced when indirect speech is being used are as follows:

confusion of pronouns: Many writers do not remember to change all the necessary pronouns when shifting from direct to indirect speech.

- When I met him he said, "You have cheated me." (direct)

needs checking	When I met him he said that you had cheated me.
revised	When I met him he said that I had cheated him.

- He will probably say to you, "I am poor. I need money."

needs checking	He will probably tell you that he is poor and that I need money.
revised	He will probably tell you that he is poor and that he needs money.

verb tenses: Remember to shift the tenses of the verbs one step back into the past when changing something into indirect speech.

- She said, "I will check my tires tomorrow."

needs checking   She said that she will check her tires the next day.
revised   She said that she would check her tires the next day.

• "Can I go with you later this afternoon?" he asked.

needs checking   He asked if he can go with us later that afternoon.
revised   He asked if he could go with us later that afternoon.

28. ELLIPSES

An ellipsis is made up of three spaced periods. In narrative writing an ellipsis may be used to indicate a pause or to show that a sentence or thought has not been completed:

"I can't think why you...." Denise left the rest unsaid.

In academic writing ellipses are frequently used with quoted material: three dots are used to indicate the omission of one or more words needed to complete a sentence or other grammatical construction. Note that when used in a quotation an ellipsis comes inside the quotation marks, and that when an ellipsis precedes a period the sentence should end with four dots. If an ellipsis is used to indicate a deletion of more than a sentence of material in the middle of a passage, a period should appear before the three ellipsis dots—again, making a total of four dots.

As a general rule, an ellipsis is not necessary at the beginning or at the end of a quotation; it is understood that a passage of quoted text will have been preceded by other material, and be followed by other material. If, however, you are changing a letter from upper case to lower case at the beginning of a quotation, MLA and some other styles specify that this should be indicated with square brackets:

Barrie conveys a vivid sense of the shadow as a physical presence:

[U]nfortunately Mrs. Darling could not leave it hanging out at the window. It looked so like the washing

> and lowered the whole tone of the house.... She
> decided to roll the shadow up and put it carefully
> away in a drawer....

In the passage quoted, the word "unfortunately" does not begin the sentence; hence the square brackets around the capital letter. In the passage quoted there is also material that follows "in a drawer" before the end of that sentence; hence the second ellipsis. (See pages 218–19 and 285 for more on MLA and APA styles and ellipses.)

It is of course vitally important that ellipses not be used to distort the meaning of a passage.

needs checking "I ... believe that these people are either English or Jewish because they are endowed with certain innate qualities," Shapiro writes in his introduction to *Shakespeare and the Jews* (4).

revised "I do not believe that these people are either English or Jewish because they are endowed with certain innate qualities," Shapiro writes in his introduction to *Shakespeare and the Jews* (4).

FORMAT
AND SPELLING

29. CAPITALIZATION

Proper nouns (naming specific persons, places, or things) should always be capitalized. Common nouns are not normally capitalized. Here are a few examples:

PROPER	COMMON
June	summer
House of Commons	a large house
Mother (used as a name)	my mother
Memorial Day	as a memorial
National Gallery	a gallery
Director of Admissions	a director
Professor Colacurcio	a professor
the Enlightenment	the eighteenth century
the Restoration (historical period in England)	the restoration (other uses of the word)
the Renaissance	a renaissance
God	a god
Catholic (belonging to that particular church)	catholic (meaning *wide-ranging* or *universal*)
a Liberal (belonging to the Liberal Party—such as the Liberal Party of Australia or the Liberal Party of Canada)	a liberal (holding liberal ideas)
a Democrat (belonging to the Democratic Party)	a democrat (believing in democratic ideals)

Names of academic subjects are not capitalized (unless they are names of languages).

Major words in the titles of books, articles, stories, poems, films, and so on should be capitalized; articles, short prepositions, and conjunctions are not normally capitalized unless they are the first word of a title or subtitle.

needs checking She became a Director of the company in 2015.
revised She became a director of the company in 2015.
or She became a member of the Board of Directors in 2015.

needs checking	Robert Boardman discusses *The Bridge On The River Kwai* extensively in his book.
revised	Robert Boardman discusses *The Bridge on the River Kwai* extensively in his book.

30. ABBREVIATIONS

Abbreviations are a convenient way of presenting information in a smaller amount of space. This section discusses conventions for using abbreviations in formal writing.

30a. Titles

Titles are normally abbreviated when used immediately before or after a person's full name.

Mr. Isaiah Thomas
Sammy Davis Jr.
Dr. Jane Phelps
Marcia Gibbs, MD

When using a title together with the last name only, the full title should be written out.

Prof. Marc Ereshefsky	Professor Ereshefsky
Sen. Keith Davey	Senator Davey

30b. Academic and Business Terms

Common abbreviations are acceptable in formal writing so long as they are likely to be readily understood. Otherwise, the full name should be written out when first used and the abbreviation given in parentheses. Thereafter, the abbreviation may be used on its own.

The Atomic Energy Commission (AEC) has broad-ranging regulatory authority.
The American Philosophical Association (APA) holds three large regional meetings annually.

30c. Latin Abbreviations

Several abbreviations of Latin terms are common in formal academic writing:

cf.	compare (Latin *confer*)
e.g.	for example (Latin *exempli gratia*)
et al.	and others (Latin *et alia*)
etc.	and so on (Latin *et cetera*)
i.e.	that is (Latin *id est*)
NB	note well (Latin *nota bene*)

31. NUMBERS

Numbers of one or two words should be written out. Use figures for all other numbers.

needs checking   The building is 72 stories tall.
     revised   The building is seventy-two stories tall.

The same principle applies for dollar figures (or figures in other currencies).

needs checking   She lent her brother 10 dollars.
     revised   She lent her brother ten dollars.

It is acceptable to combine figures and words for very large numbers:

> The government is projecting a $200 billion deficit.

In general, figures should be used in addresses, dates, percentages, and reports of scores or statistics.

needs checking   In the third game of the tournament, Sweden and the Czech Republic tied three three.
     revised   In the third game of the tournament, Sweden and the Czech Republic tied 3–3.

32. ITALICS

Italics serve several different functions. Whereas titles of short stories, poems, and other short works are set off by quotation marks, titles of longer works and the names of newspapers, magazines, and so on should appear in italics:

"The Dead"	*Dubliners*
"Burnt Norton"	*Four Quartets*
"Budget Controversy Continues"	*The Economist*
"Smells like Teen Spirit"	*Nevermind*

Italics are also used for the names of paintings and sculptures, television series, and software.

When including words or phrases from other languages into your written work, place those words in italics.

needs checking   The play ends with an appearance of a deus ex machina.

revised   The play ends with an appearance of a *deus ex machina.*

Either italics or quotation marks may be used to indicate that words are mentioned rather than used. (See above, under **quotation marks**.)

Finally, italics are often used to provide special emphasis that is not otherwise clear from the context or the structure of the sentence.

33. SPELLING

The wittiest example of the illogic of English spelling remains Bernard Shaw's famous spelling of *fish* as *ghoti*. The *gh* sounds like the *gh* in enough; the *o* sounds like the *o* in *women* (once spelled *wimmen*, incidentally); and the *ti* sounds like the *ti* in *nation* or *station*. Shaw passionately advocated a rationalization of English spelling; it still has not happened, and probably never will.

Perhaps the best way to learn correct spelling is to be tested by someone else, or to test yourself every week on a different group of words. For example, you might learn the words from the list below beginning with a and b one week, the words beginning with c and d the next week, and so on.

33a. Spell-Check and Grammar-Check

Today's spell-checkers and grammar checkers have many virtues. If you confuse *its* and *it's* or *there* and *their*, such software will often draw your attention to your mistake. Some word processing software will even silently correct the mistake for you if you type, "Its a lovely day." But it will also often suggest there is something wrong with your writing when nothing whatsoever is wrong. (Not infrequently, for example, it will suggest you change from the subjunctive mood to the indicative when the subjunctive is in fact entirely correct.) And it will do nothing to alert you to any problem if you write either of the following sentences:

> The company's literary wing compliments its academic publishing program.

> The book includes a forward as well as a preface and an introduction.

No computer software, in short, can provide a reliable substitute for careful proofreading.

What is true for spelling and grammar is even more true for matters of style. Grammar checkers will offer advice on matters such as the length of sentences and the degree to which the passive voice is used. Such issues are by their nature not readily subject to precise formulations, and one should thus take advice of this sort from software programs with more than a grain of salt.

33b. Spelling and Sound

Many spelling mistakes result from similarities in the pronunciation of words with very different meanings. These are covered in the list below. Other words that cause spelling difficulties are listed separately.

absent (adjective)	absence (noun)
absorb	absorption
accept	except
access (entry)	excess (too much)
advice (noun)	advise (verb)
affect (to influence)	effect (result)
allowed (permitted)	aloud
alter (change)	altar (in a church)
appraise (value)	apprise (inform)
base (foundation)	bass (in music)
bath (noun)	bathe (verb)
berry (fruit)	bury (the dead)
beside (by the side of)	besides (as well as)
birth	berth (bed)
bitten	beaten
bizarre (strange)	bazaar (market)
bloc (political grouping)	block
breath (noun)	breathe (verb)
buoy (in the water)	boy
buy (purchase)	by
cash	cache (hiding place)
casual (informal)	causal (to do with causes)
cause	case
ceased (stopped)	seized (grabbed)
ceiling (above you)	sealing
chick	cheek
chose (past tense)	choose (present tense)
cite (make reference to)	sight/site
climatic	climactic
cloths (fabric)	clothes
coma (unconscious)	comma (punctuation)

compliment (praise)   complement (make complete)
conscious (aware)   conscience (sense of right)
contract   construct
conventional (usual)   convectional
conversation   conservation/concentration
convinced   convicted (of a crime)
cord (rope)   chord (music)
council (group)   counsel (advice)
course   coarse (rough)
credible (believable)   creditable (deserving credit)
critic (one who criticizes)   critique (piece of criticism)
defer (show respect)   differ
deference (respect)   difference
deprecate (criticize)   depreciate (reduce in value)
desert (dry place)   dessert (sweet)
device (thing)   devise (to plan)
died/had died   dead/was dead
dissent (protest)   descent (downward motion)
distant (adjective)   distance (noun)
edition (of a book etc.)   addition (something added)
emigrant   immigrant
envelop (verb)   envelope (noun)
except   expect
fear   fair/fare (payment)
feeling   filling
fell   feel/fill
flaunt (display)   flout
formally   formerly (previously)
forth (forward)   fourth (after third)
forward   foreword (in a book)
foul   fowl (birds)
future   feature
genus (biological type)   genius (creative intelligence)
greet   great/grate (scrape)
guerrillas (fighters)   gorillas (apes)
guided (led)   guarded (protected)
had   heard/head
heat   heart/hate

heir (inheritor)	air
human	humane (kind)
illicit (not permitted)	elicit (bring forth)
illusion (unreal image)	allusion (reference)
immigrate	emigrate
independent (adjective)	independence (noun)
inhabit (live in)	inhibit (retard)
instance (occurrence)	instants (moments)
intense (concentrating)	intents
isle (island)	aisle (to walk in)
kernel	colonel
know	no/now
lack	lake
later	latter/letter
lath (piece of wood)	lathe (machine)
lead	led
leave	leaf
leave	live
leaving	living
lessen (reduce)	lesson
let	late
lightning (from clouds)	lightening (becoming lighter)
lose (be unable to find)	loose (not tight)
mad (insane)	maid (servant)
man	men
martial (to do with fighting)	marshal
mental	metal
merry	marry
met	meet/mate
minor (underage)	miner (underground)
mist (light fog)	missed
moral (ethical)	morale (spirit)
mourning (after death)	morning
new	knew
of	off
on	own
ones	once
pain	pane (of glass)

patients (sick people) — patience (ability to wait)

peer (look closely) — pier (wharf)

perpetrate (be guilty of) — perpetuate (cause to continue)

perquisite (privilege) — prerequisite (requirement)

personal (private) — personnel (employees)

perspective (vision) — prospective (anticipated)

poor — pour (liquid)/pore

precede (go before) — proceed (continue)

precedent — president

price (cost) — prize (reward)

prostate — prostrate

quay (wharf— pronounced *key*) — key

quite — quiet (not noisy)

rein (to control animals) — rain/reign

release (let go) — realize (discover)

relieve (verb) — relief (noun)

response (noun) — responds (verb)

rid — ride

ridden — written

rise — rice

rite (ritual) — right/write

rod — rode/reared

rote (repetition) — wrote

saved — served

saw — seen

saw — so/sew

scene (location) — seen

seam (in clothes etc.) — seem (appear)

secret — sacred (holy)

sell (verb) — sail (boat)

senses — census (population count)

shed — shade

shone — shown

shot — short

sit — sat/set

smell — smile

snake — snack (small meal)

soar	sore (hurt)
sole (single)	soul (spirit)
sort (type or kind)	sought (looked for)
steal (present tense)	stole (past tense)
straight (not crooked)	strait (of water)
striped (e.g., a zebra)	stripped (uncovered)
suite (rooms or music)	suit/sweet
super	supper (meal)
suppose	supposed to
sympathies (noun)	sympathize (verb)
tale (story)	tail
talk	took
tap	tape
than	then
they	there/their
thing	think
this	these
throw	threw (past tense)
tied	tired
urban (in cities)	urbane (sophisticated)
vanish (disappear)	varnish
vein (to carry blood)	vain
waist (your middle)	waste
wait	weight (heaviness)
waive (give up)	wave
wants	once
weak (not strong)	week
weather (sunny, wet, etc.)	whether (or not)
wedding	weeding
were	where
wholly (completely)	holy (sacred)/holly
woman	women
won	worn
yoke (for animals)	yolk (of an egg)

33c. American Spelling, British Spelling, Canadian Spelling

A number of words that cause spelling difficulties are spelled differently in different countries. In the following list the British spelling is on the right, the American on the left. Either is correct in Canada, so long as the writer is consistent.

behavior	behaviour
center	centre
cigaret	cigarette
color	colour
defense	defence
favor	favour
favorite	favourite
fulfill	fulfil
humor	humour
likable	likeable
maneuver	manoeuvre
marvelous	marvellous
neighbor	neighbour
omelet	omelette
program	programme
Shakespearian	Shakespearean
skeptical	sceptical
skillful	skilful
theater	theatre
traveling	travelling

33d. Other Spelling Mistakes

Following is a list of some other commonly misspelled words.

abbreviation	accommodation	acquit
absence	achieve	acre
accelerator	acknowledge	across
accident	acquire	address
accidentally	acquisition	adjacent

advertisement
affidavit
ambulance
ammonia
amoeba
among
amortize
amount
anachronism
analogous
analysis
anchor
androgynous
annihilate
antecedent
antisemitic
anxious
apocalypse
apparatus
apparently
appreciate
approach
architect
arguable
argument
arsonist
arteriosclerosis
artillery
asinine
author
auxiliary
bacteria
basically
battery
beautiful
beginning
believe
boast

boastful
breakfast
bulletin
burglar
burial
buried
business
candidate
capillary
cappuccino
Caribbean
carpentry
cautious
ceiling
changeable
character
chlorophyll
choir
cholesterol
chrome
chromosome
chronological
chrysalis
chrysanthemum
coincidence
colleague
colonel
colossal
column
commitment
committee
comparative
competition
competitor
complexion
conceive
condemn
conjunction

connoisseur
consensus
consistent
controller
convenience
cooperation
cooperative
courteous
courtesy
creator
creature
criticism
cyst
decisive
definite
delicious
description
desirable
despair
despise
destroy
develop
diesel
different
dilemma
dining
disappear
disappoint
disastrous
discrimination
disease
disintegrate
dissatisfied
dominate
dormitory
double
doubtful
drunkard

drunkenness
duchess
due
dying
eclipse
effective
efficient
eighth
embarrass
employee
encourage
enemy
enmity
enormous
entertain
enthusiasm
entitle
entrepreneur
environment
enzyme
epidermis
epididymis
erroneous
esophagus
especially
espresso
essential
exaggerate
excessive
excite
exercise
exhilaration
existence
existent
experience
extraordinary
Fahrenheit
faithful

faithfully
farinaceous
fault
financial
foreigner
foretell
forty
fourth
gamete
gauge
germination
government
grammar
grateful
gruesome
guarantee
guerrillas
guilty
happened
happiest
hatred
hectare
helpful
hyena
hypothesis
ichthyology
idiosyncratic
imaginary
imagine
immersible
immigration
impeccable
importance
impresario
inchoate
incomprehensible
independent
indestructible

indigenous
indispensable
ineffable
infinitesimal
inoculate
insufferable
intention
intentional
interrupt
irrelevant
irresponsible
isosceles
isthmus
itinerary
jealous
jeopardy
journalist
jump
junction
kneel
knowledge
knowledgeable
laboratories
laboratory
language
lazy, laziness
ledger
leisure
liaise, liaison
liberation
library
licence
lieutenant
liquid, liquefy
literature
lying
medicine
medieval

membrane
merciful
mermaid
millennia
millennium
millionaire
minuscule
mischief
mischievous
naked
naughty
necessary
necessity
noticeable
nuclear
nucleus
obscene
obsolescent
obsolete
occasion
occasional
occupy
occur
occurred
occurrence
omit
ourselves
paid
parallel
parliament
parliamentary
party
permissible
permission
perpendicular
perseverance
photosynthesis
playful

possess
possession
poultry
predictable
pregnancy
pregnant
prerogative
prescription
privilege
properly
psychiatric
psychological
punctuation
pursue
questionnaire
really
receipt
recommend
referee
reference
regret
repeat
repetition
replies
reply
residence (place)
residents (people)
restaurant
revolutionary
rheumatism
rhododendron
rhombus
rhubarb
rhyme
rhythm
saddest
sandals
scene

schedule
schizophrenic
science
scintillate
scissors
scream
scrumptious
search
seize
sense
separate
shining
shotgun
sigh
significant
simultaneous
sincerely
slippery
slogan
smart
solemn
spaghetti
speech
spongy
sponsor
stale
stingy
stomach
stubborn
studious
studying
stupefy
stupid
subordinate
subpoena
substitute
subtle, subtlety
suburbs

succeed

success, successful

sue, suing

summary

surprised

surreptitious

surrounded

survive

symbol

talkative

tarred

television

temperature

tendency

theoretical

theory

title

tough

tragedy

trophy

truly

unique

until

vacancy

vacillate

valuable

vegetable

vehicle

vicious

visitor

volume

voluntary

Wednesday

welcome

whisper

writer

writing

written

yield

RESEARCH AND
DOCUMENTATION

34. APPROACHES TO RESEARCH

How does an industrious student locate voices that she can be confident are responsible ones, regardless of whether or not she may in the end agree with their conclusions? Search engines such as Google will turn up vast amounts of material on almost any topic—more than could possibly be taken account of in a single essay, perhaps more than could be read in an entire academic year. How do you choose? And how do you judge what is likely to be reliable, and what isn't?

One important research principle is to give consideration to material that has been refereed. The term "refereed journal" (or "refereed monograph," where a book-length academic study is concerned) refers to the publishers' practice of sending all submissions to respected academic authorities to be vetted before the material is published. (Another term often used for the same process is "peer-review"—the research of one scholar is reviewed by his or her peers before it is accepted for publication.) The process of refereeing or peer review is far from foolproof, and it's often the case that refereed journal articles or monographs will come to very different conclusions. But it is one important filtering device that can help separate responsible sources from irresponsible ones.

You should be aware that most refereed journals (and the electronic copies of most academic monographs) are not accessible to anyone who goes online. It is often the case that the article will be listed by your search engine but protected by a paywall, such that only a brief abstract (or the first page of the article) will be publicly accessible, and nothing more. (A significant exception is *JSTOR*, which allows anyone to access at no charge a limited number of articles per month.) It is also often the case that outstanding academic material will be given such a low score by the search engine's algorithm that you are never likely to find it in an ordinary Google search; like other search engines, Google tends to put frequently consulted material at the head of lists—a practice that may place pieces by popular astrologers or political cranks far ahead of the less flamboyant but more reliable work of reputable scholars. For academic research, Google Scholar (scholar.google.com) is often a far better choice than the main Google search engine. But like Google, Google Scholar often gives you no more than an abstract or the first page of a scholarly article—just as Google Books (or Amazon's "Look Inside" feature) will typically provide only selected pages of monographs. It's worth making a note of anything that looks interesting from your initial search process—but to fully explore many of the articles and books that look to be interesting and relevant to your research, you'll need to be inside the paywall that protects them.

Getting inside that paywall, then, is a vitally important first step in academic research. The way to do that, of course, is through your institution's library. If you are a college or university student in good standing, you will have been given an identification number and passcode to access the library's collection. Almost all university libraries today include a vast array of electronic material: newspapers, magazines, scholarly journals, and academic monographs that cannot be accessed by anyone without a passcode. It's never a good idea to give up easily if the first indication from the university library search engine is that the library doesn't provide access to a particular scholarly journal or academic monograph. (This is one area where libraries vary quite significantly; some university libraries seem to have search engines just as good as those of Google Scholar, whereas others are clunky and unpredictable.)

Whatever combination of search engines you are using, chances are high that you will find far more material than you can easily deal with. How can you avoid spending a large amount of time merely amassing a large quantity of material, much of which may be unreliable or not relevant for your purposes?

There is no one easy answer to this question. Part of the answer is often psychological; it can be important for many writers to start actually writing even before they are sure they have all the information they will want; the very process of writing often helps them to realize what sorts of information they still need. But much of the answer is also in what priority you give to different sorts of material. Whether or not material has been reviewed is one criterion. Another is how often you find it cited. Many good researchers like to start by making a very brief list of materials to consult, working purely on the basis of what seems most relevant to the topic they are tackling. Then, as they are scanning those, they will pay attention to which other books or articles are referred to most often by the authors. If a work is frequently cited by others, it will be one that you should take into account.

Where articles are concerned, the researcher should pay attention to the journal or newspaper in which the piece was originally published. Often she will be able to pick up on clues as to whether or not it is a publication with a good reputation. So far as newspapers are concerned, *The New York Times*, *The Washington Post*, *Los Angeles Times*, and *The Wall Street Journal* are all American newspapers with strong reputations; in Canada the equivalents are *The Globe and Mail*, *The Toronto Star*, and *The National Post*; in the UK *The Times*, *The Telegraph*, *The Independent*, *The Guardian*, and *The Economist* (the latter published weekly in a magazine format, but still resolutely styling itself as a "newspaper"). Though all these are reputable publications, it is also helpful to know that some (e.g., *The Wall Street Journal*, *National Post*, *The Telegraph*) tend to be ideologically very conservative, while others (e.g., *The Washington Post*, *The Guardian*) tend to be ideologically somewhat to the left.

If you are uncertain about how reputable a source may be, it is a good idea to consult your instructor. She will be able to tell you, for example, that *The American Historical Review* and *The Journal of American History* are both highly reputable, that *The Journal of Philosophy* is a much more reputable publication than is *Animus: A Philosophical Journal for Our Time*, and so on. That should not lead you to agree with everything you find in *The Journal of Philosophy*, of course—but it should save you some time.

It's also worth thinking of the credentials of the publisher. Whether in bound or electronic form, a book or journal published by one of the world's most prestigious university presses (among them Oxford and Cambridge in Britain; California,

Chicago, Duke, Harvard, Princeton, Stanford, and Yale in the US; Toronto and McGill-Queen's in Canada) is more likely to provide reliable information than one from Pelican Publishing (a non-scholarly Louisiana publisher of books on politics, cooking, and various other topics) or from Sentinel Press (an imprint within the Penguin Group that dedicates itself to the promotion of right-wing causes). The experienced researcher will thus take account of the publisher of any book or article. But at the same time, one should never take a book's reliability for granted based on the reputation of the publisher. The university presses of Oxford and Harvard may be highly reputable, but even the most prestigious presses have published some real duds in their time. And, because librarians often have standing orders for all books from such prestigious presses as these, the chances of a real dud from such a press finding its way onto the library's shelves or databases are far greater than the chances of an inferior book from a lesser known publisher being included in the library's offerings.

With the growth of the Open Access movement in recent years, it is becoming more and more common for leading scholars and other reputable writers to bypass the traditional "gatekeepers" and post material online without it having been vetted beforehand by any process of peer review or assessment by publishers. There may often be significant advantages to this approach for both authors and readers; open access publishing makes up-to-date research available more quickly; makes available not only a larger volume of material, but also a wider range of viewpoints; and reduces the undue influence that a handful of academic journal publishers have for many years exerted over the dissemination of research. But when you are checking out material published through an open-access publisher, you should be aware that not every publisher is alike. Open access publishers such as PLOS and SSRN were founded by academics and are highly reputable. Even where there may be no formal process of peer review for self-archived pieces, basic vetting has been carried out with material published on these sites, such that articles by cranks and crackpots are few and far between. Some other open access publishers, on the other hand, operate primarily through unsupervised self-archiving, where authors of any sort post their own work. Outstanding work may certainly sometimes be found on such a site, but it is likely to constitute a much smaller percentage of the total than it does on PLOS or SSRN. Outstanding work may also be found on websites or blogs unaffiliated with any institution or aggregating site—but as a general principle, material on a site with the domain name of an accredited university is likely to be more reliable. (In some countries accredited institutions may be identified by the style of their domain names; in the US, for example, accredited universities and colleges have .edu domain names, whereas in Britain they have .ac.uk domain names.)

Think too of the credentials of the author. Is he or she an academic at a respected institution, and has he or she published widely on the topic? And think of how recent the material is; for certain sorts of research there is an obvious

---

Searching through Old Newspapers

Here's one small example of how difficult it can be for a novice to navigate the world of electronic research. Imagine you are doing an essay on some aspect of nineteenth-century British history or literature and you would like to check out what the newspapers of that era had to say about a particular figure—the poet Augusta Webster, say, or the activist and inventor Lewis Gompertz. So far as newspapers go, you might well think of *The Times* of London, and no doubt you would try to google their archives. You would quickly find that, as with most newspaper archives nowadays, they are protected by a paywall.

Luckily for you, almost every university library has a subscription to the *Times* archive. If you check your university library's website you are likely to find "The Times of London Digital Archive" quite readily—listed under "newspapers," as one would expect. It's protected by a paywall, but so long as you have your university ID and passcode you'll be able to access it easily—and utilize its very good search engine to quickly find electronic facsimiles of all articles mentioning Webster or Gompertz.

But what about other British newspapers of the nineteenth century? Chances are you won't find nineteenth-century archives for any other British newspapers listed in the same section of your library's website. Don't give up! If you root about a bit using Google or another search engine outside the library site, you are likely to find pointers to what you're looking for. Googling "Victorian newspapers" or "British Newspapers 1800–1900" will likely bring up "19th Century British Library Newspapers"—a database that brings together dozens of different British newspapers covering the years 1800 to 1913. Back on your university's library site you'll find it under "databases," not "newspapers." Like the *Times* site, it has an excellent search engine; once you are on the site you will quickly and easily be able to search those newspapers and check out all the articles in any of them that mentioned Webster or Gompertz at any time during the nineteenth century.

If Google fails you in such situations, you still need not give up; you can always ask your instructor, or your university librarian. Chances are they will either be able to point you in the direction of what you want—or, at the very least, save you from hours of fruitless searching by letting you know that there is no convenient way to find what you'd like to find!

premium to be placed on more recent material. But the most recent is not always the best, of course. Ask too if the work provides sources to back up the arguments made. And is it possible readily to check the accuracy of those sources?

Another important criterion for certain sorts of research is point of view. If you are conducting research on a controversial topic, it's important to make sure that you consult a range of different viewpoints. You should not feel obligated, though, to give equal weight to all points of view. Particularly where material on the Web is concerned, it will sometimes be the case that implausible or downright irresponsible points of view will be more widely represented than views that deserve greater respect. Such is obviously the case with websites promulgating racist, homophobic, or otherwise bigoted views, but it may also be the case with certain scientific matters. By the late 1990s, for example, the vast majority of reputable scientific opinion was in broad agreement as to the dangers of global climate change. Dissenting scientific voices comprised only a small minority among the community of reputable scientists—but for years their views received disproportionate space on the Web, where numerous sites were largely devoted to casting doubt on the consensus scientific view on climate change (and, not by coincidence, to preserving the status quo for the coal industry, the oil and gas industry, and so on). Where such ideologically charged issues as these are concerned, it is worth paying particularly close attention to accounts that run counter to the normal ideological stance of the publication. When the right-wing magazine *The Economist* accepted several years ago that the weight of evidence overwhelmingly supported the argument that global warming posed a real danger, or when the left-of-center British newspaper *The Guardian* concluded that despite its socialist rhetoric the Mugabe government in Zimbabwe was denying its people both economic justice and basic human rights, such views deserve special respect.

Finally, the experienced researcher is willing to trust her own judgement: to glance at the table of contents and skim quickly through two or three dozen works on a subject and in each case make a snap decision as to its likely usefulness. These decisions are not, of course, irreversible; she may well find that one of the books initially set aside with barely a moment's notice is generally regarded as among the most important works in the field (in which case she will, of course, return to it with more care). But she must in the first instance have some way of making the mass of material manageable.

What of the opposite problem? What if there seems to be little or nothing published on the subject? Perhaps it's an area on the border with one or more other territories; in that case, surveying those territories may be necessary. Perhaps it's a relatively new subject; in that case—as indeed for any research—it's always helpful to check the relevant indices of journal articles. Some of the most important of these for work in the arts and social sciences are as follows:

- *Humanities Index:* covers articles published from 1974 onwards in such disciplines as English, history, and philosophy.
- *MLA Bibliography:* offers articles on the English language and literature as well as on French, German, Italian, Spanish, and so on.
- *Philosopher's Index:* the most comprehensive listing of articles on philosophy.
- *Social Sciences Index:* covers articles published from 1974 onwards in such areas as anthropology, economics, political science, psychology, and sociology.

These days, virtually all indices appear in electronic form; keyword searches are indispensable for researchers. The idea is to use a single word—or a combination of words—that you consider to be the "key" or main focus of your topic. The computer system will look through every author, title, and subject heading that includes the keywords (in any order). Queen's University provides its students with the following "Basic Search Tips":

Title or journal article
- Omit initial article (*a, the, le*)
- Type just the first few words
- Use journal title for magazines, journals, newspapers

Author
- Type last name first: *einstein, a*
- Add first initial if known
- For organizations use normal word order

Keyword
- Results can include any of your words
- Use "+" to indicate essential terms
- Use "?" to truncate; use quotes for phrases: "*camp david*"

Call number
- Include punctuation and spaces

One further note about academic research in the third decade of the twenty-first century: it's worth remembering that your academic library doesn't exist only in electronic form. It still has a physical location, where you will be sure to find a number of helpful librarians. Their job is to help you understand how to do research and do it well; they really can help. And the library also provides a great deal of material that you can touch and turn the pages of. It's worth doing that for at least two reasons. One is the process of browsing in the stacks of the library can lead you to make connections and generate ideas in ways that don't always happen when you are searching and reading online. The second may surprise you: some important material is simply not available electronically. That's not only true of certain books and articles from decades or centuries ago; it's also true of some very recent material.

Whether the information comes from bound volumes of printed material or articles in an electronic database, when it comes time to use research in an essay it is essential to strike an appropriate balance between one's own ideas and those of others.

35. AVOIDING PLAGIARISM

When incorporating research into their essays, good writers are careful to document their sources accurately and completely. This is, first of all, a service to readers who would like to embark on a fuller investigation into the topic of a paper by looking up its sources themselves; every academic citation system gives readers all the information they need to access original source material. But it is also critical that there be complete clarity about which parts of an essay are the author's and which parts come from elsewhere. To allow any blurriness on this question is to be dishonest, to engage in a kind of cheating, in fact—known as plagiarism.

Most people understand that taking someone else's writing and passing it off as one's own is intellectual thievery. But it is important to be aware that you may commit plagiarism even if you do not use precisely the same words another person wrote in precisely the same order. For instance, here is an actual example of plagiarism. *Globe and Mail* newspaper columnist Margaret Wente borrowed material for one of her columns from a number of works, including an article by Dan Gardner that had appeared the previous year in another newspaper (the *Ottawa Citizen*) and a book by Robert Paarlberg called *Starved for Science* (which was the subject of Gardner's article). The similarities were brought to light by media commentator Carol Wainio, who presented a series of parallel passages, including the following, on her blog *Media Culpa* (the fonts are Wainio's—simple bold is for direct copying; the bold + italics is for "near copying"):

> Gardner: ***Many NGOs working in Africa in the area of development and the environment have been advocating against the modernization of traditional farming practices***, Paarlberg says. **"They believe that traditional farming in Africa incorporates indigenous knowledge that shouldn't be replaced by science-based knowledge introduced from the outside.** They encourage Africa to stay away from fertilizers, and be certified as organic

instead. And in the case of genetic engineering, they warn African governments against making these technologies available to farmers."

Wente: *Yet, many NGOs working in Africa have tenaciously fought the modernization of traditional farming practices.* **They believe traditional farming in Africa incorporates indigenous knowledge that shouldn't be replaced by science-based knowledge introduced from the outside.** As Prof. Paarlberg writes, "They encourage African farmers to stay away from fertilizers and be certified organic instead. And they warn African governments to stay away from genetic engineering."

Wente does not always use exactly the same words as her sources, but no one reading the passages can doubt that one writer is appropriating the phrasings of the others. Additionally, where Wente *does* quote Paarlberg directly, the quotation is lifted from Gardner's article and should be identified as such.

The penalties for such practices are not trivial; Wente was publicly reprimanded by her employer, and the CBC radio program *Q* removed her from its media panel. Other reporters have been, justifiably, fired under similar circumstances. At most colleges and universities, students are likely to receive a zero if they are caught plagiarizing—and they may be expelled from the institution. It's important to be aware, too, that penalties for plagiarism make no allowance for intent; it is no defence that a writer took someone else's words "by mistake" rather than intentionally.

How, then, can you be sure to avoid plagiarism? First of all, be extremely careful in your note-taking, so as to make it impossible to imagine, a few days later, that words you have jotted down from somewhere else are your own. This is why notes need to be in a separate file or book from your own ideas. (In her *Globe and Mail* column responding to the plagiarism charges, Wente, in fact, claimed that she had accidentally mixed a quotation into her own ideas.) If your note-taking is reliable, then you will know which words need to be credited. One way to rewrite the passage above would simply be to remove the material taken from Gardner and to credit Paarlberg by quoting him directly, if you were able to access his book and could do so: "As Robert Paarlberg has argued in his book *Starved for Science*, many NGOs 'believe that traditional farming in Africa incorporates indigenous knowledge that shouldn't be replaced by science-based knowledge introduced from the outside.'" (In an academic essay, you would look up and provide the page number as well.)

You may notice here that the quoted material is a statement of opinion rather than fact—controversial views are being given, but without any evidence provided to back them up—so a careful reader would wonder whether NGOs are really as anti-science as the quotation suggests, or whether the writer hasn't done enough research on the debate. If you were to make an assertion like this in a paper of your own it would not be enough just to quote Paarlberg; you would need to do much more research and find information to support or deny your claim. If you are including quotations in an essay, the best sources to quote are not necessarily those which express opinions that mirror the ones you are putting forward. In a case such as this, for example, the argument would have been much more persuasive if Wente had quoted an official statement from one of the NGOs she was attacking. If her article had quoted a source making this specific case against "science-based knowledge" and then argued directly against that source's argument, Wente's own position would have been strengthened. Quoting many such sources would provide proof that the article's characterization of the position of NGOs was factually accurate.

Whenever you do quote someone else, it's important to cite the source. But do you need a citation for everything that did not come from your own knowledge? Not necessarily. Citations are usually unnecessary when you are touching on common knowledge (provided it is, in fact, common knowledge, and provided your instructor has not asked you to do otherwise). If you refer to the chemical composition of water, or the date when penicillin was discovered, you are unlikely to need to provide any citation, even if you used a source to find the information, since such facts are generally available and uncontroversial. (Make sure, however, to check any "common knowledge" with several reputable sources; if your information is incorrect, it reflects poorly on you, especially if you have not cited your source.) If you have any doubts about whether something is common knowledge or not, cite it; over-cautiousness is not a serious problem, but plagiarism always is.

36. CITATION AND DOCUMENTATION

Citing sources is fundamental to writing a good research paper, but no matter how diligent you are in making your acknowledgements, your paper will not be taken seriously unless its documentation is formatted according to an appropriate and accepted referencing style. For the sake of consistency, each academic discipline has adopted a particular system of referencing as its standard, which those writing in that discipline are expected to follow. *The Broadview Pocket Guide to Citation and Documentation* outlines three of the most common of these systems. Almost all of the humanities use the documentation guidelines developed by the Modern Language Association (MLA), a notable exception being history, which tends to prefer those of the *Chicago Manual of Style* (Chicago Style). The social and some health sciences typically follow the style rules of the American Psychological Association (APA). The basic sciences most commonly use the referencing systems of the Council of Science Editors (CSE), information on which is provided on the companion website to this book. Each of these styles is exacting and comprehensive in its formatting rules; following with precision the one recommended for a given paper's discipline is one of a responsible research writer's duties.

As important as documentation is to a well-written paper, by itself it is not always enough. Writers must also be attentive to the ways in which they integrate borrowed material into their essays.

36a. Incorporating Sources

There are three main ways of working source material into a paper: summarizing, paraphrasing, and quoting directly. In order to avoid plagiarism, care must be taken with all three kinds of borrowing, both in the way they are handled and in their referencing. In what follows, a passage from page 102 of a book by Terrence W. Deacon (*The Symbolic Species: The Co-Evolution of Language and the Brain*, Norton, 1997) serves as the source for a sample summary, paraphrase, and quotation. The examples feature the MLA style of in-text parenthetical citations, but the requirements for presenting the source material are the same for all academic referencing systems. For a similar discussion with a focus on APA style, see Incorporating Sources in APA Style (starting on page 278).

original source   Over the last few decades language researchers seem to have reached a consensus that language is an innate ability, and that only a significant contribution from innate knowledge can explain our ability to learn such a complex communication system. Without question, children enter the world predisposed to learn human languages. All normal children, raised in normal social environments, inevitably learn their local language, whereas other species, even when raised and taught in this same environment, do not. This demonstrates that human brains come into the world specially equipped for this function.

● Summarizing

An honest and competent summary, whether of a passage or an entire book, must not only represent the source accurately but also use original wording and include a citation. It is a common misconception that only quotations need to be acknowledged as borrowings in the body of an essay. In fact, without a citation, even a fairly worded summary or paraphrase is an act of plagiarism. The first example below is faulty on two counts:

it borrows wording (underlined) from the source, and it has no parenthetical reference.

needs checking   Researchers agree that language learning is <u>innate</u>, <u>and that only innate knowledge can explain</u> how we are able <u>to learn</u> a <u>system</u> of <u>communication</u> that is so <u>complex</u>. <u>Normal children raised in normal</u> ways will always <u>learn their local language</u>, <u>whereas other species do not, even when taught</u> human language and exposed to the <u>same environment</u>.

The next example correctly avoids the wording of the source passage, and a signal phrase and parenthetical citation note the author and page number.

revised   As Terrence W. Deacon notes, there is now wide agreement among linguists that the ease with which human children acquire their native tongues, under the conditions of a normal childhood, demonstrates an inborn capacity for language that is not shared by any other animals, not even those who are reared in comparable ways and given human language training (102).

● Paraphrasing

Whereas a summary is a shorter version of its original, a paraphrase tends to be about the same length. However, paraphrases, just like summaries, must reflect their sources accurately, must use original wording, and must include a citation. Even though it is properly cited, the paraphrase of the first sentence of the Deacon passage, below, falls short by being too close to the wording of the original (underlined).

needs checking   Researchers in <u>language</u> have come to <u>a consensus</u> in the past <u>few decades</u> that the acquisition of language is <u>innate</u>; such <u>contributions</u> <u>from knowledge</u> <u>contribute significantly</u> to <u>our ability</u> to master <u>such a complex system</u> of <u>communication</u> (Deacon 102).

Simply substituting synonyms for the words and phrases of the source, however, is not enough to avoid plagiarism. Despite its original wording, the next example also fails but for a very different reason: it follows the original's sentence structure too closely, as illustrated in the interpolated copy below it.

needs checking Recently, linguists appear to have come to an agreement that speaking is an inborn skill, and that nothing but a substantial input from inborn cognition can account for the human capacity to acquire such a complicated means of expression (Deacon 102).

Recently (*over the last few decades*), linguists (*language researchers*) appear to have come to an agreement (*seem to have reached a consensus*) that speaking is an inborn skill (*that language is an innate ability*), and that nothing but a substantial input (*and that only a significant contribution*) from inborn cognition (*from innate knowledge*) can account for the human capacity (*can explain our ability*) to acquire such a complicated means of expression (*to learn such a complex communication system*) (Deacon 102).

What follows is a good paraphrase of the passage's opening sentence; this paraphrase captures the sense of the original without echoing the details and shape of its language.

revised Linguists now broadly agree that children are born with the ability to learn language; in fact, the human capacity to acquire such a difficult skill cannot easily be accounted for in any other way (Deacon 102).

● Quoting Directly

Unlike paraphrases and summaries, direct quotations must use the exact wording of the original. Because they involve importing outside words, quotations pose unique challenges.

Quote too frequently, and you risk making your readers wonder why they are not reading your sources instead of your paper. Your essay should present something you want to say—informed and supported by properly documented sources, but forming a contribution that is yours alone. To that end, use secondary material to help you build a strong framework for your work, not to replace it. Quote sparingly, therefore; use your sources' exact wording only when it is important or particularly memorable.

To avoid misrepresenting your sources, be sure to quote accurately, and to avoid plagiarism, take care to indicate quotations as quotations, and cite them properly. Below are two problematic quotations. The first does not show which words come directly from the source.

needs checking   Terrence W. Deacon maintains that children enter the world predisposed to learn human languages (102).

The second quotation fails to identify the source at all.

needs checking   Linguists believe that "children enter the world predisposed to learn human languages."

The next example corrects both problems by naming the source and indicating clearly which words come directly from it.

revised   Terrence W. Deacon maintains that "children enter the world predisposed to learn human languages" (102).

● Formatting Quotations

There are two ways to signal an exact borrowing: by enclosing it in double quotation marks and by indenting it as a block of text. Which you should choose depends on the length and genre of the quotation and the style guide you are following.

Short prose quotations

What counts as a short prose quotation differs among the various reference guides. In MLA style, "short" means up to four lines; in APA, up to forty words; and in Chicago Style, up to one hundred words. All the guides agree, however, that short quotations must be enclosed in double quotation marks, as in the examples below.

> *Short quotation, full sentence:*
> According to Terrence W. Deacon, linguists agree that a human child's capacity to acquire language is inborn: "Without question, children enter the world predisposed to learn human languages" (102).

> *Short quotation, partial sentence:*
> According to Terrence W. Deacon, linguists agree that human "children enter the world predisposed to learn human languages" (102).

Long prose quotations

Longer prose quotations should be double-spaced and indented, as a block, one tab space from the left margin. Do not include quotation marks; the indentation indicates that the words come exactly from the source. Note that indented quotations are often introduced with a full sentence followed by a colon.

> Terrence W. Deacon, like most other linguists, believes that human beings are born with a unique cognitive capacity:
>
> > Without question, children enter the world predisposed to learn human languages. All normal children, raised in normal social environments, inevitably learn their local language, whereas other species, even when raised and taught in this same environment, do not. This demonstrates that human brains come into the world specially equipped for this function. (102)

Verse quotations

Quoting from verse is a special case. Poetry quotations of three or fewer lines (MLA) may be integrated into your paragraph and enclosed in double quotation marks, with lines separated by a forward slash with a space on either side of it, as in the example below.

> Pope's "Epistle II. To a Lady," in its vivid portrayal of wasted lives, sharply criticizes the social values that render older women superfluous objects of contempt: "Still round and round the Ghosts of Beauty glide, / And haunt the places where their Honor dy'd" (lines 241–42).

If your quotation of three or fewer lines includes a stanza break, MLA style requires you to mark the break by inserting two forward slashes (//), with spaces on either side of them.

> The speaker in "Ode to a Nightingale" seeks, in various ways, to free himself from human consciousness, leaving suffering behind. Keats uses alliteration and repetition to mimic the gradual dissolution of self, the process of intoxication or death: "That I might drink, and leave the world unseen, / And with thee fade away into the forest dim: // Fade far away, dissolve, and quite forget" (lines 19–21).

Poetry quotations of more than three lines in MLA, or two or more lines in Chicago Style, should be, like long prose quotations, indented and set off in a block from your main text. Arrange the lines just as they appear in the original.

> The ending of Margaret Avison's "September Street" moves from the decaying, discordant city toward a glimpse of an outer/inner infinitude:
>
>> On the yellow porch
>> one sits, not reading headlines; the old eyes
>> read far out into the mild
>> air, runes.
>> See. There: a stray sea-gull. (lines 20–24)

Quotations within quotations

You may sometimes find, within the original passage you wish to quote, words already enclosed in double quotation marks. If your quotation is short, enclose it all in double quotation marks, and use single quotation marks for the embedded quotation.

> Terrence W. Deacon is firm in maintaining that human language differs from other communication systems in kind rather than degree: "Of no other natural form of communication is it legitimate to say that 'language is a more complicated version of that'" (44).

If your quotation is long, keep the double quotation marks of the original.

> Terrence W. Deacon is firm in maintaining that human language differs from other communication systems in kind rather than degree:
>
> > Of no other natural form of communication is it legitimate to say that "language is a more complicated version of that." It is just as misleading to call other species' communication systems *simple* languages as it is to call them languages. In addition to asserting that a Procrustean mapping of one to the other is possible, the analogy ignores the sophistication and power of animals' non-linguistic communication, whose capabilities may also be without language parallels. (44)

● Adding to or Deleting from a Quotation

While it is important to use the original's exact wording in a quotation, it is allowable to modify a quotation somewhat, as long as the changes are clearly indicated and do not distort the meaning of the original.

Using square brackets to add to a quotation

You may want to add to a quotation in order to clarify what would otherwise be puzzling or ambiguous to someone who does not know its context; in that case, put whatever you add in square brackets.

> Terrence W. Deacon writes that children are born "specially equipped for this [language] function" (102).

Using an ellipsis to delete from a quotation

If you would like to streamline a quotation by omitting anything unnecessary to your point, insert an ellipsis (three spaced dots) to show that you've left material out.

When the quotation looks like a complete sentence but is actually part of a longer sentence, you should provide an ellipsis to show that there is more to the original than you are using.

> Terrence W. Deacon says that ". . . children enter the world predisposed to learn human languages" (102).

Note that if the quotation is clearly a partial sentence, ellipses aren't necessary.

> Terrence W. Deacon writes that children are born "specially equipped" to learn human language (102).

When the omitted material runs over a sentence boundary or constitutes a whole sentence or more, insert a period plus an ellipsis.

> Terrence W. Deacon, like most other linguists, believes that human children are born with a unique ability to acquire their native language: "Without question, children enter the world predisposed to learn human languages. . . . [H]uman brains come into the world specially equipped for this function" (102).

Be sparing in modifying quotations; it is all right to have one or two altered quotations in a paper, but if you find yourself changing quotations often, or adding to and omitting from one quotation more than once, reconsider quoting at all. A paraphrase or summary is very often a more effective choice.

Integrating quotations

Quotations must be worked smoothly and grammatically into your sentences and paragraphs. Always, of course, mark quotations as such, but for the purpose of integrating them into your writing, treat them as if they were your own words. The boundary between what you say and what your source says should be grammatically seamless.

needs checking   Terrence W. Deacon points out, "whereas other species, even when raised and taught in this same environment, do not" (102).

revised   According to Terrence W. Deacon, while human children brought up under normal conditions acquire the language they are exposed to, "other species, even when raised and taught in this same environment, do not" (102).

Avoiding "dumped" quotations

Integrating quotations well also means providing a context for them. Don't merely drop them into your paper or string them together like beads on a necklace; make sure to introduce them by noting where the material comes from and how it connects to whatever point you are making.

needs checking   For many years, linguists have studied how human children acquire language. "Without question, children enter the world predisposed to learn human language" (Deacon 102).

revised   Most linguists studying how human children acquire language have come to share the conclusion articulated here by Terrence W. Deacon: "Without question, children enter the world predisposed to learn human language" (102).

needs checking   "Without question, children enter the world predisposed to learn human language" (Deacon 102). "There is . . . something special about human brains that enables us to do with ease what no other species can do even minimally without intense effort and remarkably insightful training" (Deacon 103).

revised   Terrence W. Deacon bases his claim that we "enter the world predisposed to learn human language" on the fact that very young humans can "do with ease what no other species can do even minimally without intense effort and remarkably insightful training" (102–03).

● Signal Phrases

To leave no doubt in your readers' minds about which parts of your essay are yours and which come from elsewhere, identify the sources of your summaries, paraphrases, and quotations with signal phrases, as in the following examples.

- As Carter and Rosenthal have demonstrated, . . .
- In the words of one researcher, . . .
- In his most recent book McGann advances the view that, as he puts it, . . .
- As Nussbaum observes, . . .
- Kendal suggests that . . .
- Freschi and others have rejected this claim, arguing that . . .
- Morgan has emphasized this point in her recent research: . . .
- As Sacks puts it, . . .
- To be sure, Mtele allows that . . .
- In his later novels Hardy takes a bleaker view, frequently suggesting that . . .

In order to help establish your paper's credibility, you may also find it useful at times to include in a signal phrase information that shows why readers should take the source seriously, as in the following example:

In her landmark work, biologist and conservationist Rachel Carson warns that . . .

Here, the signal phrase mentions the author's professional credentials; it also points out the importance of her book, which is appropriate to do in the case of a work as famous and as respected as Carson's *Silent Spring*.

Below is a fuller list of words and expressions that may be useful in the crafting of signal phrases:

according to _____,	endorses
acknowledges	finds
adds	grants
admits	illustrates
advances	implies
agrees	in the view of _____,
allows	in the words of _____,
argues	insists
asserts	intimates
attests	notes
believes	observes
claims	points out
comments	puts it
compares	reasons
concludes	refutes
confirms	rejects
contends	reports
declares	responds
demonstrates	suggests
denies	takes issue with
disputes	thinks
emphasizes	writes

Additional Material
The discussion above of
"Your Arguments, Others' Arguments" (pages 43–46)
may also be helpful.

CONTENTS

37. MLA STYLE

"MLA style" refers to the referencing guidelines of the Modern Language Association, which are favoured by many disciplines in the humanities. The main components of the MLA system are in-text author-page number citations, which appear in the body of an essay, and a bibliography giving publication details—the list of "Works Cited"—at the end of the essay.

This section outlines the key points of MLA style. Sample essay pages appear at the end of this section, and additional sample essays can be found on the Broadview website; go to sites.broadviewpress.com/writingcdn. Consult the *MLA Handbook* (9th edition, 2021) if you have questions not answered here; you may also find answers at the website of the MLA, www.mla.org.

37a. About In-text Citations

in-text citations: Under the MLA system a quotation or specific reference to another work is followed by a parenthetical page reference:

- Bonnycastle refers to "the true and lively spirit of opposition" with which Marxist literary criticism invigorates the discipline (204).

  The work is then listed under "Works Cited" at the end of the essay:

- Bonnycastle, Stephen. *In Search of Authority: An Introductory Guide to Literary Theory.* 3rd ed., Broadview Press, 2007.

  (See below for information about the "Works Cited" list.)

no signal phrase (or author not named in signal phrase): If the context does not make it clear who the author is, that information must be added to the in-text citation. Note that no comma separates the name of the author from the page number.

- Even in recent years some have continued to believe that Marxist literary criticism invigorates the discipline with a "true and lively spirit of opposition" (Bonnycastle 204).

placing of in-text citations: Place in-text citations at the ends of clauses or sentences in order to keep disruption of your writing to a minimum. The citation comes before the period or comma in the surrounding sentence. (If the quotation ends with punctuation other than a period or comma, include it in the quotation, and place a period or comma after the in-text citation.)

- Ricks refuted this point early on (16), but the claim has continued to be made in recent years.
- In "The Windhover," on the other hand, Hopkins bubbles over; "the mastery of the thing!" (8), he enthuses when he thinks of a bird, exclaiming shortly thereafter, "O my chevalier!" (10).

When a cited quotation is set off from the text, however, the in-text citation should be placed after the concluding punctuation.

- Muriel Jaeger draws on the following anecdote in discussing the resistance of many wealthy Victorians to the idea of widespread education for the poor:

> In a mischievous mood, Henry Brougham once told [some well-off acquaintances who were] showing perturbation about the likely results of educating the "lower orders" that they could maintain their superiority by working harder themselves. (105)

in-text citation when text is in parentheses: If an in-text citation occurs within text in parentheses, square brackets are used for the reference.

- The development of a mass literary culture (or a "print culture," to use Williams's expression [88]) took several hundred years in Britain.

page number unavailable: Many web sources lack page numbers. If your source has no page or section numbers, no number should be given in your citation. Do not count paragraphs yourself, as the version you are using may differ from others.

- In a recent web posting a leading critic has clearly implied that he finds such an approach objectionable (Bhabha).

If the source gives explicit paragraph or section numbers, as many websites do, cite the appropriate abbreviation, followed by the number.

- Early in the novel, Austen makes clear that the "business" of Mrs. Bennet's life is "to get her daughters married" (ch. 1).

- In "The American Scholar" Emerson asserts that America's "long apprenticeship to the learning of other lands" is drawing to a close (par. 7).

Note that (as is not the case with page numbers), MLA style requires a comma between author and paragraph or section numbers in a citation.

- Early in the novel, Mrs. Bennet makes it clear that her sole business in life is "to get her daughters married" (Austen, ch. 1).

one page or less: If a source is one page long or less, it is advisable to still provide the page number (though MLA does not require this).

- In his *Chicago Tribune* review, Bosley calls the novel's prose "excruciating" (1).

multiple authors: If there are two authors, both authors should be named either in the signal phrase or in the in-text citation, connected by *and*.

- Chambliss and Best argue that the importance of this novel is primarily historical (233).

- Two distinguished scholars have recently argued that the importance of this novel is primarily historical (Chambliss and Best 233).

If there are three or more authors, include only the first author's name in the in-text citation, followed by *et al.*, short for the Latin *et alia*, meaning *and others*.

- Meaning is not simply there in the text, but in the complex relationships between the text, the reader, and the Medieval world (Black et al. xxxvi).

corporate author: The relevant organization or the title of the piece should be included in the in-text citation if neither is included in the body of your text; make sure enough information is provided for readers to find the correct entry in your Works Cited list. Shorten a long title to avoid awkwardness, but take care that the shortened version begins with the same word as the corresponding entry in "Works Cited" so that readers can move easily from the citation to the bibliographic information. For example, *Comparative Indo-European Linguistics: An Introduction* should be shortened to *Comparative Indo-European* rather than *Indo-European Linguistics*. The first two examples below cite unsigned newspaper or encyclopedia articles; the last is a corporate author in-text citation.

- As *The New York Times* reported in May 2021, many of the new voting laws being enacted were driven by disinformation about election integrity ("Perpetual Motion Machine").

- In the 1990s Sao Paulo began to rapidly overtake Mexico City as the world's most polluted city ("Air Pollution" 21).

- There are a number of organizations mandated "to foster the production and enjoyment of the arts in Canada" (Canada Council for the Arts 2).

more than one work by the same author cited: If you include more than one work by the same author in your list of Works Cited, you must make clear which work is being cited each time. This may be done either by mentioning the work in a signal phrase or by including in the citation a short version of the title.

- In *The House of Mirth*, for example, Wharton writes of love as keeping Lily and Selden "from atrophy and extinction" (282).

- Wharton sees love as possessing the power to keep humans "from atrophy and extinction" (*House of Mirth* 282).

- Love, as we learn from the experience of Lily and Selden, possesses the power to keep humans "from atrophy and extinction" (Wharton, *House of Mirth* 282).

multi-volume works: Note, by number, the volume you are referring to, followed by a colon and a space, before noting the page number. Use the abbreviation "vol." when citing an entire volume.

- Towards the end of *In Darkest Africa* Stanley refers to the Victoria Falls (2: 387).

- In contrast with those of the medieval period, Renaissance artworks show an increasing concern with depicting the material world and less and less of an interest in metaphysical symbolism (Hauser, vol. 2).

two or more authors with the same last name: If the Works Cited list includes two or more authors with the same last name, the in-text citation should supply both first initials and last names, or, if the first initials are also the same, the full first and last names:

- One of the leading economists of the time advocated wage and price controls (Harry Johnston 197).

- One of the leading economists of the time advocated wage and price controls (H. Johnston 197).

indirect quotations: When an original source is not available but is referred to by another source, the in-text citation includes *qtd. in* (an abbreviation of *quoted in*) and a reference to the second source. In the example below, Casewell is quoted by Bouvier; the in-text citation directs readers to an entry in Works Cited for the Bouvier work.

- Casewell considers Lambert's position to be "outrageously arrogant" (qtd. in Bouvier 59).

short poems: For short poems, cite line numbers rather than page numbers.

- In "wont you celebrate with me," Clifton describes a speaker who forges her identity "here on this bridge between / starshine and clay" (lines 8–9).

If you are citing the same poem repeatedly, use just the numbers for subsequent references.

- Clifton asks the reader to celebrate that "everyday / something has tried to kill me / and has failed" (12–14).

longer poems: For longer poems with parts, cite the part (or section, or "book") as well as the line (where available). Use Arabic numerals, and use a period for separation.

- In "Ode: Intimations of Immortality" Wordsworth calls human birth "but a sleep and a forgetting" (5.1).

novels or short stories: When a work of prose fiction has chapters or numbered divisions the citation should include first the page number, and then book, chapter, and section numbers as applicable. (These can be very useful in helping readers of a different edition to locate the passage you are citing.) Arabic numerals should be used. A semi-colon should be used to separate the page number from the other information.

- When Joseph and Fanny are by themselves, they immediately express their affection for each other, or, as Fielding puts it, "solace themselves" with "amorous discourse" (151; ch. 26).

- In *Tender Is the Night* Dick's ambition does not quite crowd out the desire for love: "He wanted to be loved too, if he could fit it in" (133; bk. 2, ch. 4).

plays: Almost all plays are divided into acts and/or scenes. For plays that do not include line numbering throughout, cite the page number in the edition you have been using, followed by act and/or scene numbers as applicable:

- As Angie and Joyce begin drinking together Angie pronounces the occasion "better than Christmas" (72; act 3).

- Near the conclusion of Inchbald's *Wives as They Were* Bronzely declares that he has been "made to think with reverence on the matrimonial compact" (62; act 5, sc. 4).

For plays written entirely or largely in verse, where line numbers are typically provided throughout, you should omit the reference to page number in the citation. Instead, cite the act, scene, and line numbers, using Arabic numerals. For a Shakespeare play, if the title isn't clear from the introduction to a quotation, an abbreviation of the title may also be used. The in-text citation below is for Shakespeare's *The Merchant of Venice*, Act 2, Scene 3, lines 2–4:

- Jessica clearly has some fondness for Launcelot: "Our house is hell, and thou, a merry devil, / Dost rob it of some taste of tediousness. / But fare thee well; there is a ducat for thee" (*MV* 2.3.2–4).

works without page numbers: If you are citing literary texts where you have consulted editions from other sources (on the Web or in an e-book, for instance), the principles are exactly the same, except that you need not cite page numbers. For example, if the online Gutenberg edition of Fielding's *Joseph Andrews* were being cited, the citation would be as follows:

- When Joseph and Fanny are by themselves, they immediately express their affection for each other, or, as Fielding puts it, "solace themselves" with "amorous discourse" (ch. 26).

Students should be cautioned that online editions of literary texts are often unreliable. Typically there are far more typos and other errors in online versions of literary texts than there are in print versions, and such things as the layout of poems are also frequently incorrect. It is often possible to exercise judgement about such matters, however. If, for example, you are not required to base your essay on a particular copy of a Thomas Hardy poem but may find your own, you will be far better off using the text you will find on the Representative Poetry Online site run out of the University of Toronto than you will using a text you might find on a "World's Finest Love Poems" site.

sacred texts: The Bible and other sacred texts that are available in many editions should be cited in a way that enables the reader to check the reference in any edition. For the Bible, book, chapter, and verse should all be cited, using periods for separation. The reference below is to Genesis, chapter 2, verse 1.

- According to the Judeo-Christian story of creation, at the end of the sixth day "the heavens and the earth were finished" (Gen. 2.1).

works in an anthology or book of readings: In the in-text citation for a work in an anthology, use the name of the author of the work, not that of the editor of the anthology. The page number, however, should be that found in the anthology. The following citation refers to an article by Frederic W. Gleach in an anthology edited by Jennifer Brown and Elizabeth Vibert.

- One of the essays in Brown and Vibert's collection argues that we should rethink the Pocahontas myth (Gleach 48).

In your list of Works Cited, this work should be alphabetized under Gleach, the author of the piece you have consulted, not under Brown. If you cite another work by a different author from the same anthology or book of readings, that should appear as a separate entry in your list of Works Cited—again, alphabetized under the author's name.

tweets: Cite tweets by giving the author's name in your text rather than in an in-text citation.

- Stephen King has written about the elusive nature of artistic inspiration, tweeting for example in May 2021 that "[g]ood writing is a delight to those who read it and a mystery to those who write it."

37b. About Works Cited: MLA Core Elements

The Works Cited list in MLA style is an alphabetized list at the end of the essay (or article or book). The entire list, like the main part of the essay, should be double-spaced throughout, and each entry should be given a hanging indent: the first line is flush with the left-hand margin, and each subsequent line is indented one tab space.

The Works Cited list should include information about all the sources you have cited. Do not include works that you consulted but did not cite in the body of your text.

MLA style provides a set of citation guidelines that the writer follows and adapts, regardless of whether the source being cited is print, digital, audio, visual, or any other form of media. All sources share what the MLA call "Core Elements," and these, listed in order, create the citation for all your entries: Author, Title of Source, Title of Container (larger whole), Contributor, Version, Number, Publisher, Publication Date, and Location. Each element is followed by the punctuation marks shown in the table below, unless it is the last element, which should always close with a period. (There are a few exceptions to this rule, which are outlined below.) Most sources don't have all the elements (some don't have an author, for example, or a version, or a location); if you find that this is the case, omit the element and move on to the next.

1. Author.
2. Title of source.
3. Title of container,
4. Contributor,
5. Version,
6. Number,
7. Publisher,
8. Publication Date,
9. Location.

The table can function as a guide when creating citations. Once you have found all the publication details for your source, place them in order and punctuate according to the table, leaving out any elements for which you don't have information. It is common for a source to have more than one "container"—such as an article printed in a journal and found on an online database. For sources like these, the table above can be filled out a second time, beginning with item 3 for the second container. Please see the section on "Title of Container" for details and examples.

In the sections below, you will discover how to identify the core elements of MLA style and how to use them across media. For a list of examples, please see 37c below.

Author

This element begins your citation. For a **single author**, list the author's last name first, followed by a comma, and then the author's first name or initials (use whatever appears on the work's title page or copyright page), followed by a period.

Graham, Jorie. *From the New World*. Ecco, 2015.

Johnson, George M. *All Boys Aren't Blue*. Farrar, Straus and Giroux, 2020.

If a source has **two authors**, the first author's name should appear with the last name first, followed by a comma and *and*. Note also that the authors' names should appear in the order they are listed; sometimes this is not alphabetical.

Rectenwald, Michael, and Lisa Carl. *Academic Writing, Real World Topics*. Broadview Press, 2015.

If there are **three or more authors**, include only the first author's name, reversed, followed by a comma and *et al.* (the abbreviation of the Latin *et alia*, meaning *and others*).

Waldron, Janice L., et al. *The Oxford Handbook of Social Media and Music Learning*. Oxford UP, 2020.

Sources that are **edited** rather than authored are usually cited in a similar way; add "editor" or "editors" after the name(s) and before the title.

Renker, Elizabeth, editor. *Poems: A Concise Anthology*. Broadview Press, 2016.

When referring to an edited version of a work written by another author or authors, list the editor(s) after the title, in the Contributor element.

Trollope, Anthony. *The Eustace Diamonds*. 1873. Edited by Stephen Gill and John Sutherland, Penguin, 1986.

Authors can be organizations, institutions, associations, or government agencies ("corporate authors"). If a work has been issued by a **corporate author** and no author is identified, the entry should be listed by the name of the organization that produced it.

Ontario, Ministry of Natural Resources. *Achieving Balance: Ontario's Long-Term Energy Plan*. Queen's Printer for Ontario, 2016, www.energy.gov.on.ca/en/ltep/achieving-balance-ontarios-long-term-energy-plan. Accessed 10 June 2021.

If the work is published by the same organization that is the corporate author, skip the author element and list only the publisher. The citation will begin with the source title.

2020 Annual Report. Broadview Press, 2021.

"History of the Arms and Great Seal of the Commonwealth of Massachusetts." Commonwealth of Massachusetts, www.sec.state.ma.us/pre/presea/sealhis/htm. Accessed 5 May 2021.

"Our Mandate." Art Gallery of Ontario, www.ago.net/mandate. Accessed 10 May 2022.

Works with an **anonymous author** should be alphabetized by title, omitting the author element.

Sir Gawain and the Green Knight. Edited by Paul Battles, Broadview Press, 2012.

Works under a **pseudonym**, or **works that are by an author that has published under more than one name**, can be treated in several ways. The pseudonym or name that your source records as author may simply be used as-is in the author element. If you are citing an older work by someone who has since changed their name, you may substitute in the current name the person is using. For trans authors, for example, use an author's chosen name—do not mention former names in either your citations or your prose, regardless of the name that is listed by your source. MLA calls this "consolidating"—this way, all works by one person can be cited under one name. For example, if you are citing the novelist Agatha Christie (who also wrote under the name Mary Westmacott), it is fine to consolidate the titles under "Agatha Christie" (unless the pseudonym is relevant to your writing, in which case see other options below):

Christie, Agatha. *Absent in the Spring*. 1944. HarperCollins, 1997.

---. *Murder on the Orient Express*. 1934. HarperCollins, 2011.

If a writer uses more than one pseudonym, it may be useful to cite their works using the writer's better-known name. In this case, you may use the better-known name in the author element, followed by the lesser-known name in square brackets and preceded by *published as* (in italics).

Oates, Joyce Carol [*published as* Lauren Kelly]. *Take Me, Take Me with You*. HarperCollins, 2005.

You may also simply place the author's more well-known name in square brackets and omit the lesser-known pseudonym, indicating that the name has been supplied by you and was originally published under another name.

[Oates, Joyce Carol]. *Take Me, Take Me with You*. HarperCollins, 2005.

Online usernames are copied out exactly as they appear on the screen.

@newyorker. "With the resignation of Turkey's Prime Minister, the country's President now stands alone and unchallenged." *Twitter*, 6 May 2016, twitter.com/NewYorker/status/728676985254379520.

Note that the author element is flexible. If you are discussing the work of a film director, for example, the director's name should be placed in the author element, with a descriptor.

Hitchcock, Alfred, director. *The Lady Vanishes*. United Artists, 1938.

If, on the other hand, you are discussing film editing, you would place the film editor in the author element. In this case, you might also include Hitchcock's name in the "Other Contributors" element.

Dearing, R.E., film editor. *The Lady Vanishes*, directed by Alfred Hitchcock, United Artists, 1938.

If no single contributor's work is of particular importance in your discussion of a film or television source, omit the author element altogether.

"The Buys." *The Wire*, created by David Simon and Ed Burns, directed by Peter Medak, season 1, episode 3, HBO, 16 June 2002, disc 1.

If you are citing a **translated source** and the translation itself is the focus of your work, the translator or translators can be placed in the author element.

Lodge, Kirsten, translator. *Notes from the Underground*. By Fyodor Dostoevsky, edited by Kirsten Lodge, Broadview Press, 2014.

When the work itself is the focus, as is usually the case, the author should remain in the author element, and the translator moved to the "other contributors" element:

Dostoevsky, Fyodor. *Notes from the Underground*. Translated and edited by Kirsten Lodge, Broadview Press, 2014.

This principle holds true across media and elements. Adapt the MLA structure to create citations that are clear, most relevant to your work, and most useful to your reader.

Title of Source

The title of your source follows the author element. Copy the title as you find it in the source, but with MLA-standard capitalization and punctuation. Capitalize the first word, the last word, and all key words, but not articles, prepositions, coordinating conjunctions, or the *to* in infinitives.

Carson, Anne. *The Albertine Workout*. New Directions, 2014.

If there is a **subtitle**, include it after the main title, following a colon.

Bök, Christian. *The Xenotext: Book 1*. Coach House Books, 2015.

Your title gives the reader information about the source. Italicized titles indicate that the source is a complete, independent whole. A title enclosed in quotation marks tells the reader that the source is part of a larger work.

A **book** is an independent whole, so the title is italicized.

Sowerby, Githa. *Three Plays*. Edited by J. Ellen Gainor, Broadview Press, 2021.

Other examples include **long poems** (*In Memoriam*), **magazines** (*The New Yorker*), **newspapers** (*The Guardian*), **journals** (*The American Poetry Review*), **websites** (*The Camelot Project*), **films** (*Memento*), **television shows** (*The X-Files*), and **compact discs** or **record albums** (*Dark Side of the Moon*).

A **poem**, **short story**, or **essay** within a larger collection is placed in quotation marks.

Wordsworth, William. "The Solitary Reaper." *Poems, in Two Volumes*, edited by Richard Matlak, Broadview Press, 2016, p. 153.

Other examples include **chapters in books** ("The Autist Artist" in *The Man Who Mistook His Wife for a Hat and Other Clinical Tales*), **encyclopedia articles** ("Existentialism"), **essays in books or journals** ("Salvation in the Garden: Daoism and Ecology" in *Daoism and Ecology: Ways within a Cosmic Landscape*), **short stories** ("Young Goodman Brown"), **short poems** ("Daddy"), **pages on websites** ("The Fisher King" from *The Camelot Project*), **episodes of television shows** ("Small Potatoes" from *The X-Files*), and **songs** ("Eclipse" from *Dark Side of the Moon*). Put the titles of **public lectures** in double quotation marks as well ("Walls in *The Epic of Gilgamesh*").

These formatting rules apply across media forms. A website is placed in italics; a posting on the website is placed in quotation marks.

Stein, Sadie. "Casting the Runes." *The Daily: The Paris Review Blog*, 9 Oct. 2015, www.theparisreview.org/blog/2015/10/09/casting -the-runes/.

If the title of a stand-alone work contains the title of a work that is not independent, the latter is put in double quotation marks, and the entire title is put in italics (*"Self-Reliance" and Other Essays*). If the title of a stand-alone work appears within the title of another independent work, MLA recommends that the latter be put in italics and the former not (*Chaucer's House of Fame: The Poetics of Skeptical Fideism*). If the title of a non-independent work is embedded in another title of the same kind, put the inner title into single quotation marks and the outer title in double quotation marks ("The Drama of Donne's 'The Indifferent'").

When a stand-alone work appears in a **collection**, the work's title remains in italics.

James, Henry. *The American. Henry James: Novels 1871–1880*, edited by William T. Stafford, Library of America, 1983.

Title of Container

Very often your source is found within a larger context, such as an **anthology**, **periodical**, **newspaper**, **digital platform**, or **website**. When this is the case, the larger whole is called the "container." For an article in a newspaper, for example, the article is the "source" and the newspaper is the "container." For a song in an **album**, the song is the "source" and the album is the "container."

The title of the container is usually italicized and followed by a comma.

Russell, Anna. "The Beguiling Legacy of *Alice in Wonderland*." *The New Yorker*, 11 July 2021, www.newyorker.com/culture/ culture-desk/the-beguiling-legacy-of-alice-in-wonderland.

The container is anything that contains another work: a website; a book that is a collection of stories, poems, plays, or essays; a magazine; a journal; an album; or a database.

When doing research, particularly online, one often comes across nested containers, in which, for example, an article is found in a collection of essays, which is itself found on a database. All containers are recorded in the citation, so your reader knows exactly how to find your source. Add more container elements as needed. Additional containers should follow the period at the end of the information given for the preceding container (usually after the date or location element).

It can be helpful to see this process charted out. Notice that the publication information for the container follows that of the source.

Here is an example of an **article from a periodical**, accessed from an online database.

1. Author.	Lamothe, Daphne.
2. Title of source.	"The City-Child's Quest: Spatiality and Sociality in Paule Marshall's *The Fisher King*."
CONTAINER 1:	
3. Title of container,	*Meridians*,
4. Contributor,	
5. Version,	
6. Number,	vol. 15, no. 2,
7. Publisher,	
8. Publication Date,	2017,
9. Location.	pp. 491–506.
CONTAINER 2:	
3. Title of container,	*JSTOR,*
4. Contributor,	
5. Version,	
6. Number,	
7. Publisher,	
8. Publication Date,	
9. Location.	www.jstor.org/stable/10.2979/meridians.15.2.10.

MLA Style

Citation as It Would Appear in the Works Cited List:

Lamothe, Daphne. "The City-Child's Quest: Spatiality and Sociality in Paule Marshall's *The Fisher King*." *Meridians*, vol. 15, no. 2, 2017, pp. 491–506. *JSTOR*, www.jstor.org/stable/10.2979/meridians.15.2.10.

The next example is an **e-book** accessed from a digital platform.

1. Author.	Copeland, Edward, and Juliet McMaster, editors.
2. Title of source.	*The Cambridge Companion to Jane Austen.*
CONTAINER 1:	
3. Title of container,	
4. Contributor,	
5. Version,	2nd ed.,
6. Number,	
7. Publisher,	Cambridge UP,
8. Publication Date,	2010.
9. Location.	
CONTAINER 2:	
3. Title of container,	*Cambridge Core,*
4. Contributor,	
5. Version,	
6. Number,	
7. Publisher,	
8. Publication Date,	2011,
9. Location.	https://doi.org/10.1017/CCO9780521763080.

Citation as It Would Appear in the Works Cited List:

Copeland, Edward, and Juliet McMaster, editors. *The Cambridge Companion to Jane Austen*. 2nd ed., Cambridge UP, 2010. *Cambridge Core*, 2011, https://doi.org/10.1017/CCO9780521763080.

The elements are recorded sequentially to create your citation. Notice that any elements that don't apply to this source are left out. Note that for a **self-contained e-book** that you access on an e-reader or in a proprietary web app, you may treat the citation as you would a print book, adding "e-book ed." in the Version element.

1. Author.	Austen, Jane.
2. Title of source.	*Pride and Prejudice.*
CONTAINER 1:	
3. Title of container,	
4. Contributor,	Edited by Robert P. Irvine,
5. Version,	2nd ed., e-book ed.,
6. Number,	
7. Publisher,	Broadview Press,
8. Publication Date,	2020.
9. Location.	

Citation as It Would Appear in the Works Cited List:

Austen, Jane. *Pride and Prejudice*. Edited by Robert P. Irvine, 2nd ed., e-book ed., Broadview Press, 2020.

Here is an example citation of a **performance in a television series**, accessed on Hulu.

1. Author.	Washington, Kerry, performer.
2. Title of source.	"The Spark."
CONTAINER 1:	
3. Title of container,	*Little Fires Everywhere,*
4. Contributor,	directed by Lynn Shelton,
5. Version,	
6. Number,	season 1, episode 1,
7. Publisher,	Best Day Ever Productions et al.,
8. Publication Date,	2020.
9. Location.	
CONTAINER 2:	
3. Title of container,	*Hulu,*
4. Contributor,	
5. Version,	
6. Number,	
7. Publisher,	
8. Publication Date,	
9. Location.	www.hulu.com/series/little-fires-everywhere-bce24897-1a74-48a3-95e8-6cdd530dde4c.

Citation as It Would Appear in the Works Cited List:

Washington, Kerry, performer. "The Spark." *Little Fires Everywhere*, directed by Lynn Shelton, season 1, episode 1, Best Day Ever Productions et al., 2020. *Hulu*, www.hulu.com/series/little-fires-everywhere-bce24897-1a74-48a3-95e8-6cdd530dde4c.

Contributor

There may be other key people who should be credited in your citation as contributors. This element follows the title of the source and the container (if there is one). The MLA recommends that you include the names of contributors who are important to your research, or if they help your reader to identify the source. Before each name, place a description of the role (do not abbreviate):

adapted by	introduction by
directed by	narrated by
edited by	performance by
illustrated by	translated by

If your listing of a contributor follows the source title, it is capitalized (following a period). If the contributor follows a container, it will be lower-case (following a comma).

James, Henry. *The American. Henry James: Novels 1871–1880*, edited by William T. Stafford, Library of America, 1983.

Mechain, Gwerful. *The Works of Gwerful Mechain*. Translated by Katie Gramich, Broadview Press, 2018.

In the Contributor element, include the most relevant contributors not already mentioned in the author element. If you are writing about a television episode and a certain performance is one of the elements you discuss, for example, include the performer's name in the Contributor element, along with any other contributors you wish to include.

Medak, Peter, director. "The Buys." *The Wire*, created by David Simon and Ed Burns, performance by Dominic West, season 1, episode 3, HBO, 16 June 2002.

Note that the MLA guidelines are flexible; for this part of the citation especially, consider what your readers most need to know about your source and include that information. Note also that there is some flexibility in the author element; if a particular performance or other contribution is the major focus in your discussion of source, it can be cited in the author element instead.

Version

If your source is **one of several editions**, or if it is a **revised version**, record those details in this element of your citation, followed by a comma. The word "edition" is abbreviated in your citation (ed.).

Edgeworth, Maria, et al. *Moral Tales: A Selection*. Edited by Robin Runia, e-book ed., Broadview Press, 2021.

Fowles, John. *The Magus*. Rev. ed., Jonathan Cape, 1977.

Shelley, Mary. *Frankenstein*. Edited by D.L. Macdonald and Kathleen Sherf, 3rd ed., Broadview Press, 2012.

You may also come across **expanded editions**, **revised editions**, and **updated editions**, all of which can be noted in this element of your citation. Different media might use different terminology. For example in film you may find a **director's cut**, or in music an **abridged version** of a concerto: use the same principles as above, providing the relevant information in the Version element of your citation.

Coen, Ethan, and Joel Coen, directors. *Blood Simple*. Director's cut, Universal, 2001.

Number

If your source is part of a **multi-volume work**, or if it is part of a journal that is issued in numbers and/or volumes, include the volume information in this Number element of your citation.

If you are citing **two or more volumes** of a multi-volume work, the entry should note the total number of volumes. If you cite only one of the volumes, list it after the title.

Jeeves, Julie, editor. *A Reference Guide to Spanish Architecture*. 3 vols, Hackett, 2005.

Mercer, Bobby, editor. *A Reference Guide to French Architecture*. Vol. 1, Hackett, 2002.

Include the **volume and issue numbers** for journals. Use the abbreviations *vol.* for volume and *no.* for issue number.

Gregory, Elizabeth. "Marianne Moore's 'Blue Bug': A Dialogic Ode on Celebrity, Race, Gender, and Age." *Modernism/Modernity*, vol. 22, no. 4, 2015, pp. 759–86.

Some journals do not use volume numbers and give only an issue number.

Sanger, Richard. "Goodbye, Seamus." *Brick*, no. 93, summer 2014, pp. 153–57.

The Number element is also where you record issue numbers for comic books, or the season and episode numbers for a television series.

Washington, Kerry, performer. "The Spark." *Little Fires Everywhere*, directed by Lynn Shelton, season 1, episode 1, Best Day Ever Productions et al., 2020. *Hulu*, www.hulu.com/series/little-fires-everywhere-bce24897-1a74-48a3-95e8-6cdd530dde4c.

Publisher

In this element of your citation, record the organization that produced the source, whether it be publisher of a book, the organization running a website, or the studio producing a film. (In the case of a secondary container, include the organization that produced the container.) Do not abbreviate, except in the case of university presses, which may be abbreviated as *UP*.

To find the publisher of a **book**, look on the title page or on the copyright page.

Joyce, James. *Exiles*. Edited by Keri Walsh, Oxford UP, 2021.

Rush, Rebecca. *Kelroy*. Edited by Betsy Klimasmith, Broadview Press, 2016.

For a **film** or **television series**, the studio or company that produced the show is recorded in the information on the back of a DVD or in the opening and closing credits.

Simon, David, creator. *The Wire*. HBO, 2002–2008.

For **websites**, the publisher's information can often be found in the copyright notice at the bottom of the page.

Bogan, Louise. "Women." 1922. *Representative Poetry Online*, edited by Ian Lancashire, University of Toronto, 2000.

You may omit a publisher's name in the following kinds of publications:

- A periodical (journal, magazine, newspaper).
- A work published by its author or editor.
- A website whose title is essentially the same as the name of the publisher.
- A website not involved in producing the works it is making available (YouTube, JSTOR, ProQuest). These are listed as containers, but not as publishers.

If **two or more publishers** are listed for your source, cite them both and separate them with a forward slash (/).

Banting, Keith G., editor. *Thinking Outside the Box: Innovation in Policy Ideas*. School of Policy Studies, Queen's University / McGill–Queen's University Press, 2015.

Publication Date

In this element of your citation, record the date of publication for your source. For **books**, this date is found on the copyright page (and sometimes on the title page). If several editions are listed, use the date for the edition you have consulted.

Stevenson, Robert Louis. *Strange Case of Dr. Jekyll and Mr. Hyde*. Edited by Martin A. Danahay, 3rd ed., Broadview Press, 2015.

Online sources almost always have a date posted, and this is the date you should record in this element.

Heller, Nathan. "The Big Uneasy: What's Roiling the Liberal-Arts Campus?" *The New Yorker*, 30 May 2016, www.newyorker.com/ magazine/2016/05/30/the-new-activism-of-liberal-arts-colleges.

A source may be associated with **more than one publication date**. An article online may have been previously published in print, or an article printed in a book may have been published previously in a periodical. In this case, the MLA recommends that you record the date that is most relevant to your use of the source. If you consulted the online version of an article, for example, ignore the date of print publication and cite the online publication date.

For books, we record the year of publication. For other sources, whether to include a year, month, and day depends on your source and the context in which you are using it. If you are citing an **episode from a television series**, for example, it is usually enough to record the year it aired.

Medak, Peter, director. "The Buys." *The Wire*, created by David Simon and Ed Burns, season 1, episode 3, HBO, 2002.

If, however, the context surrounding the episode is being discussed in your work, you should be more specific about the date:

Medak, Peter, director. "The Buys." *The Wire*, created by David Simon and Ed Burns, season 1, episode 3, HBO, 16 June 2002.

For a **video posted on a website**, include the date on which the video was posted. In the example below, the posting date should be included in the second container, which records the details for the digital platform. The date the video was released is included in the publication details for the source.

McDonald, Emily, director. *Looking Back with Pride*. Forever Pictures, 2021. *Vimeo*, uploaded by Emily McDonald, 21 June 2021, www.vimeo.com/565585933.

If you are citing a **comment posted on a web page**, and the time the content was posted is indicated, include the time in your entry.

Evan. Comment on "Another Impasse on Gun Bills, Another Win for Hyperpolitics." *The New York Times*, 21 June 2016, 9:02 a.m., www.nytimes.com/2016/06/22/us/politics/washington-congress -gun-control.html.

Larger projects are created over a longer span of time. If you are documenting a web project as a whole, include the full range of years during which it was developed.

Secord, James A., et al., editors. *Darwin Correspondence Project*. 1974–2016, www.darwinproject.ac.uk/.

The dates of publication for **periodicals** vary. Include in full the information provided by the copyright page, whether it be indicated by season, year, month, week, or day.

Gander, Forrest. "A Most Ingenious Work of Literature." *Brick*, no. 107, summer 2021, pp. 11–18.

Salenius, Sirpa. "Transatlantic Interracial Sisterhoods: Sarah Remond, Ellen Craft, and Harriet Jacobs in England." *Frontiers: A Journal of Women Studies*, vol. 38, no. 1, 2017, pp. 166–96. *JSTOR*, www.jstor.org/stable/10.5250/fronjwomestud.38.1.0166.

Location

The content of the Location element varies considerably between print, digital, and other sources.

For **print sources** within a periodical or anthology, record a page number (preceded by p.) or a range of page numbers (preceded by pp.).

Gregory, Elizabeth. "Marianne Moore's 'Blue Bug': A Dialogic Ode on Celebrity, Race, Gender, and Age." *Modernism/Modernity*, vol. 22, no. 4, 2015, pp. 759–86.

An **online work** is located by its DOI or URL. If a DOI (Digital Object Identifier) is available, it is a more reliable and preferred option, as DOIs do not change when the source moves (whereas URLs do). If your source has no DOI but offers a "stable" URL, choose that one to include in your citation. The publisher in this case has agreed not to change the URL. Note that the MLA considers the inclusion of URLs to be optional, as there are downsides to including them (such as their instability and their tendency to create messier citations). In general, however, it is advisable to include them, unless your instructor advises otherwise. When copying a URL into your citation, remove the *http://*; this means that usually the URL will begin with *www*. For excessively long URLs, the MLA recommends truncating them, leaving readers enough of the address to find the source but avoiding an unruly citation. If you need to break a URL or DOI over two or more lines, do not insert any hyphens at the break point; instead, when possible, break after a colon or slash or before other marks of punctuation.

Jesse, Tom. "John Ashbery's Unexceptional Politics." *Pacific Coast Philology*, vol. 55, no. 2, 2021, pp. 171–90. *JSTOR*, www.jstor.org/stable/10.5325/pacicoasphil.55.2.0171.

Yearling, R. "*Hamlet* and the Limits of Narrative." *Essays in Criticism: A Quarterly Journal of Literary Criticism,* vol. 65, no. 4, 2015, pp. 368–82. *Proquest,* https://doi:dx.doi.org/10.1093/escrit/cgv022.

We find a **television episode** on a DVD by its disc number. Place the disc number in the Location element.

"The Buys." *The Wire*, created by David Simon and Ed Burns, directed by Peter Medak, season 1, episode 3, HBO, 2002, disc 1.

For a **work of art** that you have seen in person, cite the name of the institution and city where you saw it in the Location element. Leave out the name of the city if the city name is part of the institution name (e.g., The Art Institute of Chicago).

Sargent, John Singer. *Henry James.* 1913, National Portrait Gallery, London.

Some **archived sources** have a different system for locating objects in the archive. Where this is the case, include the code or number in the Location element.

Blake, William. *The Marriage of Heaven and Hell.* 1790–1793. The Fitzwilliam Museum, Cambridge, 123-1950. Illuminated printed book.

If you are citing a **live performance** or **lecture**, name the location and the city. Omit the city name if it is part of the location name.

Royal Winnipeg Ballet. *The Princess and the Goblin.* Directed and choreographed by Twyla Tharp, performances by Paloma Herrera and Dmitri Dovgoselets, 17 Oct. 2012, Centennial Concert Hall, Winnipeg.

Supplemental Elements

You may include any of the following elements in your citation if you think they are helpful to your reader. Supplemental elements are typically inserted into two possible places in your citation—after the title of your source, if it applies primarily to the source (such as an original publication date), or at the end of the citation, if it applies to the citation as a whole (such as a date of access). Add a period at the end of a supplemental element, regardless of its placement.

Date of Original Publication

If your source has been republished, it may give your reader some important context if you include the date of original publication. If you do so, place the date immediately after the source title and close with a period.

Trollope, Anthony. *The Eustace Diamonds.* 1873. Edited by Stephen Gill and John Sutherland, Penguin, 1986.

City of Publication

Including the city of publication is not very useful these days, so the MLA has decided to remove this element from citations. There are two situations, however, where you may wish to include the city. If the book was published before 1900, the city of publication is associated more closely with the source than the publisher. For these books, you may substitute the city of publication for the publisher.

Dickens, Charles. *Our Mutual Friend.* Vol. 1, New York, 1865.

Some publishers release more than one version of a text in different countries (a British and an American edition, for example). If you are reading an unexpected version of a text, or the version you are reading has historical significance, place the name of the city in front of the publisher.

Lawrence, D.H. *Lady Chatterley's Lover.* London, Penguin, 1960.

Books in a Series

If your source is a book in a series, you may add the series name in roman (i.e., without italics) at the end of your citation, preceded by a period.

Klooster, Wim, editor. *Spanish American Independence Movements: A History in Documents*. Broadview Press, 2021. Broadview Sources Series.

Unexpected Type of Work

If your source needs further explanation, place a descriptive term (e-mail, transcript, broadcast, street performance, talk, address) at the end of the citation, preceded by a period.

Rosenheim, Jeff. "Diane Arbus." Art Gallery of Ontario, 6 May 2016, Toronto. Lecture.

Date of Access

It is optional to include a date of access for your online citations, and the MLA recommends you do so when the work lacks a publication date or if the website has ceased to exist.

Crawford, Isabella Valancy. "The Canoe." *Representative Poetry Online*, edited by Ian Lancashire, Web Development Group, Information Technology Services, University of Toronto Libraries, www.tspace.library.utoronto.ca/html/1807/4350/poem596 .html. Accessed 24 Nov. 2022.

37c. Examples

The following are examples of MLA-style citations for sources across various media. While these examples can offer useful guidance, remember that the MLA guidelines may be adapted to suit the details of the sources you are documenting, as well as the context in which you are using them.

single author:

Graham, Jorie. *From the New World*. Ecco, 2015.

Ingalls, Rachel. *Mrs Caliban*. 1982. Faber & Faber, 2021.

two authors:

Davis, Lydia, and Eliot Weinberger. *Two American Scenes*. New Directions, 2013. Pamphlets Series.

Rectenwald, Michael, and Lisa Carl. *Academic Writing, Real World Topics*. Broadview Press, 2015.

three or more authors:

Fantuzzi, Marco, et al., editors. *Reception in the Greco-Roman World: Literary Studies in Theory and Practice.* Cambridge UP, 2021.

Fromkin, Victoria, et al. *An Introduction to Language.* 4th Canadian ed., Nelson, 2010.

corporate author:

2020 Annual Report. Broadview Press, 2021.

"History of the Arms and Great Seal of the Commonwealth of Massachusetts." Commonwealth of Massachusetts, www.sec .state.ma.us/pre/presea/sealhis/htm.

Ontario, Ministry of Natural Resources. *Achieving Balance: Ontario's Long-Term Energy Plan.* Queen's Printer for Ontario, 2016, www.energy.gov.on.ca/en/ltep/achieving-balance-ontarios -long-term-energy-plan.

works with an anonymous author: Works with an anonymous author should be alphabetized by title.

Pearl. Edited and translated by Jane Beal, Broadview Press, 2020.

two or more works by the same author: The author's name should appear for the first entry only; for subsequent entries substitute three hyphens for the name of the author.

Menand, Louis. "Bad Comma: Lynne Truss's Strange Grammar." Review of *Eats, Shoots and Leaves,* by Lynne Truss. *The New Yorker,* 28 June 2004, www.newyorker.com/magazine/2004/06/ 28/bad-comma.

---. *The Metaphysical Club: A Story of Ideas in America.* Farrar, Straus and Giroux, 2001.

works under a pseudonym: These are given using the same formatting as author's names. Online usernames are given as they appear.

@TheAtlantic. "The president is loath to acknowledge that many Americans support the recent attacks on democracy, 'and those who don't face a system stacked against them,' @GrahamDavidA writes." *Twitter,* 14 July 2021, www.twitter.com/TheAtlantic/ status/1415363709950701572.

edited works:

Renker, Elizabeth, editor. *Poems: A Concise Anthology*. Broadview Press, 2016.

When referring to an edited version of a work written by another author or authors, list the editor(s) after the title.

Trollope, Anthony. *The Eustace Diamonds*. 1873. Edited by Stephen Gill and John Sutherland, Penguin, 1986.

works in translation:
The translator is normally listed in the Contributor element of the citation.

Bolaño, Roberto. *By Night in Chile*. Translated by Chris Andrews, New Directions, 2003.

If your work focuses on the translation itself, you may list the translator in the author element, moving the author to the Contributor element.

Andrews, Chris, translator. *By Night in Chile*. By Roberto Bolaño, New Directions, 2003.

selections from anthologies or collections of readings: A selection from a collection of readings or an anthology should begin with the name of the author of the selection. If they are available, be sure to add the selection's inclusive page numbers after the anthology's publication date.

Crawford, Isabella Valancy. "The Canoe." *Representative Poetry Online*, edited by Ian Lancashire, U of Toronto, 1997, www.rpo.library.utoronto.ca/poems/canoe. Accessed 20 Apr. 2022.

Skelton, John. *Magnificence. The Broadview Anthology of Tudor Drama*, edited by Alan Stewart, Broadview Press, 2021, pp. 125–80.

Whitman, Walt. "Song of the Redwood-Tree." *Leaves of Grass*, Boston: James R. Osgood and Co., 1881–82. *The Walt Whitman Archive*, edited by Matt Cohen et al., www.whitmanarchive.org/published/LG/1891/poems/93.

cross-references for works from the same collection or anthology: It can be more efficient to create a full entry for the collection or anthology, and then to list each cited item in its own entry. Position the entries in the Works Cited list alphabetically, as you normally would, and use a short form for the collection or anthology, as in the following example:

Brown, Jennifer S.H., and Elizabeth Vibert, editors. *Reading Beyond Words: Contexts for Native History*. Broadview Press, 1996.

Cruikshank, Julie. "Discovery of Gold on the Klondike: Perspectives from Oral Tradition." Brown and Vibert, pp. 433–59.

Gleach, Frederic W. "Controlled Speculation: Interpreting the Saga of Pocahontas and Captain John Smith." Brown and Vibert, pp. 21–42.

multi-volume works: If you are citing one or more of the volumes, list them after the title. The entry may note the total number of volumes at the end of the citation (this is optional).

Jeeves, Julie, editor. *A Reference Guide to Spanish Architecture*. 3 vols., Hackett, 2005.

Mercer, Bobby, editor. *A Reference Guide to French Architecture*. Vol. 1, Hackett, 2002. 3 vols.

different editions: The edition should be specified whenever it is not the first edition. Include whatever the title page indicates about the particular edition, and use abbreviations (e.g., *rev. ed.* for *revised edition*, *2nd ed.* for *second edition*, and so on).

Acheson, Katherine O. *Writing Essays about Literature: A Guide for University and College Students*. 2nd ed., Broadview Press, 2021.

The Bible. Authorized King James Version, Oxford UP, 2008.

Fowles, John. *The Magus*. Rev. ed., Jonathan Cape, 1977.

republished sources: When a source was previously published in a different form, you may include information about the prior publication. This is an optional element; include this information at your discretion, if you feel it would give your reader important context for the source.

MacMillan, Margaret. "Hubris." *History's People: Personalities and the Past, Massey Lectures*, CBC Radio, 3 Nov. 2015, www.cbc.ca/radio/ideas/history-s-people-personalities-the-past -lecture-2-1.3301571. Podcast. Originally delivered at the Arts and Culture Centre, St. John's, NL, 25 Sept. 2015, 7:00 p.m. Lecture.

reference work entries: List by the author of the entry, if known; otherwise, list by the entry itself. The citation of a well-known reference work (because such works are frequently updated) should not have full publication details; provide the edition number, date, and location only. Don't include page numbers for works that arrange their entries alphabetically.

"Artificial." *Oxford English Dictionary.* 2nd ed., 1989.

"Baldwin, James, 1924–1987." *ProQuest Biographies*, 2006. *Literature Online*, www-proquest-com./encyclopedias-reference -works/baldwin-james-1924-1987.

Fowler, H.W. "Unique." *The King's English*, 2nd ed., 1908. *Bartleby. com*, bartleby.com/116/108.html#2.

works with a title in the title: A title that is usually italicized should remain italicized when it appears within quotation marks:

Yearling, R. "*Hamlet* and the Limits of Narrative." *Essays in Criticism: A Quarterly Journal of Literary Criticism,* vol. 65, no. 4, 2015, pp. 368–82. *Proquest*, https://doi:dx.doi.org/10.1093/escrit/cgv022.

Titles that are in quotation marks that appear within other titles in quotation marks are enclosed by single quotation marks:

Berndt, Katrin. "Trapped in Class? Material Manifestations of Poverty and Prosperity in Alice Munro's 'Royal Beatings' and 'The Beggar Maid.'" *Neohelicon*, vol. 47, 18 Aug. 2020, pp. 521–35. *Springer-Link Journals*, https://doi.org/10.1007/s11059-020-00550-1.

An italicized title that is included within another italicized title is neither italicized nor placed in quotation marks. It appears in roman:

Morelli, Stefan. *Stoppard's* Arcadia *and Modern Drama*. Ashgate, 2004.

If a title normally enclosed in quotation marks appears in an italicized title, keep the quotation marks:

Runzo, Sandra. *"Theatricals of Day": Emily Dickinson and Nineteenth-Century American Popular Culture*. U of Massachusetts P, 2019.

material from prefaces, introductions, etc.: If you refer to something from a work's preface, introduction, or foreword, the reference under Works Cited should begin with the name of the author of that preface, introduction, or foreword. Add inclusive page numbers after the date of publication.

Stage, Kelly. Introduction. *The Roaring Girl*, by Thomas Middleton and Thomas Dekker, Broadview Press, 2019, pp. 7–17.

magazine articles: The title of the article should appear in quotation marks, the title of the magazine in italics. If no author is identified, the title of the article should appear first. If the magazine is published monthly or every two months, give the date as month and year. For magazines published weekly or every two weeks, give the date as day, month, and year. Abbreviate the names of months (except for *May*, *June*, and *July*).

Enright, Robert. "Ways of Looking, Ways of Not Seeing: An Interview with Shaan Syed." *Border Crossings*, no. 156, May 2021, www.bordercrossingsmag.com/article/ways-of-looking-ways -of-not-seeing.

"Greens in Pinstriped Suits." *The Economist*, 21 May 2016, www.economist.com/news/business/21699141-climate-con-scious-shareholders-are-putting-big-oil-spot-greens-pinstriped-suits.

If the website is hosted by a body other than the magazine itself, include it as a second container with its accompanying publication details.

Kreimer, Julian. "Mernet Larsen." *Art in America*, vol. 104, no. 4, 2016, pp. 115–16. *Academic Search Complete*, www.search.ebscohost .com/login.aspx?direct=true&db=a9hAN=114088897&site =ehost-live.

newspaper articles: The basic principles to follow with newspaper articles or editorials are the same as with magazine articles (see above). Note, however, that when the newspaper's sections are paginated separately, section as well as page numbers are often required. If an article is not printed on consecutive pages, include only the first page number followed by a plus sign. In the following reference the article begins on page 3 of the first section:

Jackson, David, et al. "Comey's Ouster Stuns Washington." *USA Today*, 10 May 2017, p. A3+.

If you are citing an online version of a newspaper article you should include the date the article was posted. The site name, if it is different from the container title, should also be included.

Kaplan, Thomas. "Bernie Sanders Wins Oregon; Hillary Clinton Declares Victory in Kentucky." *The New York Times*, 17 May 2016, www.nytimes.com/2016/05/18/us/politics/bernie-sanders-oregon-results.html.

journal articles: The basic principles are the same as with magazine articles, but entries for journal articles include the volume and issue numbers.

Belcourt, Billy-Ray. "Meditations on Reserve Life, Biosociality, and the Taste of Non-Sovereignty." *Settler Colonial Studies*, vol. 8, no. 1, Jan. 2018, pp. 1–15, https://doi.org/10.1080/22014 73X.2017.1279830.

If you are citing an online version of a journal article you should include any additional containers and their publication details (databases, for example).

Sohmer, Steve. "12 June 1599: Opening Day at Shakespeare's Globe." *Early Modern Literary Studies: A Journal of Sixteenth- and Seventeenth-Century English Literature*, vol. 3, no. 1, 1997. *ProQuest*, www.extra.shu.ac.uk/emls/emlshome.html.

book reviews: The name of the reviewer (if it has been provided) should come first, followed by the title of the review (if there is one), and then by the information on the book itself.

Leiter, Brian, and Michael Weisberg. "Do You Only Have a Brain? On Thomas Nagel." Review of *Why the Materialist Neo-Darwinian Conception of Nature Is Almost Certainly False*, by Thomas Nagel, *The Nation*, 22 Oct. 2012, www.thenation.com/article/do-you-only-have-brain-thomas-nagel/.

Lennon, J. Robert. "I Was Trying to Find the Edge." Review of *Second Place*, by Rachel Cusk, *London Review of Books*, vol. 43, no. 11, 3 June 2021, www.lrb.co.uk/the-paper/v43/n11/j.-robert -lennon/i-was-trying-to-find-the-edge.

periodical publications in online databases:

Moy, Olivia Loksing. "Reading in the Aftermath: An Asian American *Jane Eyre*." *Victorian Studies*, vol. 62, no. 3, 2020, pp. 406–20. *Project MUSE*, muse.jhu.edu/article/771238.

illustrated books: Include the illustrator's name as well as the author's name.

Juster, Norman. *The Phantom Tollbooth*. Illustrated by Jules Feiffer, Yearling-Random House, 1961.

graphic narratives: In many graphic narratives, both the illustrations and the text are created by one person; these kinds of works should be documented as in the second example below. Use the first example's format for works whose text is by one person and illustrations by another.

Butler, Octavia E. *Kindred: A Graphic Novel Adaptation*. Art by John Jennings, adapted by Damian Duffy, Abrams Books, 2017.

Leavitt, Sarah. *Tangles: A Story about Alzheimer's, My Mother, and Me*. Freehand Books, 2010.

films or television episodes: These entries may be tailored to the context in which you are citing the work. If you are discussing the work of a director, for example, place the director's name in the Author element:

Medak, Peter, director. "The Buys." *The Wire*, created by David Simon and Ed Burns, season 1, episode 3, HBO, 16 June 2002.

Zhao, Chloé, director. *Nomadland*. Performances by Frances McDormand, Gay DeForest, Patricia Grier, and Linda May, Searchlight Pictures, 2020. *Hulu*, www.hulu.com/nomadland-movie.

If you are discussing a particular performance, place the actor's name in the Author element.

Moss, Elizabeth, performer. "A Little Kiss." *Mad Men*, directed by Jennifer Getzinger, AMC, 25 Mar. 2012.

Washington, Kerry, performer. "The Spark." *Little Fires Everywhere*, directed by Lynn Shelton, season 1, episode 1, Best Day Ever Productions et al., 2020. *Hulu*, www.hulu.com/series/little-fires-everywhere-bce24897-1a74-48a3-95e8-6cdd530dde4c.

online videos: If your source is a video on a website, cite, if you can, who uploaded the video, and the date on which the video was posted.

McDonald, Emily, director. *Looking Back with Pride*. Forever Pictures, 2021. *Vimeo*, uploaded by Emily McDonald, 21 June 2021, www.vimeo.com/565585933.

radio broadcasts:

"Glenn Gould Special." *The Sunday Edition*, narrated by Robert Harris and Michael Enright, CBC Radio One, 23 Sept. 2012.

podcasts:

"Are Young People Losing Faith in Democracy?" *Talking Politics*, hosted by David Runciman, 2 Nov. 2020, www.talkingpoliticspodcast.com/blog/2020/285-are-young-people-losing-faith-in-democracy.

recorded music:

Bridgers, Phoebe. "Motion Sickness." *Stranger in the Alps*, Dead Oceans, 2017.

live performances: If you are citing a live performance or lecture, include the physical location and the city where the performance or lecture was delivered, as well as the date. Omit the city name if it is part of the location name. Include other information about the performance—the names of the director, the conductor, and/or lead performers, for instance—where such information is relevant. If your work focuses on the contribution of a performance's director, for example, cite that person in the Author element. Other important contributors follow the title in the Contributor element.

Bedford, Brian, director. *The Importance of Being Earnest*. By Oscar Wilde, performances by Brian Bedford, Santino Fontana, David Furr, Charlotte Parry, and Sarah Topham, Roundabout Theatre Company, 3 July 2011, American Airlines Theatre, New York.

MacMillan, Margaret. "Hubris." *History's People: Personalities and the Past*, 25 Sept. 2015, 7:00 p.m., Arts and Culture Centre, St. John's, NL. Massey Lecture.

works of visual art: When citing a physical object you have experienced, such as a work of art, provide in the Location element the name of the institution and city where you experienced it. Leave out the name of the city if the city name is part of the institution name (e.g., Art Institute of Chicago).

Belmore, Rebecca. *Fringe*. 2008, National Gallery of Canada, Ottawa.

Sargent, John Singer. *Henry James*. 1913, National Portrait Gallery, London.

If you access a work of art online or in a book, you should include full information about the website or volume you consulted.

Colquhoun, Ithell. *Scylla*. 1938, Tate Gallery, London. *Tate Women Artists*, by Alicia Foster, Tate, 2004, p. 85.

Giotto di Bondone. *Lamentation*. 1304–06, Capella Scrovegni, Padua, *Web Gallery of Art*, www.wga.hu/frames-e.html?/html/g/giotto/. Accessed 29 Jan. 2022.

interviews: Begin all entries for interviews with the name of the person being interviewed, and if there is a title for the interview, include it (in quotation marks if it is part of another work, or in italics if it has been published by itself). If there is no title, or if the title does not make clear that the work is an interview, write *Interview*, and give the name of the interviewer, if known. Finish with whatever publication information is appropriate. If you conducted the interview yourself, give the name of the person you interviewed, the medium (*Personal interview*, *Telephone interview*), and the date.

Lockwood, Patricia. "Patricia Lockwood Is a Good Reason to Never Log Off." Interview by Gabriella Paiella, *GQ*, 15 Feb. 2021, www.gq.com/story/patricia-lockwood-book-interview.

Rankine, Claudia. "The Art of Poetry No. 102." Interview by David L. Ulin, *Paris Review*, no. 219, winter 2016, www.theparisreview.org/interviews/6905/the-art-of-poetry-no-102-claudia-rankine.

Rosengarten, Herbert. Personal interview, 21 Jan. 2017.

online projects: In the case of large projects, cite the full range of years during which the project has been developed:

Secord, James A., et al., editors. *Darwin Correspondence Project.* 1974–2016, www.darwinproject.ac.uk/.

Willett, Perry, editor. *Victorian Women Writers Project.* Indiana University Digital Library Program, 1995–2016, webapp1.dlib.indiana.edu/vwwp/welcome.do. Accessed 26 Nov. 2017.

e-books: E-book citations should follow the basic pattern for physical books, with the format recorded in the Version element.

Edgeworth, Maria, et al. *Moral Tales: A Selection.* Edited by Robin Runia, e-book ed., Broadview Press, 2021.

Note that the above formatting applies to publications formatted for e-book web readers or e-readers. If you have accessed or downloaded an e-book from a website, digital platform, or database, format your citation as you would any other source found online, by adding a Container element and by citing a DOI or stable URL in the Location element.

Austen, Jane. *Pride and Prejudice.* 1813. *Project Gutenberg*, 2008, www.gutenberg.org/files/1342/1342-h/1342-h.htm. Accessed 20 Feb. 2021.

information databases:

Morissette, René, et al. "Working from Home: Potential Implications for Public Transit and Greenhouse Gas Emissions." *Statistics Canada*, 22 Apr. 2021, https://doi.org/10.25318/362800012021004005-eng.

entry in a wiki: Wikis are online sites that can be added to and edited by any site user; as such, they may be subject to frequent changes made by any number of authors and editors. Do not, therefore, provide any authors' names. Start with the entry's title; then give the name of the wiki, the site publisher, the date of the entry's last update, the medium, and the date you accessed the site.

"William Caxton." *Wikipedia*. Wikimedia Foundation, 20 Oct. 2012, www.en.wikipedia.org/wiki/William_Caxton. Accessed 26 Oct. 2021.

blog post: Include the title of the posting as your source title, the blog title as the first container, and the name of the blog host as a publisher.

Gluck, Heather. "Brontë Society Fights to Keep 'Lost' Emily Brontë Poems Available for the Public." *MobyLives*, Melville House, 14 June 2021, www.mhpbooks.com/bronte-society-fights-to-keep -lost-emily-bronte-poems-available-for-the-public/.

e-mail message: Use the subject as the title and place it within quotation marks.

Milton, Frank. "Thoughts on Animal Rights." Received by the author, 15 Jan. 2013.

If it is not clear from the context of your work that the source being cited is an e-mail, you may wish to add an optional element to the end of your citation that indicates the type of work.

Stuart, Jennifer. "My Experience of the Attack." Received by the author, 17 May 2016. E-mail.

tweet: Copy the full, unchanged text of the tweet in the title element and enclose it in quotation marks. The username is included as the Author element.

@TheAtlantic. "The president is loath to acknowledge that many Americans support the recent attacks on democracy, 'and those who don't face a system stacked against them,' @GrahamDavidA writes." *Twitter*, 14 July 2021, www.twitter.com/TheAtlantic/ status/1415363709950701572.

comment posted on a web page: Usernames are given in full, unchanged. If the comment is anonymous, skip the author element. If the comment does not have its own title, provide instead a description of the comment that includes the title of the work being commented on (e.g., Comment on "Trump's Tweets after Comey Firing"). If it is available, include the exact time of posting in the Publication Date element.

Evan. Comment on "Another Impasse on Gun Bills, Another Win for Hyperpolitics." *The New York Times*, 21 June 2016, 9:02 a.m., www.nytimes.com/2016/06/22/us/politics/washington-congress -gun-control.html.

37d. MLA Style Sample Essay Pages

Following are sample pages from an essay written in MLA style; the full essay is posted on the companion site. Note that further sample essays, some of which also employ MLA style, are also available on the companion website associated with this book.

Among the details to notice in this referencing system:

- MLA style focuses on the process of documentation, not the prescriptive following of specific guidelines (though consistent formatting according to MLA principles is still vital to communicate clearly with your reader).

- To create a citation, list the relevant elements in the order prescribed by MLA (see the table on page 232). Any elements that don't apply to a given source are left out (placeholders for unknown information like *n.d.* ("no date") are not required).

- Follow the punctuation guidelines in the table on page 232. Any elements recorded after a period should be capitalized; elements following a comma should be lower-case.

- Your citation should give your reader a map to your exact source. If you are documenting an article found in a periodical, for example, which was itself found on a database, you should include the publication details of both "containers" (periodical and database) as part of your citation. See the "Title of Container" section above for details.

- Terms such as *editor*, *edited by*, *translator*, *translated by*, and *review* are not abbreviated.

- If there are three or more authors or editors, only the first name is given, reversed, followed by *et al.*

- Citations for journals include abbreviations for volume and issue ("vol. 40, no. 3").

- Give the publisher's name in full, but drop business words such as "Company." For University presses, use the abbreviations *U*, *P*, and *UP*.

- City names are not required as part of the publication details.

- The date of access for an online source is optional.

- Page numbers are preceded by *p.* for a single page reference, or *pp.* for a range of pages.

- Include the URL (with *http:* removed) or the DOI in the location element for digital sources. Do not surround the address with angle brackets and do conclude with a period.

- You do not have to identify the media type of your source, unless it is required for clarity.

MLA Style

cover page (not required in MLA style, but may be required by some instructors)

Monumental Problems:

Setting the Criteria for Decisions in Political Aesthetics

By Robin Lee

Prof. K. D. Smith

Humanities 205

20 October 2021

all text centred

MLA Style

Robin Lee

Professor Smith

Humanities 205

20 October 2021

Lee 1

Monumental Problems:

Setting the Criteria for Decisions in Political Aesthetics

first line of all paragraphs indented

In recent years the level of political controversy over public monuments has greatly increased. Heated disagreements have arisen in America (over monuments honouring Confederate leaders and supporters of slavery); in Canada (over monuments honouring John A. Macdonald and other leaders of the past who were complicit in the ill-treatment of Indigenous Canadians); in Britain (over monuments honouring James Colston and other leaders of the past who were involved in the slave trade); and elsewhere around the world. Should these controversial monuments be removed? Should they be preserved but locked away, accessible only to historians and art historians? Should they be accessible to all, but be displayed in low-key fashion in museums or art galleries (with full contextualization provided) rather than be raised on pedestals in public places? Should they simply be destroyed as relics of a past we have moved beyond? Or should hard choices be made in individual cases, with some works preserved, some not? In the heat of claims and counter-

text left-justified and ragged right

text double-spaced throughout

Lee 2

claims it can be difficult to sort out what criteria are truly
relevant for such decisions. This essay will examine issues of
relevance from several angles and will argue that one criterion
in particular deserves to be considered more frequently—the
aesthetic value of a work of art. Debates on these issues
rightly include considerable discussion of historical, political, and ethical issues, but too often entirely neglect aesthetic
considerations.

first
paragraph
ends with
a state-
ment of
the essay's
thesis

It is important at the outset to recognize that cities,
nations, and cultures have been removing public monuments
for almost as long as they have been erecting them. In ancient
Rome, for example, it was common to remove and destroy
monuments honouring one leader as soon as the next one
came to power; the Romans termed this process *damnatio
memoriae* or "condemnation of memory/legacy" (Byrne).
The notion that societies can and should periodically
re-assess the leaders of the past and revise their assessment
of who deserves to be honoured with public monuments
is not an idea dreamed up in the disrespectful twenty-first
century; it has been with us for millennia.

2

if your
source has
no num-
bered pages
or sections,
no number
is given

Nor is it an idea that should be associated with any
particular part of the political spectrum. Some have suggested
that it is predominantly those on the political left who want to
remove public monuments honouring figures they feel do not

3

M LA Style

Lee 3

endnote inserted to give additional information

deserve to be honoured.[1] But the left has no monopoly on such practices—far from it. Anti-communists joyously took down thousands of statues of Soviet leaders after the fall of the Soviet Union in 1990. The Communist government of East Germany tore down statues of Wilhelm I (the first German Emperor) in 1950. Militaristic Canadians tore down a statue of the Kaiser in 1914, as Canada was going to war with Germany. Countries throughout Africa have removed public memorials to European colonial and imperialist figures. Back in 1912 the Kentucky

for a source listed by title, use a shortened title for parenthetical citation

chapter of the Daughters of the Confederacy was keen not only to erect a statue honouring Confederate leader Jefferson Davis but also to remove a statue of Abraham Lincoln in order to make way for Davis ("Objectionable"). And so it has gone; the idea of removing public monuments of discredited leaders is decidedly not something the radical left has dreamed up in our own era.

4

Nor is it a "freedom of speech" or "freedom of expression" issue, much as some have suggested that to be the case.[2] In Canada and the United States, as in democracies around the world, any individual remains free to commission and display in their front yard a statue of Robert E. Lee, of Joseph Stalin, or of whomever they like; the issue is whom governments decide (on behalf of the people as a whole) to honour with public monuments in civic squares, in public parks, or in front of leg-islatures and courthouses. Inevitably, views as to who deserves

Lee 4

or does not deserve to be so honoured change over time, and
are often highly charged politically; consensus is often elusive.

One of the greatest mistakes of the debate over public   5
monuments is to suppose that such monuments are intended
primarily in order to preserve the historical record. On the
contrary, statues placed on pedestals in prominent public places
are placed there in order to honour those represented—and to
invite the public to look up to them, both literally and figu-
ratively.[3] The controversial Robert E. Lee monument in New
Orleans, for example, "rose 109 feet. The bronze figure of Lee
alone stood 16 feet tall and was hailed at the time as 'the
largest bronze statue ever cast in New York'" (Cox 43).[4] Out-
sized statues of figures raised and presented in this
fashion, then, are not *merely* statues of historical figures; they
have become public monuments as well as statues. Such a
statue is inevitably, as Benedito Machava of Yale University
puts it, "a political statement" (Machava 00:03).

for audio and visual media works, use a time-stamp to locate the citation

Conversely, the act of removing a public monument   6
in itself says nothing about history; there is no claim more
absurd in the ongoing debate over public monuments than the
frequently-made suggestion that removing a statue from a public place is tantamount to "erasing history."[5] The ways in which
Jefferson Davis and Robert E. Lee shaped American history,
and in which John A. Macdonald shaped Canadian history, are
entirely unaffected by whether or not their statues are displayed

Lee 5

in places of honour in our cities; their actions continue to
be remembered, written about, and extensively discussed in
schools and universities.

7   The reality is that arguments over the degree to which we
may want to honour leaders of the past with public monuments
today are first and foremost arguments about our political and
ethical views and values today—not arguments about what
happened decades or centuries ago. To be sure, those seeking
to defend Macdonald downplay the policies that were designed
to "do away with the tribal system and assimilate the Indian
people in all respects" (qtd. in Beazley), just as those seeking to
defend Lee and Davis downplay the extent to which these leaders were defenders of enslaving what Davis called "the servile
race." But unrepentant racists aside (and it should be admitted
that their numbers are not negligible), everyone acknowledges
both that Macdonald played a central role in Canada's Confed-
eration, *and* that his policies towards the Indigenous people in
Canada were oppressive. The substantial disagreement is as to
which values should be accorded more emphasis in our own
time. Do we value the knitting together of a nation more than
we deplore the oppression of its native peoples? Similarly, it
is broadly agreed *both* that Robert E. Lee and Jefferson Davis
were defenders of slavery who were themselves enslavers *and*
that they were well-mannered and behaved graciously in defeat.
The substantial disagreement is again as to what values should

for
indirect
sources,
use the
abbre-
viation
"qtd. in"
("quoted
in")

Lee 6

be accorded more emphasis in our own time. Do we value graciousness in defeat more than we deplore the slavery and subsequent oppression of a substantial portion of a nation's people?

Other values too are at stake in these controversies. In fighting for slavery (and "states' rights"),[6] for example, Davis and Lee were also fighting against federal interference in an economic system according to the principles of which those with vast amounts of capital should be allowed to do what they wish with it.[7] That fight too has a powerful echo in debates in America today (and, indeed, around the world); to what degree should a belief in the desirability of all humans being treated equitably outweigh a belief that capitalism should be allowed free rein?

Not everything, of course, can or should be seen only through the lens of today. Those who say we should not assess historical figures entirely by the standards of today make a fair point; we need to understand the ways in which earlier eras differed from our own. It would be obviously absurd to argue that John A. Macdonald or Woodrow Wilson should be disparaged because they did not support gay rights, when no one in late nineteenth- or early twentieth-century North America contemplated equal rights on the basis of sexual orientation. We need to understand too that "the standards of the past" are never uniform. During the same decade that Woodrow Wilson

Lee 7

was doing everything in his power while President of Princeton to keep African Americans from attending that university, the presidents of Columbia and Yale were for the first time welcoming African Americans into those institutions. On the matter of Macdonald's Conservative government setting up the oppressive system of Indigenous residential schools, it seems fair to point out that very few in mainstream white society at the time opposed his action; when Wilfrid Laurier's Liberals came to power, indeed, they greatly expanded the system (and it was under Laurier's successor, Robert Borden, that it was made compulsory under the Indian Act for all Indigenous children to attend either industrial or residential schools). It seems fair to point out too that the attitudes adopted by Macdonald and other Canadian politicians of the 1870s were in many respects considerably less oppressive than those adopted by their American counterparts at the time; no one in Macdonald's government was making statements as extreme as American Congressman James Michael Cavanaugh's 1868 assertion: "I have never in my life seen a good Indian except when I have seen a dead Indian" (Mieder 42). When it comes to the matter of public monuments, discussion will inevitably focus less on achieving entirely balanced assessments of how individuals behaved in the context of their own time than on questions of who (and of what sorts of behaviour) we wish to *honour* in the present. ...

parenthetical references at end of short quotations followed by punctuation

Notes

1   Limbaugh, for example, links the movement to remove monuments to "the American and the worldwide left."

2   Donald Trump is a notable example. As Macaya et al. report, he made the following statement about the removal of Confederate monuments during a speech he delivered in Tulsa: "This cruel campaign of censorship and exclusion violates everything we hold dear as Americans." When Virginia's governor announced the state's intention to take down a prominent public memorial to Robert E. Lee, state senator Amanda Chase argued that, because such monuments are a form of artistic expression, removing them raises "First Amendment concerns" (Carrington and Strother). In Canada, former journalist Robert Roth is among those who contend that taking down public monuments honouring former prime ministers is "to suppress free speech" (Llana).

notes numbered as in text

each note indented

3   An exception is John Dann's statue of Sir John A. Macdonald, which was removed from its place in front of Victoria's City Hall in 2017. Dann has drawn attention to the fact that in this case the statue was not raised high above the street level but rather placed at eye level with passers-by: "It's not a sculpture on a pedestal, it's not a monument. It's a portrait of a man and that man is accessible to the people who go in and out of the building" (Canadian Press).

…

Lee 23

Works Cited

Ainsworth, Fred C., and Joseph W. Kirkley, eds. *The War of the Rebellion: A Compilation of the Official Records of the Union and Confederate Armies.* Series 4, vol. 1, Government Printing Office, 1900, www.books.google.ca/books.

American Museum of Natural History. "Addressing the Statue." Statement. *American Museum of Natural History*, June 2020, www.amnh.org/exhibitions/addressing-the -theodore-roosevelt-statue#statement.

——. "Perspectives on the Statue." *American Museum of Natural History*, www.amnh.org/exhibitions/addressing-the -theodore-roosevelt-statue/perspectives-today.

——. "What Did the Artists and Planners Intend?" *American Museum of Natural History*, www.amnh.org/exhibitions/ addressing-the-theodore-roosevelt-statue/making-the -statue.

Bagehot [Adrian Woolridge]. "Britain's Academic Split: Problem-solving v Problem-wallowing." *The Economist,* 19 June 2021, www.economist.com/britain/2021/06/19/britains -academic-split-problem-solving-v-problem-wallowing.

Beazley, Doug. "Decolonizing the Indian Act." *National Magazine*, Canadian Bar Association, 18 Dec. 2017, www .nationalmagazine.ca/en-ca/articles/law/in-depth/2017/ decolonizing-the-indian-act.

each entry begins at left margin; subsequent lines are indented

MLA recommends truncating excessively long URLs after host location

works cited are listed alphabetically by author

Bromwich, Jonah Engel. "What Does It Take to Tear Down a Statue?" Interview with Erin L. Thompson, *New York Times*, 11 June 2020, www.nytimes.com/2020/06/11/style/confederate-statue-columbus-analysis.html.

Byrne, Patrick. "Americans Channel Ancient Rome in Condemning Confederate Statues." *The Hill*, 23 Aug. 2017, www.thehill.com/blogs/pundits-blog/state-local-politics/347562-americans-channel-ancient-rome-in-erecting-statues.

Canadian Press. "Vancouver Artist of Removed Macdonald Statue Says It Was Never Intended as a Monument." 15 Aug. 2018, www.lethbridgenewsnow.com/2018/08/15/artist-behind-macdonald-statue-says-it-was-never-intended-as-a-monument/.

Caplan, Talia. "Huckabee: Erasing American History Is 'Dangerous,' Can Lead to a Lost Civilization." *Fox News*, 23 June 2021, www.foxnews.com/media/huckabee-erasing-history-dangerous-can-lead-lost-civilization.

Carrington, Nathan T., and Logan Strother. "Legally, Confederate Statues in Public Spaces Aren't a Form of Free Speech." *Newsday*, 20 June 2020, www.newsday.com/opinion/commentary/confederate-statues-free-speech-black-lives-matter-protests-racism-1.45750735.

...

double spacing used throughout

italics used for titles of books, journals, magazines, etc.

CONTENTS

38. APA STYLE

The American Psychological Association (APA) style is used in many behavioural and social sciences. Like MLA style, APA style calls for parenthetical references in the body of a paper, although the main components in these are author and date rather than author and page number. APA also requires that full bibliographical information about the sources be provided in a list called "References" at the end of the essay.

This section outlines the key features of APA style and includes, at the end, a sample excerpt using APA citation. Additional full sample essays in APA style are available on the Broadview website; go to http://sites.broadviewpress.com/writingcdn/. If you have more detailed questions, consult *Concise Rules of APA Style* (7th edition, 2020). You may also find answers at www.apastyle.org.

38a. Incorporating Sources in APA Style

The following material should be read in conjunction with the introductory discussion of citation, documentation, and plagiarism (see pages 198–221).

There are three main ways of working source material into a paper: summaries, paraphrases, and direct quotations. In order to avoid plagiarism, care must be taken with all three kinds of borrowing, both in the way they are handled and in their referencing. In what follows, a passage from page 102 of a book by Terrence W. Deacon (*The Symbolic Species: The Co-Evolution of Language and the Brain*, published in New York City by Norton in 1997) serves as the source for a sample summary, paraphrase, and quotation. The examples feature the APA style of in-text parenthetical citations, but the requirements for presenting the source material are the same for all academic referencing systems.

original source   Over the last few decades language researchers seem to have reached a consensus that language is an innate ability, and that only a significant contribution from innate knowledge can explain our ability to learn such a complex communication system. Without question, children enter the world predisposed to learn human languages. All normal children, raised in normal social environments, inevitably learn their local language, whereas other species, even when raised and taught in this same environment, do not. This demonstrates that human brains come into the world specially equipped for this function.

● Summarizing

An honest and competent summary, whether of a passage or an entire book, must not only represent the source accurately but also use original wording and include a citation. It is a common misconception that only quotations need to be acknowledged as borrowings in the body of an essay, but without a citation, even a fairly worded summary or paraphrase is an act of plagiarism. The first example below is faulty on two counts: it borrows wording (underlined) from the source, and it has no parenthetical reference.

needs checking Researchers agree that language learning is innate, and that only innate knowledge can explain how we are able to learn a system of communication that is so complex. Normal children raised in normal ways will always learn their local language, whereas other species do not, even when taught human language and exposed to the same environment.

The next example avoids the wording of the source passage, and a parenthetical citation notes the author and date (but note that no page number is provided, as APA does not require these in citations of summarized material).

revised There is now wide agreement among linguists that the ease with which human children acquire their native tongues, under the conditions of a normal childhood, demonstrates an inborn capacity for language that is not shared by any other animals, not even those who are reared in comparable ways and given human language training (Deacon, 1997).

● Paraphrasing

Whereas a summary is a shorter version of its original, a paraphrase tends to be about the same length. However, paraphrases, like summaries, must reflect their sources accurately while using original wording, and must include a citation. The original material's page number (or paragraph number for a nonpaginated online source) is not absolutely essential for a paraphrase, but APA suggests it be added as an aid to any reader who would like to refer to the original text. What follows is a paraphrase of the first sentence of the Deacon passage, which despite having a proper citation, falls short by being too close to the wording of the original (underlined).

needs checking   Researchers in language have come to a consensus in the past few decades that the acquisition of language is innate; such contributions from knowledge contribute significantly to our ability to master such a complex system of communication (Deacon, 1997, p. 102).

Simply substituting synonyms for the words and phrases of the source, however, is not enough to avoid plagiarism. Even with its original wording, the next example also fails but for a very different reason: it follows the original's sentence structure, as illustrated in the interpolated copy below it.

needs checking   Recently, linguists appear to have come to an agreement that speaking is an in-born skill, and that nothing but a substantial input from in-born cognition can account for the human capacity to acquire such a complicated means of expression (Deacon, 1997, p. 102).

> Recently (*over the last few decades*), linguists (*language researchers*) appear to have come to an agreement (*seem to have reached a consensus*) that speaking is an in-born skill (*that language is an innate ability*), and that nothing but a substantial input (*and that only a significant contribution*) from in-born cognition (*from innate knowledge*) can account for the human capacity (*can explain our ability*) to acquire such a complicated means of expression (*to learn such a complex communication system*) (Deacon, 1997, p. 102).

What follows is a good paraphrase of the passage's opening sentence; this paraphrase captures the sense of the original without echoing the details and shape of its language.

> *revised* Linguists now broadly agree that children are born with the ability to learn language; in fact, the human capacity to acquire such a difficult skill cannot easily be accounted for in any other way (Deacon, 1997, p. 102).

● Quoting Directly

Unlike paraphrases and summaries, direct quotations must use the exact wording of the original. Because they involve importing outside words, quotations pose unique challenges. Quote too frequently, and you risk making your readers wonder why they are not reading your sources instead of your paper. Your essay should present something you want to say—informed and supported by properly documented sources, but forming a contribution that is yours alone. To that end, use secondary material to help you build a strong framework for your work, not to replace it. Quote sparingly, therefore; use your sources' exact wording only when it is important or particularly memorable.

To avoid misrepresenting your sources, be sure to quote accurately, and to avoid plagiarism, take care to indicate quotations as quotations, and cite them properly. If you use the author's name in a signal phrase, follow it with the date in parentheses, and be sure the verb of the phrase is in the past tense (*demonstrated*) or present perfect tense (*has demonstrated*). For all direct quotations, you must also include the page number (or paragraph number for a nonpaginated online source) of the original in your citation, as in the following examples.

Below are two problematic quotations. The first does not show which words come directly from the source.

needs checking Deacon (1997) maintained that children enter the world predisposed to learn human languages (p. 102).

The second quotation fails to identify the source at all.

needs checking Many linguists have argued that "children enter the world predisposed to learn human languages."

The next example corrects both problems by naming the source and indicating clearly which words come directly from it.

revised Deacon (1997) maintained that "children enter the world predisposed to learn human languages" (p. 102).

● Formatting Quotations

There are two ways to signal an exact borrowing: by enclosing it in double quotation marks and by indenting it as a block of text. Which you should choose depends on the length and genre of the quotation and the style guide you are following.

Short Quotations

What counts as a short quotation differs among the various reference guides. In MLA style, "short" means up to four lines; in APA, up to forty words; and in Chicago Style, up to one hundred words. All the guides agree, however, that short quotations must be enclosed in double quotation marks, as in the examples below.

Short quotation, According to Deacon (1997), linguists agree that a
full sentence: human child's capacity to acquire language is
inborn: "Without question, children enter the
world predisposed to learn human languages" (p.
102).

Short quotation, According to Deacon (1997), linguists agree that
partial sentence: human "... children enter the world predisposed
to learn human languages" (p. 102).

Long Quotations

In APA style, longer quotations of forty words or more should
be double-spaced and indented, as a block, about one-half
inch from the left margin. Do not include quotation marks;
the indentation indicates that the words come exactly from
the source. Note that indented quotations are often introduced with a full sentence followed by a colon.

Deacon (1997) maintained that human beings are born
with a unique cognitive capacity:

> Without question, children enter the world predis-
> posed to learn human languages. All normal children,
> raised in normal social environments, inevitably learn
> their local language, whereas other species, even when
> raised and taught in this same environment, do not.
> This demonstrates that human brains come into the
> world specially equipped for this function. (p. 102)

Quotations within Quotations

You may sometimes find, within the original passage you wish
to quote, words already enclosed in double quotation marks.
If your quotation is short, enclose it all in double quotation
marks, and use single quotation marks for the embedded
quotation.

Deacon (1997) was firm in maintaining that human language differs from other communication systems in kind

rather than degree: "Of no other natural form of communication is it legitimate to say that 'language is a more
complicated version of that'" (p. 44).

If your quotation is long, keep the double quotation marks
of the original. Note as well that in the example below, the
source's use of italics (*simple*) is also faithfully reproduced.

Deacon (1997) was firm in maintaining that human language differs from other communication systems in kind
rather than degree:

Of no other natural form of communication is it
legitimate to say that "language is a more complicated version of that." It is just as misleading to call
other species' communication systems *simple* languages as it is to call them languages. In addition to
asserting that a Procrustean mapping of one to the
other is possible, the analogy ignores the sophistica-
tion and power of animals' non-linguistic communication, whose capabilities may also be without language parallels. (p. 44)

● Adding to or Deleting from a Quotation

While it is important to use the original's exact wording in a
quotation, it is allowable to modify a quotation somewhat, as
long as the changes are clearly indicated and do not distort
the meaning of the original. You may want to add to a quotation in order to clarify what would otherwise be puzzling or
ambiguous to someone who does not know its context; put
whatever you add in square brackets.

Using Square Brackets to Add to a Quotation

Deacon (1997) concluded that children are born "specially
equipped for this [language] function" (p. 102).

If you would like to streamline a quotation by omitting anything unnecessary to your point, insert an ellipsis (three spaced
dots) to show that you've left material out.

Using an Ellipsis to Delete from a Quotation

When the quotation looks like a complete sentence but is actually part of a longer sentence, you should provide an ellipsis to show that there is more to the original than you are using.

> Deacon (1997) concluded that "… children enter the world predisposed to learn human languages" (p. 102).

Note the square brackets example above; if the quotation is clearly a partial sentence, ellipses aren't necessary.

When the omitted material runs over a sentence boundary or constitutes a whole sentence or more, insert a period plus an ellipsis.

> Deacon (1997) claimed that human children are born with a unique ability to acquire their native language: "Without question, children enter the world predisposed to learn human languages…. [H]uman brains come into the world specially equipped for this function" (p. 102).

Be sparing in modifying quotations; it is all right to have one or two altered quotations in a paper, but if you find yourself changing quotations often, or adding to and omitting from one quotation more than once, reconsider quoting at all. A paraphrase or summary is very often a more effective choice.

Integrating Quotations

Quotations must be worked smoothly and grammatically into your sentences and paragraphs. Always, of course, mark quotations as such, but for the purpose of integrating them into your writing, treat them otherwise as if they were your own words. The boundary between what you say and what your source says should be grammatically seamless.

needs checking Deacon (1997) pointed out, "whereas other species, even when raised and taught in this same environment, do not" (p. 102).

revised   According to Deacon (1997), while human children brought up under normal conditions acquire the language they are exposed to, "other species, even when raised and taught in this same environment, do not" (p. 102).

Avoiding "Dumped" Quotations

Integrating quotations well also means providing a context for them. Don't merely drop them into your paper or string them together like beads on a necklace; make sure to introduce them by noting where the material comes from and how it connects to whatever point you are making.

needs checking   For many years, linguists have studied how human children acquire language. "Without question, children enter the world predisposed to learn human language" (Deacon, 1997, p. 102).

revised   Most linguists studying how human children acquire language have come to share the conclusion articulated by Deacon (1997): "Without question, children enter the world predisposed to learn human language" (p. 102).

needs checking   "Without question, children enter the world predisposed to learn human language" (Deacon, 1997, p. 102). "There is ... something special about human brains that enables us to do with ease what no other species can do even minimally without intense effort and remarkably insightful training" (Deacon, 1997, p. 103).

revised   Deacon (1997) based his claim that we "enter the world predisposed to learn human language" on the fact that very young humans can "do with ease what no other species can do even minimally without intense effort and remarkably insightful training" (pp. 102–103).

● Signal Phrases

To leave no doubt in your readers' minds about which parts of your essay are yours and which come from elsewhere, identify the sources of your summaries, paraphrases, and quotations with signal phrases, as in the following examples.

- As Carter and Rosenthal (2016) demonstrated, …
- According to Ming et al. (2014), …
- In his latest article McGann (2015) advanced the view that, …
- As Beyerstein (2000) observed, …
- Kendal and Ahmadi (1998) have suggested that …
- Freschi (2004) was not alone in rejecting these claims, arguing that …
- Cabral et al. (2017) have emphasized this point in their recent research: …
- Sayeed (2016) has maintained that …
- In a landmark study, Mtele (1992) concluded that …
- In her later work, however, Hardy (2005) overturned previous results, suggesting that …

In order to help establish your paper's credibility, you may also find it useful at times to include in a signal phrase information that shows why readers should take the source seriously, as in the following example:

> In this lucid and groundbreaking work, psychologist and economist Daniel Kahneman (2011) described …

Here, the signal phrase mentions the author's professional credentials; it also points out the importance of his book, which is appropriate to do in the case of a work as famous as Kahneman's *Thinking Fast and Slow*.

Below is a fuller list of words and expressions that may be useful in the crafting of signal phrases:

according to _____	endorsed
acknowledged	found
added	granted
admitted	illustrated
advanced	implied
agreed	in the view of _____,
allowed	in the words of _____,
argued	insisted
asserted	intimated
attested	noted
believed	observed
claimed	pointed out
commented	put it
compared	reasoned
concluded	refuted
confirmed	rejected
contended	reported
declared	responded
demonstrated	suggested
denied	thought
disputed	took issue with
emphasized	wrote

38b. About In-text Citations

in-text citation: The APA system emphasizes the date of publication, which must appear within an in-text citation. Whenever a quotation is given, the page number, preceded by the abbreviation *p.*, must also be provided. Note that when two authors are mentioned in the body of the text, it is necessary to spell out the word "and":

- Rahman and Gilman (2020) argue that democratic participation needs to be "understood as a constant, sustained practice that outlives election cycles and stretches beyond voting or other formal, governmental channels for citizen imput" (p. 107).

It is common to mention in the body of your text the surnames of authors that you are citing, as is done in the example above. If author names are not mentioned in the body of the text, however, they must be provided within the in-text citation. In the example below, note the comma between the name and date of publication.

- One analysis of democratic participation (Rahman & Gilman, 2020) emphasizes that civic engagement needs to be an ongoing process that "stretches beyond voting or other formal, governmental channels for citizen input" (p. 107).

If the reference does not involve a quotation (as it commonly does not in social science papers), only the date need be given as an in-text citation, provided that the author's name appears in the signal phrase. For paraphrases, APA encourages, though does not require, a page number reference as well. The in-text citation in this case must immediately follow the author's name:

- Rahman and Gilman (2020) argue that true democratic participation needs to be an ongoing process that extends beyond the process of formal voting (p. 107).

A citation such as this connects to a list of references at the end of the paper. In this case the entry under "References" at the end of the paper would be as follows:

- Rahman, K. S., & Gilman, H. R. (2020). *Civic power: Rebuilding American democracy in an era of crisis*. Cambridge University Press.

Notice here that the date of publication is again foregrounded, appearing immediately after the authors' names. Notice too that the formatting of titles must follow APA style; the details are in the section below.

no signal phrase (or author not named in signal phrase): If the context does not make it clear who the author is, that information must be added to the in-text citation. Note that commas separate the name of the author, the date, and the page number elements:

- Some political scientists are urging that democratic participation needs to be seen as an ongoing process that "stretches beyond voting or other formal, governmental channels for citizen input" (Rahman & Gilman, 2020, p. 107).

titles of stand-alone works: Stand-alone works are those that are published on their own rather than as part of another work. The titles of stand-alone works (e.g., journals, magazines, newspapers, books, and reports) should be in italics. Writers in the social and behavioural sciences do not normally put the titles of works in the bodies of their papers, but if you do include the title of a stand-alone work, all major words and all words of four letters or more should be capitalized. For book and report titles in the References list, however, capitalize only the first word of the title and subtitle (if any), plus any proper nouns. Journal, magazine, and newspaper titles in the list of References are exceptions; for these, capitalize all major words.

In-text: Such issues are treated at length in *Ethical and Legal Issues in Nursing* (DeMarco et al., 2019).

References list: DeMarco, J. P., Jones, G. E., & Daly, B. J. (2019). *Ethical and legal issues in nursing.* Broadview Press.

titles of articles and chapters of books: The titles of these works, and anything else that is published as part of another work, are also not usually mentioned in the body of an essay, though if they are, they should be put in quotation marks, with all major words capitalized. In the References, however, titles of these works should *not* be put in quotation marks or italicized, and no words should be capitalized, with the exception of any proper nouns, and the first word in the title and the first in the subtitle, if any.

In-text: In "End of Life and the Refusal of Treatment," the role of nurses in end-of-life care is analyzed in depth (DeMarco et al., 2019, pp. 139–191).

References list: DeMarco, J. P., Jones, G. E., & Daly, B. J. (2019). End of life and the refusal of treatment. *Ethical and legal issues in nursing* (pp. 139–191). Broadview Press.

placing of in-text citations: When the author's name appears in a signal phrase, the in-text citation comes directly after the name. Otherwise, the citation follows the paraphrased or quoted material. If a quotation ends with punctuation other than a period or comma, then this should precede the end of the quotation, and a period or comma should still follow the parenthetical reference, if this is grammatically appropriate.

- The claim has been convincingly refuted by Ricks (2010), but it nevertheless continues to be put forward (Dendel, 2015).
- One of Berra's favourite coaching tips was that "ninety per cent of the game is half mental" (Adelman, 2007, p. 98).
- Adelman (2007) notes that Berra at one point said to his players, "You can observe a lot by watching!" (p. 98).
- Vieira (2020) considers the legitimacy of politicians claiming to represent silent constituencies.

citations when text is in parentheses: If a parenthetical reference occurs within text in parentheses, commas are used to set off elements of the reference.

- (See Figure 6.1 of Harrison, 2014, for data on transplant waiting lists.)

electronic source—page number unavailable: If online material is in PDF format, the page numbers are stable and may be cited as one would the pages of a printed source. Many online sources, however, lack page numbers altogether. In such cases you should provide a section or paragraph number if a reference is needed. For paragraphs, use the abbreviation "para."

- In a recent Web posting a leading theorist has clearly stated that he finds such an approach "thoroughly objectionable" (Bhabha, 2012, para. 7).
- Carter and Zhaba (2009) describe this approach as "more reliable than that adopted by Perkins" (Method section, para. 2).

For ebooks, do not include location numbers, but provide the chapter, section, and/or paragraph numbers instead. If you are citing longer texts from electronic versions, chapter references may be more appropriate. For example, if the online

Gutenberg edition of Darwin's *On the Origin of Species* were being cited, the citation would be as follows:

- Darwin refers to the core of his theory as an "ineluctable principle" (1859, Chapter 26).

Notice that *chapter* is capitalized and not abbreviated.

Students should be cautioned that online editions of older or classic works are often unreliable; typically there are far more typos and other errors in such versions than there are in print versions. It is often possible to exercise judgement about such matters, however. If, for example, you are not required to base your essay on a particular edition of Darwin's *Origin of Species* but may find your own, you will be far better off using the text you will find on the reputable Project Gutenberg site than you will using a text you might find on a site such as "Manybooks.com."

audiovisual works: Audio books, online lectures, YouTube videos, TV shows, or movies should include a time stamp marking the relevant quotation instead of a page number.

- Adichie (2012) believes that people can and should act to create deep cultural change: "Culture does not make people; people make culture" (27.06–27.09).

two or more dates for a work: If you have consulted a re-issue of a work (whether in printed or electronic form), you should provide both the original date of publication and the date of the re-issue (the date of the version you are using).

- Emerson (1837/1909) asserted that America's "long apprenticeship to the learning of other lands" was "drawing to a close" (para. 1).

The relevant entry in the list of references would look like this:

- Emerson, R. W. (1909). *Essays and English traits*. P. F. Collier & Son. (Original work published 1837)

If you are citing work in a form that has been revised by the author, however, you should cite the date of the revised publication, not the original.

- In a preface to the latest edition of his classic work, Watson (2004) discusses its genesis.

two authors: If there are two authors, both authors should be named either in the signal phrase or in the in-text citation. Use *and* in the signal phrase but *&* in parentheses.

- Chambliss and Best (2013) have argued that the nature of this research is practical as well as theoretical.
- Two distinguished scholars have argued that the nature of this research is practical as well as theoretical (Chambliss & Best, 2013).

three or more authors: In the body of the text and in the in-text citation, list the first author's name, followed by "et al." (short for the Latin *et alia*: *and others*).

- Chambliss et al. (2015) have argued that the nature of this research is practical as well as theoretical.
- Six distinguished scholars have argued that the nature of this research is practical as well as theoretical (Chambliss et al., 2015).

If you are citing more than one work with similar groups of authors, you will need to write out more names to avoid confusion. If for example you are citing works with these two sets of authors:

> Haley, Caxaj, George, Hennebry (2020)
> Haley, Caxaj, Diaz, Cohen (2020)

You would cite them in-text as follows:

> (Haley, Caxaj, George, et al., 2020)
> (Haley, Caxaj, Diaz, et al., 2020)

organization as author: As you would with an individual human author, provide the name of a corporate author either in the body of your text or in a parenthetical citation. Recommended practice is to provide the full name of an organization on the first occasion, followed by an abbreviation, and then to use the abbreviation for subsequent references:

- Blindness has decreased markedly but at an uneven pace since the late 1800s (National Institute for the Blind [NIB], 2013).

author not given: If the author of the source is not given, it may be identified in the parenthetical reference by the title, which may be represented by a short form if the title is long.

- Confusion over voting reform is widespread ("Results of National Study," 2018).

date not given: Some sources, particularly electronic ones, do not provide a date of publication. Where this is the case, use the abbreviation *n.d.* for *no date*.

- Some still claim that evidence of global climate change is difficult to come by (Sanders, n.d.; Zimmerman, 2018).
- Sanders (n.d.) and Zimmerman (2018) still claim that evidence of global climate change is difficult to come by.

two or more works in the same citation: In this case, the works should appear in in-text citations in the same order they do in the list of references. If the works are by different authors, arrange the sources alphabetically by author's last name and separate the citations with a semi-colon. If the works are by the same authors, arrange the sources by publication date. Add *a*, *b*, *c*, etc. after the year to distinguish works written by the same authors in the same year.

- Various studies have established a psychological link between fear and sexual arousal (Aikens et al., 1998; Looby & Cairns, 2008).
- Various studies appear to have established a psychological link between fear and sexual arousal (Looby & Cairns, 1999, 2002, 2005).
- Looby and Cairns (1999a, 1999b, 2002, 2005a, 2005b) have investigated extensively the link between fear and sexual arousal.

two or more authors with the same last name: If the References list includes two or more authors with the same last name, the in-text citation should supply an initial:

- One of the leading economists of the time advocated wage and price controls (H. Johnston, 1977).

works in a collection of readings or anthology: In the in-text citation for a work in an anthology or collection of readings, use the name of the author of the work, not that of the editor of the anthology. If the work was first published in the collection you have consulted, there is only the one date to cite. But if the work is reprinted in that collection after having first been published elsewhere, cite the date of the original publication and the date of the collection you have consulted, separating these dates with a slash. The following citation refers to an article by Ana S. Iltis that was reprinted in a collection of readings edited by Elisabeth Gedge and Wilfrid Waluchow.

- One of the essays in Gedge and Waluchow's collection argues that we should restrict, but not prohibit, placebo-controlled trials (Iltis, 2004/2012).

In your list of references, this work should be alphabetized under Iltis, the author of the piece you have consulted, not under Gedge.

The next example is a lecture by Georg Simmel first published in 1903, which a student consulted in an edited collection by Roberta Garner that was published in 2001.

- Simmel (1903/2001) argues that the "deepest problems of modern life derive from the claim of the individual to preserve the autonomy and individuality of his existence" (p. 141).

The reference list entry would look like this:

Simmel, G. (2001). The metropolis and mental life. In R. Garner (Ed.), *Social theory–Continuity and confrontation: A reader* (pp. 141–153). Peterborough, ON: Broadview Press. (Original work published in 1903)

As you can see, in your reference list these works are listed under the authors of the pieces (Iltis or Simmel), not under the compilers, editors, or translators of the collection (Gedge & Waluchow or Garner). If you cite another work by a different author from the same anthology or book of readings, that should appear as a separate entry in your list of references—again, alphabetized under the author's name.

indirect source: If you are citing a source from a reference other than the source itself, you should use the phrase "as cited in" in your in-text citation.

- In de Beauvoir's famous phrase, "one is not born a woman, one becomes one" (as cited in Levey, 2017, para. 3).

In this case, the entry in your reference list would be for Levey, not de Beauvoir.

personal communications: These are any communications that cannot be found by your reader, such as emails, classroom lectures, messages on online discussion groups, text messages, unrecorded speeches, personal interviews, and conversations (among others). This type of communication should not be added to your list of references but documented only as an in-text citation. Provide the initials and surname of the person you communicated with as well as the date of communication.

- K. Montegna (personal communication, January 21, 2017) has expressed scepticism over this method's usefulness.

Indigenous traditional knowledge and oral traditions: APA guidelines suggest that before including Indigenous traditional knowledge in your paper, it should be confirmed to be both accurate and permitted—some Indigenous stories, for example, are to be told only at certain times and by certain people, and some are only to be told orally and are not meant to be printed. If the material you are citing can be found in a source discoverable by your readers, add it to your reference list following the formatting for the source type and cite in-text accordingly. If you spoke with an Indigenous person yourself or are citing materials that cannot be found by your readers, you can tailor the format for personal communications (see above) to create an in-text citation. In this case, give the person's full name and the Indigenous group to which they belong, as well as any other details that you think are important, followed by "personal communication" and the date or range of dates. It is also vital to communicate with the Indigenous person being cited, so they can confirm both that your citation is accurate and that they have agreed to be included in your work. Here is an example of how to format an in-text citation of a personal communication with an Indigenous writer:

- We spoke with Jeannette Armstrong (Sylix Nation, lives on the Penticton Indian Band Reserve, British Columbia, Canada, personal communication, June 1991) about her work as director of the En'owkin Centre ...

38c. About References

The list of references in APA style is an alphabetized listing of sources that appears at the end of an essay, article, or book. This list, entitled References, includes all the information necessary to identify and retrieve each of the sources you have cited, and only the works you have cited. Lists that include all the sources you have consulted are called Bibliographies, but these are not required by APA. The list of references should include only sources that can be accessed by your readers, and so it should not include private communication, such as private letters, memos, e-mail messages, and telephone or personal conversations. Those should be cited only in your text (see the section above).

Entries should be ordered alphabetically by author surname, or, if there is no known author, by title. The first line of each entry should be flush with the left-hand margin, with all subsequent lines indented about one half inch. Double-space throughout the list of references.

The basic format for all entries consists of four major elements, all of which are somewhat flexible and can be customized to suit your source. The four elements (in the order they appear in your reference entry) are author, date, title, and source. Remember that one function of the list of references is to provide the information your readers need if they wish to locate your sources for themselves; APA allows any "non-routine" information that could assist in identifying the sources to be added in square brackets to any entry (e.g., [Sunday business section], [Film], [Interview with O. Sacks]).

In the References examples that follow, information about entries for electronic sources has been presented in an integrated fashion alongside information about referencing sources in other media, such as print, audiovisual, and so on. Note that the DOI (Digital Object Identifier) or URL is the last element of your reference entry for digital sources, and a crucial one for readers when they want to use your reference to find the source. Include the DOI or URL as a hyperlink in your document, beginning "http://" or "https://". DOIs must be formatted "https://doi.org/xxxxx" (the "xxxxx" being the DOI number). Any articles with older DOI formatting should be reformatted to this new standard. This means that the label "DOI" is no longer needed before the link; it is also unnecessary to include the words "Accessed from" or "Retrieved from" before DOI and URL links. The only exception to this rule is if the material is unarchived and frequently updated—in this case you may want to add a retrieval date, as the content could differ if your reader seeks access at a later time. Copy and paste the DOI or URL directly into your References list; do not add line breaks, even if the hyperlink is moved onto its own line by your word-processing software. Do not add any other punctuation, including periods, as it may interfere with link functionality.

work with single author: For a work with one author the entry should begin with the last name, followed by a comma, and then the author's initials as applicable, followed by the date of publication in parentheses. Note that initials are generally used rather than first names, even when authors are identified by first name in the work itself. After the title of the work, add the publisher's name, leaving out abbreviations such as *Inc.* and *Co.* (but keeping *Press* and *Books*). If a DOI is available, APA requires that it be included, whether you are using the print or digital version.

> Hueglin, T. O. (2021). *Federalism in Canada: Contested concepts and uneasy balances.* University of Toronto Press.

two authors: List both authors by their last names and initials, separated by a comma and ampersand:

> Caxaj, S., & Diaz, L. (2018). Migrant workers' (non)belonging in rural British Columbia, Canada: Storied experiences of marginal living. *International Journal of Migration, Health and Social Care, 14*(2), 208–220. https://doi.org/10.1108/ijmhsc-05-2017-0018

three to twenty authors: Last names should in all cases come first, followed by initials. Use commas to separate the authors' names, and use an ampersand rather than *and* before the last author. Note that the authors' names should appear in the order they are listed; sometimes this is not alphabetical.

> Warne, R. T., Astle, M. C., & Hill, J. C. (2018). What do undergraduates learn about human intelligence? An analysis of introductory psychology textbooks. *Archives of Scientific Psychology, 6*(1), 32–50. https://doi.org/10.1037/arc0000038

more than twenty authors: List the names of the first nineteen authors, add an ellipsis, and then give the last author's name.

> Akerboom, J., Chen, T., Wardill, T. J., Tian, L., Marvin, J. S., Mutlu, S., Calderón, N. C., Esposti, F., Borghuls, B. G., Sun, X. R., Gordus, A., Orger, M. B., Portugues, R., Engert, F., Macklin, J. J., Filosa, A., Aggarwal, A., Kerr, R. A., Takagi, R., ... Looger, L. L. (2012). Optimization of a GCaMP calcium indicator for neural activity imaging. *Journal of Neuroscience, 32*(40), 13819–13840. https://doi.org/10.1523/JNEUROSCI.2601-12.2012

works with an organization as author: If a work has been issued by a government body, a corporation, or some other organization and no author is identified, the entry should be listed by the name of the group. If this group is also the work's publisher, do not include the publisher in the source element of the citation.

> Broadview Press. (2019). *Annual report.* https://sec.report/Document/0001398344-19-016555/
> Canadian Nurses Association. (2017). *Code of ethics.* https://cna-aiic.ca/nursing-practice/nursing-ethics
> Environment and Climate Change Canada. (2016). *Pan-Canadian framework on clean growth and climate change: Canada's plan to address climate change and grow the economy.* http://publications.gc.ca/pub?id=9.828774&sl=0

APA Style

works with unknown author: When a work does not have an author, move the title to the author position in your citation. Only if the work is signed "Anonymous" do you begin the citation with "Anonymous" in the author position. Alphabetize the entry in your References list according to "Anonymous" (if applicable), or to the first important word in the title (ignoring articles such as "The," "A," and "An").

For in-text citations, once the title has been stated in full either in the narrative or in a parenthetical citation, you may from then on use an abbreviated version, italicized or in quotation marks, as appropriate. For example, the *Oxford English Dictionary* could be abbreviated as OED, and italicized in your in-text citation as (*OED*, 2019). The reference list entry would be as follows:

> *Oxford English Dictionary.* (2020). https://www.oed.com

two or more works by the same author: The author's name should appear for all entries. Entries should be ordered by year of publication, beginning with the earliest.

> Mouffe, C. (2019). *For a left populism.* Verso.
> Mouffe, C. (2020). *The return of the political.* Verso.

two or more works by the same author in the same year: If two or more cited works by the same author or group of authors have been published in the same year, see if they have more specific dates: if they do, list the works chronologically. If works are listed only by year, list them before the ones with a specific date. If two of the works have the same date, arrange these alphabetically according to the title and use letters to distinguish them: (2020a), (2020b), and so on.

> Employment and Social Development Canada. (2019a). *Temporary Foreign Worker Program 2012–2019.* https://open.canada.ca/data/en/dataset/76defa14-473e-41e2-abfa-60021c4d934b
> Employment and Social Development Canada. (2019b). *What we heard: Primary agriculture review.* https://www.canada.ca/en/employment-social-development/services/foreign-workers/reports/primary-agriculture.html

prefaces, introductions, forewords, afterwords: Cite these sections of a work as you would a chapter title:

> DeMarco, J. P., Jones, G. E., & Daly, B. J. (2019). Introduction. *Ethical and legal issues in nursing.* Broadview Press.

edited works: Entries for edited works include the abbreviation *Ed.* or *Eds.* The second example below is for a book with both an author and an editor; since the original work in this entry was published earlier than the present edition, that information is given in parentheses at the end.

> Armstrong, C. L., & Morrow, L. A. (Eds.). (2019). *Handbook of medical neuropsychology: Applications of cognitive neuroscience* (2nd ed.). Springer.
>
> Sapir, E. (1981). *Selected writings in language, culture, and personality.* D. G. Mandelbaum (Ed.). Berkeley, CA: University of California Press. (Original work published 1949)

works with an author and a translator: The translator's name, along with the designation *Trans.*, is included in parentheses after the title; the original publication date is given in parentheses following the present edition's publication information.

> Jung, C. G. (2006). *The undiscovered self* (R. F. C. Hull, Trans.). New York, NY: Signet. (Original work published 1959)

selections from edited books and collections of readings: An article reprinted in an edited collection of readings should be listed as follows:

> Holmes, S., & Buchbinder, L. (2020). In a defunded health system, doctors and nurses suffer near-impossible conditions. In M. C. Schwartz (Ed.), *The ethics of pandemics* (pp. 25–27). Broadview Press.

selections from multivolume works:

> Truth, S. (2008). Speech delivered at the Akron, Ohio convention on women's rights, 1851. In A. Bailey, S. Brennan, W. Kymlicka, J. T. Levy, A. Sager, & C. Wolf (Eds.), *The Broadview anthology of social and political thought: Vol. 1. From Plato to Nietzsche* (pp. 964–965). Broadview Press. (Original work published 1851)

302 | RESEARCH AND DOCUMENTATION

ebooks and audiobooks: If the ebook content is the same as an existing physical book, you do not need to specify which version you cited (APA style states that if a DOI is available, that information should be included whether you use the print or the electronic version). If the electronic version is different from the print, then you should specify that you are using the ebook version. Similarly, you do not need to state that you are using an audiobook version, unless it differs from the print version or you want to add narrator information.

Atkins, J. W. (2013). *Cicero on politics and the limits of reason: The* Republic *and* Laws. Cambridge University Press. https://doi.org/10.1017/CBO9781107338722

Herman, E. S., & Chomsky, N. (2017). *Manufacturing consent* (J. Pruden, Narr.) [Audiobook]. Random House. https://www.audible.ca/pd/Manufacturing-Consent-Audiobook/B072BSNQ9K (Original work published 1988)

periodical articles (with and without DOIs): Articles from journals, magazines, online platforms, and newspapers follow the same pattern of citation. Notice that article titles are not enclosed in quotation marks, and that both the periodical title and the volume number (if applicable) are in italics. If all issues of a given volume of a periodical begin with page 1, include the issue number as well, directly after the volume number, in parentheses and not italicized. Page ranges for periodicals should follow after a comma, be separated by an en dash, and close with a period. If there are discontinuous page numbers (in a print newspaper, for example), separate the page numbers with commas (for example 25–34, 45). The citation should finish with a period, unless it ends with a DOI or URL, in which case no period should be added. Include the DOI or URL as a hyperlink, beginning "http://" or "https://". DOIs must be formatted "https://doi.org/xxxxx" (the "xxxxx" being the DOI number). Note that if a DOI is available, APA asks that you add it to the citation, even if you consulted the print version.

Li, J., Osher, D. E., Hansen, H. A., & Saygin, Z. M. (2020). Innate connectivity patterns drive the development of the visual word form area. *Scientific Reports, 10*, Article 18039. https://doi.org/10.1038/s41598-020-75015-7

Luque, J. S., & Castañeda, H. (2012). Delivery of mobile clinic services to migrant and seasonal farmworkers: A review of practice models for community-academic partnerships. *Journal of Community Health, 38*(2), 397–407. https://doi.org/10.1007/s10900-012-9622-4

Pinquart, M., & Kauser, R. (2018). Do the associations of parenting styles with behavior problems and academic achievement vary by culture? Results from a meta-analysis. *Cultural Diversity and Ethnic Minority Psychology, 24*(1), 75–100. https://doi.org/10.1037/cdp0000149

Example from a periodical only available in print form (no DOI or URL):

Bowlin, B. (2019). Still alive, mostly. *The Fiddlehead, 281*, 47–48.

abstract of a periodical article: Cite as you would the journal article itself, adding *Abstract* in square brackets.

Yang, C., Sharkey, J. D., Reed, L. A., Chen, C., & Dowdy, E. (2018). Bullying victimization and student engagement in elementary, middle, and high schools: Moderating role of school climate [Abstract]. *School Psychology Quarterly, 33*(1), 54–64. https://doi.org/10.1037/spq0000250

magazine articles: The basic principles are the same as for journal articles. Note that neither quotation marks nor italics are used for the titles of articles. If no author is identified, the title of the article should appear first. For monthly magazines, provide the month as well as the year; for magazines issued more frequently, give the day, month, and year.

Aziza, S. (2020, October 30). For Persian Gulf migrant workers, the pandemic has amplified systemic discrimination. *The Nation.* https://www.thenation.com/article/world/migrants-coronavirus-persian-gulf/

Dyer, A. (2012, November/December). The end of the world ... again. *SkyNews, 18*(4), 38–39.

The rise of the yuan: Turning from green to red. (2012, October
    20). *The Economist, 405*(42), 67–68.

newspaper articles: The basic principles to follow with newspaper articles or editorials are the same as with magazine articles (see above). Notice that if there is no letter assigned to a
newspaper section, you should give the section's title in square
brackets.

Bennett, J. (2012, December 16). How to attack the gender pay
    gap? *The New York Times* [Sunday business section], 1, 6.
Waldbieser, J. (2020, November 3). Escape the bore-
    dom trap. *New York Times*. https://www.nytimes.
    com/2020/11/03/parenting/boredom-kids-pandemic.
    html?searchResultPosition=7

reviews: Reviews of any type of media—books, TV shows,
podcasts, films, albums—can be found in many different
publications, including websites, newspapers, blogs, and
magazines. Your reference should be formatted according to
the citation format of the publication in which the review is
found, with the name of the reviewer (if it has been provided)
listed first, followed by the date and title of the review, and the
information on the source itself, as follows:

Semuels, A. (2020, January 14). Soon a robot will be writing
    this headline [Review of the book *A world without work:
    Technology, automation, and how we should respond*, by
    D. Susskind]. *New York Times*. https://www.nytimes.
    com/2020/01/14/books/review/a-world-without-work-
    daniel-susskind.html

reference work entries with an individual author: List by
the author of the entry, if known; otherwise, list by the entry
itself.

Toole, B. A. (2017). Byron, (Augusta) Ada King, countess of
    Lovelace (1815–1852). In D. Cannadine (Ed.), *Oxford
    dictionary of national biography* (September 1, 2017
    ed.). Oxford University Press. https://doi.org.10.1093/
    ref:odnb/37253

reference work entries with an organization as author: List the organization name in the author element of your citation. Note that if a reference work accessed online is continuously updated, you should use "n.d." as the publication year ("no date"). In this case, you should add a retrieval date in your citation.

> American Psychological Association. (n.d.). Sample standard deviation. In *APA dictionary of psychology.* Retrieved November 12, 2020, from https://dictionary.apa.org/sample-standard-deviation

diagnostic manuals (*DSM* and *ICD*): If the publisher and author are the same, you do not need to include the publisher in your reference list citation.

> American Psychiatric Association. (2013). *Diagnostic and statistical manual of mental disorders* (5th ed.). https://doi-org.10.1176/appi.books.9780890425596
>
> World Health Organization. (2019). *International statistical classification of diseases and related health problems* (11th ed.). https://icd.who.int/browse11/l-m/en

Note that when citing these manuals in your text, they may be abbreviated; it is also customary to create an in-text citation for a manual on the first mention of it:

• *Diagnostic and Statistical Manual of Mental Disorders* (5th ed.; DSM-5; American Psychiatric Association, 2013)

After this first instance, it is not necessary to repeat citations of these manuals in your paper (they can be referred to by their abbreviations), unless you are quoting or paraphrasing, in which case you should provide further in-text citations.

articles from databases: Some databases—such as the Cochrane Database of Systematic Reviews and UpToDate—make their articles available only within the databases. Format these citations as you would an article from a periodical (see above).

Martin-McGill, K. J., Bresnahan, R., Levy, R. G., & Cooper, P. N. (2020). Ketogenic diets for drug-resistant epilepsy. *Cochrane Database of Systematic Reviews.* https://doi. org/10.1002/14651858.CD001903.pub5

For the UpToDate database, include a retrieval date, because these articles are continually edited, and the different versions are not archived:

Meyer, T. E. (2022). Rheumatic mitral stenosis: Overview of management. *UpToDate.* Retrieved October 20, 2022, from https://www.uptodate.com/contents/rheumatic-mitral-stenosis-overview-of-management#H2400009337

dissertations from a database, published and unpublished: Published theses and dissertations can be found on databases such as ProQuest. For these references, the title of the thesis or dissertation should be followed by a description ("Doctoral dissertation" or "Master's thesis," for example) and name of the institution that granted the degree in square brackets.

Porteny, T. (2019). *Improving migrant health policies and programs: From the normative to the positive* [Doctoral dissertation, Harvard University]. DASH: Digital Access to Scholarship at Harvard. http://nrs.harvard.edu/urn-3:HUL. InstRepos:42029506

If you are citing an unpublished thesis or dissertation, the university granting the degree appears as the source element rather than in square brackets after the title:

Arthur, K. (2017). *We are having all kinds of fun: Fluidity in shoebox project* [Unpublished doctoral dissertation]. University of Waterloo.

data sets: Entries for data sets in your references list should include the date of publication or of collection, as well as the version number. A retrieval date should only be included if the data is still being gathered. As with many of the APA bracketed descriptions, the one following the title is flexible, and you can use it to specify the kind of data you are citing (data set, code book, etc.).

Statistics Canada. (2019). *Life expectancy, at birth and at age 65, by sex, three-year average, Canada, provinces, territories, health regions and peer groups* (Table 13100389) [Dataset]. https://open.canada.ca/data/en/dataset/00c99f50-4f07-4e8c-b61d-9e188a51ed82

software and reference apps: References to commonly used software and apps do not need to be cited in your paper unless you quote directly or paraphrase information from such a source. Below is an example of a reference list entry for information found on a reference app:

Unbound Medicine, Inc. (2020). Anemia, in *Nursing Central* (Version 1.44) [Mobile app]. Apple App Store, https://apps.apple.com/ca/app/nursing-central/id300420397

films and video recordings: Begin entries for motion pictures with the name of the director, followed by the date of release, the film's title, the medium in square brackets, and the name of the studio. In most cases, the director of the film is stated in the author position of the citation; this element is flexible, however, and you can list the name of a host, producer, or composer if more appropriate.

Attenborough, D. (Narrator). (2017). *Blue Planet II* [Nature Documentary Series]. BBC.

Nolan, C. (Director). (2020). *Tenet* [Film]. Warner Bros; Syncopy.

episodes from television series: Entries for television show episodes should begin with the names of the writer and director, followed by the date, episode title, medium, series title, and production company's name. Identify the role, in parentheses, of each person listed. While the writers' and director's names are given in the example below, this element is flexible and you can include other relevant names if needed, along with their role descriptions.

Lindelof, D., (Writer), Jefferson, C. (Writer), & Williams, S. (Director). (2019, November 24). This extraordinary being (Season1, Episode 6) [Television series episode]. In D. Lindelof (Executive Producer), *The Watchmen*. HBO; WarnerMedia.

TED Talks: If you are citing a TED Talk from the TED website, the author should be the speaker of the talk. If you are citing a version from YouTube, list the account owner as the author for ease of retrieval:

Jauhar, S. (2019, July). How your emotions change the shape of your heart [Video]. TEDSummit. https://www.ted.com/talks/sandeep_jauhar_how_your_emotions_change_the_shape_of_your_heart?

TED. (2019, October 5). Sandeep Jauhar: How emotions change the shape of your heart [Video]. YouTube. https://www.youtube.com/watch?v=mwoLhdHRt_0

YouTube and other streaming videos: As mentioned above, videos accessed on streaming services such as YouTube or Vimeo should have the person who uploaded the video listed as author. If that person is simply a username, place the username in the author position; if the person's real name is known, place the name (inverted as usual) in the author position, followed by the username in square brackets.

Blank, D. (2009). Timelapse: Los Angeles wildfire [Video]. Vimeo. https://vimeo.com/6356422

University of Oxford. (2010, October 21). An introduction to general philosophy [Video lecture by Peter Millican]. YouTube. https://www.youtube.com/watch?v=hdCBGWcd4qw

podcasts: The host of the podcast should be listed as author, along with the role description in parentheses. The podcast should be specified as audio or visual in square brackets after the title. Add the URL when available—if you have accessed the podcast through an app, you may omit adding the URL.

Runciman, D. (Host). (2020, November 2). Are young people losing faith in democracy? (No. 285) [Audio podcast episode]. In *Talking Politics*. https://www.talkingpoliticspodcast.com/blog/2020/285-are-young-people-losing-faith-in-democracy

music recordings: Arrange an entry for a music recording as follows: give the writer's name, the copyright date of the piece of music, its title, the album title, the medium in square brackets, and the label name. If the piece is recorded by someone other than the writer, note that in square brackets after the piece's title. Add the recording date at the end of the entry if it differs from the copyright date. If the music is available only online, include a URL for ease of retrieval.

Cardi B. (2017). Bodak yellow [Song]. On *Invasion of Privacy* [Album]. Atlantic Records.

Chopin, F. (1996). *Nocturnes* [Recorded by Maria João Pires]. Deutsche Grammophon. (Original works written between 1827–1846)

Pass, J. (1988, February 3). Cheek to cheek [Song]. On *Blues for Fred* [Album; CD]. Pablo Records. (Original song by Irving Berlin published 1935)

recorded webinars: The following format should only be used for retrievable webinars; to cite unrecorded webinars, follow the formatting listed above for personal communications.

Chodos, H., & Caron, L. (Guest speakers). (2019, January 31). *Best advice; Recovery-oriented mental health and addiction care in the patient's medical home* [Webinar]. Mental Health Commission of Canada. https://www.mentalhealthcommission.ca/English/media/4240

interviews: How you format an entry for an interview will depend on where it is located. If you watched or listened to a recording of the interview, use the format appropriate to the medium. The first example below is for an interview of Jane Goodall posted on YouTube. The second example is for an interview with Willie Nelson printed in a periodical. Here, the entry follows the format for a newspaper article, with the interviewer in the author position, and information about the interviewee in square brackets. Notice as well that, although the periodical is called a magazine, this publication goes by date only, not volume and issue number, and so the newspaper article format is the appropriate choice. These guidelines apply only to published interviews; unpublished interviews you have conducted yourself are considered private correspondence and should not be included in your References list.

> CBC News: The National. (2016, April 22). *Jane Goodall interview* [Video]. YouTube. https://www.youtube.com/watch?v=3h1UbYZV-IU
>
> Goldman, A. (2012, December 16). The silver-headed stranger [Interview with W. Nelson]. *New York Times Magazine*, 12.

blog posts: Start with the writer's name; then give the full date, entry title, blog title, and URL.

> Accetti, C. I., & Oskian, G. (2020, November 17). What is a consultative referendum? The democratic legitimacy of popular consultations. *Political Science Now*. https://politicalsciencenow.com/what-is-a-consultative-referendum-the-democratic-legitimacy-of-popular-consultations/

Wikipedia article: Because Wikipedia pages can be revised by anyone, their content tends to change over time. In order for your readers to be able to access the same version of the article you are citing, use the archived version for your citation. To do this, go to the "View History" tab on the Wikipedia page and click on the date you accessed the article. The URL for that archived version is a permanent link that you can cite as the location in your reference. If the link is not labelled as permanent, include the retrieval date.

> Behaviorism. (2020, August 4). In *Wikipedia*. https://en.wikipedia.org/w/index.php?title=Behaviorism&oldid=971230907

social media: When you use social media to discover content located elsewhere, cite the location of the original posting (for example if you find a news article via Twitter, cite the article itself, not the Tweet). Only create references for social media posts when you cite the content directly. If the author's real name is known, place the name (inverted as usual) in the author position, followed by the username in square brackets. If you only have the username, place it in the author position (including the symbol @, if applicable). Your reference should include all the non-standard spelling, capitalization, acronyms, and emojis that can be found in social media posts. If you cannot recreate an emoji in your word-processing software, include square bracketed descriptions "[smiling face with heart-eyes]" for example. A complete list of descriptions for the various emojis can be found at https://unicode.org/emoji/charts/emoji-list.html. The title of a social media post should be the text of the first 20 words. If there are any audiovisuals, include a square bracketed note to that effect after the title.

The following format for a Facebook post reference can be used for most social media platforms; further examples for Instagram and Twitter are included below.

Facebook posts:

College of Nurses of Ontario. (2020, November 13). *What is "reflective practice"? Why do I need an action plan? Reflection should be part of a nurse's everyday routine* [Video]. Facebook. https://www.facebook.com/collegeofnurses/posts/2773432936208758

Peltier, A. (2020, September 4). *For everyone who does work protecting the waters and the lands and to everyone we cross paths with, keep doing* [Link attached to notice of documentary screening featuring Peltier]. Facebook. https://www.facebook.com/Waterwarrior1/posts/901124333712126

Instagram photos or videos:

Art Gallery of Ontario [@agotoronto]. (2020, August 23). *In the late 1950s and '60s, when artists felt pressure to live and work in the metropolitan centres of the world* [Photograph]. Instagram. https://www.instagram.com/p/CEPtIubAUmS/?utm_source=ig_web_copy_link

tweets: If the author's real name is known, provide it first, followed by the author's screen name in square brackets. If the author's real name cannot be determined, provide only the screen name, without the square brackets. Include only the date, not the time. Include the entire tweet.

> Johnson Space Center [@NASA_Johnson]. (2020, November 17). Let the science begin! [Test tube emoji]. *Astronaut Kate Rubins has been conducting science experiments on the @Space_Station, and with NASA's SpaceX Crew-1* [Gif and link attached]. https://twitter.com/NASA_Johnson/status/1328751028242587649?s=20

other webpages and websites: In the case of websites and webpages that are not part of an overarching publication, create a reference for each page that you cite. If you are not quoting or paraphrasing the website in your text, but are discussing it generally, you do not need to create a reference for it—simply place the URL in parentheses as an in-text citation. If you are quoting or paraphrasing material from a webpage, and an author or editor is indicated, list by author; otherwise, list by title. If the source is undated or its content is likely to change, you should include the date on which you accessed the material. Use square brackets to include information that will help identify the source.

> Fox, L. (2020, November 17). *Fate of the stimulus looks bleak as lawmakers turn attention to spending deadline.* CNN. https://www.cnn.com/2020/11/17/politics/stimulus-negotiations-latest-congress/index.html
>
> World Health Organization. (2020, November 13). *WHO establishes council on the economics of health for all.* https://www.who.int/news/item/13-11-2020-who-establishes-council-on-the-economics-of-health-for-all

visual works: When creating references for visual works such as paintings, maps, infographics, and photographs, include the medium in square brackets after the title.

work of art in a gallery or gallery website: Note that in this case the name of the gallery or museum, as well as the city, province, and country where it is located, are listed in the source element, in addition to the URL. If the work is not available on a website, omit the URL.

Belmore, R. (1987–1991). *Rising to the occasion* [Sculpture]. Art Gallery of Ontario, Toronto, Ontario, Canada. https://ago.ca/collection/object/95/173

stock images or clip art:

oksmith. (2020). *Doctor with mask #4* [Clip art]. Openclipart. https://openclipart.org/detail/325362/doctor-with-mask-4

infographics:

The Economist. (2020, November 13). *Against the clock: Performance of world chess champions and their opponents* [Infographic]. https://www.economist.com/graphic-detail/2020/11/13/the-queens-gambit-is-right-young-chess-stars-always-usurp-the-old

maps:

Pew Research Center. (2019, April 11). *Immigrant share in U.S. is lower than in many other countries* [Map]. https://www.pewresearch.org/fact-tank/2019/04/11/6-demographic-trends-shaping-the-u-s-and-the-world-in-2019/ft_19-01-31_foreignbornshare_immigrantshareinus_2-2/

photographs:

Adams, A. (1943). *Manzanar from Guard Tower, view west (Sierra Nevada in background), Manzanar Relocation Center, California* [Photograph]. Library of Congress. https://www.loc.gov/pictures/collection/manz/item/2002695970/

PowerPoint slides, lecture notes, recorded Zoom lectures: If the slides, lecture notes, or recorded Zoom lectures you are citing are available online, create a reference such as the first example listed below. If the material is on a closed learning management system or intranet and your readers have access, include the name of the site and the URL for the login page in your reference (see the second example below). If your audience does *not* have access to the materials, cite these resources as personal communications (see above).

University of British Columbia. (2011, November 24). *The social side of mobile health* [PowerPoint slides by D. Hooker]. SlideShare. https://www.slideshare.net/ubc/the-social-side-of-mobile-health-10314829

The following is a reference citation for a recorded Zoom class posted on an internal university learning management system:

Ruddock, J. (2020, June 3). *Lecture 5: ENGL 234* [Archived recording of Zoom class]. Moodle. https://moodle.concordia.ca/moodle/course/view.php?id=125464

conference presentations: To cite a conference session that you attended in person, include the names of presenters in the author element, the date and title, and the name of the conference and location. If you accessed the discussion online, add the URL or DOI in the location element.

Felher, B. (Chair), Cook, J., Johnson, P., & Lentschke, L. (Speakers). (2019, March 13–16). *Performing protest: Resistance rhetorics and the minoritarian response* [Panel]. Conference on College Composition and Communication, Pittsburgh, PA, United States.

38d. APA Style Sample Essay Pages

Following are sample pages from an essay written in APA style. Note that full essays in APA style appear on the adjunct website associated with this book.

Among the details to notice in this reference system:

- Where two or more works by the same author are included in References, they are ordered by date of publication.

- APA style prefers author initials rather than first names.

- Only the first words of titles and subtitles are capitalized, except for proper nouns.

- The date appears in parentheses near the beginning of each entry in References.

- The in-text citation comes directly after the name of the author or after the end quotation mark. Often, these citations fall just before the period or comma in the surrounding sentence.

- If an in-text citation occurs within text in parentheses, commas are used to set off elements of the reference.

- When a work has appeared in an edited collection, information on the editors must be included in the reference.

- Authors' first and last names are reversed; note the use of the ampersand (&) in place of *and* between author names.

- Translators should be included where appropriate in the References list.

- Publisher should be given in References entries for print works.

- Months and publisher names are not abbreviated; the day of the month follows the name of the month.

- Online references include the date of publication or of last revision in parentheses immediately after the author's name. Note that, if a URL ends a reference entry, there is no period at the end of the entry.

1

top right-
hand corner
pagination
begins with
title page

Resistance to Vaccination: A Review of the Literature

Jeremy P. Yap

Psychology Department, Wagner College

PS 252: Health Psychology

Dr. J.B. Martin

February 25, 2021

author's
name may
appear
either just
below the
title (as
shown) or
at the bot-
tom of the
page with
course and
instructor
information

AIPA Style

Resistance to Vaccination: A Review of the Literature

title should
be centred
and bolded

Since the late 1990s, vaccination has become highly controversial. This paper will review the literature on the subject, with a particular focus on the vaccination of children, by posing and responding to three key questions:

1. How effective is the practice of vaccination—and how safe?

2. Why have vaccination rates declined?

3. What are the best ways to increase rates of vaccination?

This is an area in which medical science must engage with the research findings of social psychologists; there is an urgent need to find effective solutions. The problems are sufficiently complex, however, that it seems unlikely that any single approach will be sufficient to resolve them.

How Effective Is the Practice of Vaccination—and How Safe?

There is overwhelming evidence on a variety of fronts that vaccination is one of the great triumphs of modern medical science. Thanks to the spread of vaccination, smallpox and polio have been eliminated in most of the world. The Centers for Disease Control and Prevention (2020) reports that diseases such as measles, mumps, and rubella, for which a combined vaccine has for generations been routinely given to children, are almost unknown in areas where vaccination is near-

3

universal. The example of measles is an instructive one. Before the practice of vaccination was introduced, measles infected several million children every year in the United States alone, and killed more than 500 annually. After vaccination became common practice, measles almost entirely disappeared in North America—until recently. Now it is a threat once again in the United States and Canada—and not a threat to be taken lightly. According to the World Health Organization (2020), measles still kills over 100,000 worldwide each year; for 2018 the figure was 142,300.

Evidence for the effectiveness of vaccination is very strong in the case of polio and smallpox, and in the case of "childhood diseases" such as measles and rubella. There is also strong evidence that vaccination against influenza has been successful in bringing about significantly reduced rates of infection (Atwell et al., 2019). Importantly, though, the success of vaccination depends in large part on so-called "herd immunity." So long as approximately 95% or thereabouts of a population have been vaccinated, the incidence of a disease catching on in that population is negligible. When vaccination rates dip below that level, however, the risk for those who have not been vaccinated increases dramatically. Despite this, some communities where vaccination is readily available nonetheless

for citation of work with three or more authors use "et al."

4

have vaccination rates dramatically below the percentage required for herd immunity. In California, for example, where a 2015 outbreak of measles has received wide attention, Maimuna et al. (2015) have estimated that in the relevant population clusters vaccination rates have dropped below 50%.

What about the other side of the ledger? Have there been cases of patients suffering adverse effects after taking a vaccine? And if so, do the benefits of vaccination outweigh the risks? Here too the answers seem clear. Yes, there have been cases of adverse effects (notably, fever and allergic reactions for some individuals). But as Schmid et al. (2017) and others have concluded, these are rare, and on balance vastly outweighed by the benefits of mass vaccination. Perhaps the broadest study of vaccines, their effectiveness, and their occasional side effects was that conducted by the Institute of Medicine (2011), which reviewed vaccines used against chickenpox, influenza, hepatitis B, human papillomavirus, measles, mumps, rubella, meningitis, and tetanus. Their conclusion was clear:

> Vaccines offer the promise of protection against a variety of infectious diseases … [and] remain one of the greatest tools in the public health arsenal. Certainly, some vaccines result in adverse effects that must be acknowledged. But the latest evidence shows

square brackets used for a word not in the original quotation

5

that few adverse effects are caused by the vaccines
reviewed in this report. (p. 4)

Except in rare cases, then (as with certain individuals
susceptible to severe allergic reactions), the benefits of vaccines
clearly far outweigh the risks.

centred
headings
for sections

Why Have Vaccination Rates Declined?

Near the end of the last century, British medical researcher
Andrew Wakefield and his colleagues (1998) published a
study linking the vaccination of children against diseases
such as measles, mumps, and rubella to increased incidence
of gastrointestinal disease, and also to increased incidence
of "developmental regression"—notably, autism. The study
appeared in *The Lancet,* one of the world's leading medical
journals, and had a major impact—but an entirely unfortunate
one. News of the study's findings spread widely, with thousands
of articles in the popular press in 2001 and 2002 questioning
the safety of vaccination. Parents whose children suffered
from autism started to blame vaccination, and many of them
launched lawsuits.

It was not until six years later that serious doubts were
publicly raised. Investigative journalist Brian Deer (2004)
revealed that Wakefield's study was compromised by a serious
conflict of interest; he had received financial compensation

6

from parties intending to sue vaccine manufacturers before he embarked on the research. And, as was gradually discovered, the research itself had been fabricated. In 2010 *The Lancet* finally retracted the 1998 article, and Wakefield himself was censured. By that time, a very great deal of damage had been done; public confidence in vaccines had dropped precipitously.

Fabricated research results are not the sole cause of the lack of confidence in vaccination that many continue to express. To some extent, confidence in vaccination among the general public has always been shaky. The very nature of vaccination— giving the patient a very small, modified dose of an illness in order to prevent further harm—seems counterintuitive to many. As Brendan Nyhan observed in an interview with Julia Belluz (2015), "people have always been suspicious of vaccines. There has always been an instinctive response to the idea of using a disease to protect yourself against the disease. It gives people the heebie jeebies" (para. 8). In a meta-analysis, Atwell et al. (2019) report that humans are far more likely to get vaccinated when they believe the disease in question to pose a serious threat—a finding which should not come as surprising, and which explains why doubts about vaccines have found fertile ground in places where the vaccines themselves have largely or entirely succeeded. ...

provide paragraph number when page numbers are unavailable

References

list of references alphabetized by author's last name

Anderson, M. G., Ballinger, E. A., Benjamin, D., Frenkel, L. D., Hinnant Jr., C. W., & Zucker, K. W. (2020). A clinical perspective of the U.S. anti-vaccination epidemic: Considering marginal costs and benefits, CDC best practices guidelines, free riders, and herd immunity. *Vaccine, 38*(50), 7877–7879. https://doi.org/10.1016/j. vaccine.2020.10.068

author initials used—not first names

Atwell, K., Dube, E., Gagneur, A., Omer, S. B., & Suggs, L. S. (2019). Vaccine acceptance: Science, policy, and practice in a "post-fact" world. *Vaccine, 37*(5), 677–682. https:// doi.org/10.1016/j.vaccine.2018.12.014

Belluz, J. (2015, February 7). Debunking vaccine junk science won't change people's minds. Here's what will [Interview with B. Nyhan]. *Vox.* http://www.vox. com/2015/2/7/7993289/vaccine-beliefs

Callaghan, T., Motta, M., Sylvester, S., Trujillo, K., & Blackburn, C. C. (2019). Parent psychology and the decision to delay childhood vaccination. *Social Science & Medicine, 238*(112407). https://doi.org/10.1016/j. socscimed.2019.112407

Centers for Disease Control and Prevention. (2020, November 5). *Measles History.* https://www.cdc.gov/measles/about/

history.html

Chapin, A. (2015, February 13). How to talk to anti-vaxxers. *Ottawa Citizen*. http://ottawacitizen.com/opinion/columnists/how-to-talk-to-anti-vaxxers

Deer, B. (2004, February 22). Revealed: MMR research scandal. *The Sunday Times* (London). http://www.thesunday-times.co.uk/sto/

El-Amin, A. N., Parra, M. T., Kim-Farley, R., & Fielding, J. E. (2012). Ethical issues concerning vaccination requirements. *Public Health Reviews, 34*(1), 1–20. http://www.publichealthreviews.eu/upload/pdf_files/11/00_El_Amin.pdf

Groopman, J. (2015, March 5). There's no way out of it [Review of the book *On immunity: An introduction*]. *The New York Review of Books*, 29–31.

Haverkate, M., D'Ancona, F., Giambi, C., Johansen, K., Lopalco, P. L., Cozza, V., & Appelgren, E. (2012, May). Mandatory and recommended vaccination in the EU, Iceland and Norway: Results of the VENICE 2010 survey on the ways of implementing national vaccination programmes. *Eurosurveillance, 17*(22), 31. http://www.eurosurveillance.org/ViewArticle.aspx?ArticleId=20183

Institute of Medicine. (2011, August 25). Adverse effects of vaccines: Evidence and causality [Report brief]. http:// …

provide URL for web-sourced material when DOI not available

CONTENTS

39. CHICAGO STYLE

39a. About Chicago Style

The University of Chicago's massively comprehensive *Chicago Manual of Style* (17th edition, 2017) provides full information on two documentation systems: an author-date system of citation that is similar to APA style, and a traditional foot- or end-noting system. The latter, which this book refers to as Chicago Style, and which is often used in the history and philosophy disciplines, is outlined below. This chapter also includes, at the end, a short essay excerpt using Chicago Style documentation. Full sample essays in Chicago Style are available on the Broadview website. Go to sites.broadviewpress.com/writingcdn. You can also find additional information at Chicago Style's online site (www.chicagomanualofstyle.org).

In the pages that follow, information about electronic sources has been presented in an integrated fashion, with information about referencing hard copies of print sources presented alongside information about referencing online versions. General guidelines covering entries for online sources are as follows. Begin each note and bibliography entry for an electronic source as you would for a non-electronic source, including all relevant publication information that the source makes available. Then provide either the website's URL, followed by the usual end punctuation for the note or entry, or, if available, the source's digital object identifier (DOI): a string of numbers, letters, and punctuation, beginning with *10*, usually located on the first or copyright page. If both a URL and DOI are available, provide only the latter; DOIs are preferred because they are stable links to sources, whereas URLs are often not permanent. If you need to break a URL or DOI over two or more lines, do not insert any hyphens at the break point; instead, break after a colon or double slash or before other marks of punctuation. Note that Chicago Style does not put angle brackets around URLs. Except when there is no publication or modification date available, Chicago Style does not require the addition of access dates for online material, but your instructors may wish you to include them. If so, put them before the URL or DOI, after the word *accessed*.

notes: The basic principle of Chicago Style is to create a note each time one cites a source. The note can appear at the foot of the page on which the citation is made, or it can be part of a separate list, titled *Notes*, situated at the end of the essay and before the bibliography. For both foot- and endnotes, a superscript number at the end of the clause in which the reference appears points to the relevant note:

- Levy and Mole suggest that the emotional attachment some people feel for print books is "historically and culturally constructed, and it could be constructed differently in the future."[1]

The superscript number [1] here is linked to the information provided where the same number appears at either the foot of the page or in the list of notes at the end of the main text of the paper:

1. Michelle Levy and Tom Mole, *The Broadview Introduction to Book History* (Peterborough, ON: Broadview Press, 2017), 138.

Notice that the author's name is in the normal order, elements of the note are separated by commas, publication information is in parentheses, and the first line of the note is indented. The note ends with a page number for the citation.

In addition, all works cited, as well as works that have been consulted but are not cited in the body of your essay, must be included in an alphabetically arranged list, titled *Bibliography*, that appears at the end of the essay. The entry there would in this case be as follows:

Levy, Michelle, and Tom Mole. *The Broadview Introduction to Book History*. Peterborough, ON: Broadview Press, 2017.

In the entry in the bibliography, notice that the first author's name is inverted, elements of the entry are separated by periods, and no parentheses are placed around the publication information. Also, the entry is given a hanging indent: the first line is flush with the left-hand margin, and subsequent lines are indented. Notice as well that the province or state of publication is included in both notes and bibliography entries if the city of publication is not widely known.

In the various examples that follow, formats for notes and bibliography entries for each kind of source are shown together.

titles: italics/quotation marks: Notice in the above example that the title is in italics. Titles of short works (such as articles, poems, and short stories) should be put in quotation marks. In all titles key words should be capitalized. For more details, see the Title of Source section in the chapter on MLA documentation above (pages 236–38).

multiple references to the same work: For later notes referencing an already-cited source, use the author's last name, title (in shortened form if it is over four words long), and page number only.

> 1. Levy and Mole, *Broadview Introduction to Book History*, 154.

If successive references are to the same work, you may omit the title of the work just cited, in order to avoid repetition.[1]

> 1. Sean Carver, "The Economic Foundations for Unrest in East Timor, 1970–1995," *Journal of Economic History* 21, no. 2 (2011): 103.
> 2. Carver, 109.
> 3. Carver, 111.
> 4. Jennifer Riley, "East Timor in the Pre-Independence Years," *Asian History Online* 11, no. 4 (2012): par. 18, http://www.aho.ubc.edu/prs/text-only/issue.45/16.3jr.txt.
> 5. Riley, par. 24.

---

1   This recommendation represents a change from previous editions, which had recommended using *ibid.* (an abbreviation of the Latin *ibidem*, meaning *in the same place*) for successive references. The 17th edition discourages the use of *ibid.*

Carver, Sean. "The Economic Foundations for Unrest in East Timor, 1970–1995." *Journal of Economic History* 21, no. 2 (2011): 100–21.

Riley, Jennifer. "East Timor in the Pre-Independence Years." *Asian History Online* 11, no. 4 (2012). http://www.aho .ubc.edu/prs/text-only/issue.45/16.3jr.txt.

page number or date unavailable: If an Internet document is in PDF format, the page numbers are stable and may be cited in the same way that one would the pages of a printed book or journal article. Many Internet pages are unstable, however, and many more lack page numbers. Instead, provide a section number, paragraph number, or other identifier if available.

2. Hanif Bhabha, "Family Life in 1840s Virginia," *Southern History Web Archives* 45, no. 3 (2013): par. 14, accessed March 3, 2021, http://shweb.ut.edu/history/american.nineteenthc /bhabha.html.

Bhabha, Hanif. "Family Life in 1840s Virginia." *Southern History Web Archives* 45, no. 3 (2013). Accessed March 3, 2021. http://shweb.ut.edu/history/american.nineteenthc /bhabha.html.

If you are citing longer texts from electronic versions, and counting paragraph numbers is impracticable, chapter references may be more appropriate. For example, if the online Gutenberg edition of Darwin's *On the Origin of Species* were being cited, the citation would be as follows:

• Darwin refers to the core of his theory as an "ineluctable principle."[1]

1. Charles Darwin, *On the Origin of Species* (1859; Project Gutenberg, 2001), chap. 26, http://www.gutenberg.darwin .origin.frrp.ch26.html.

Darwin, Charles. *On the Origin of Species.* 1859. Project Gutenberg, 2001. http://www.gutenberg.darwin.origin.frrp.ch26 .html.

Students should be cautioned that online editions of older or classic works are often unreliable; typically there are far more typos and other errors in online versions of literary texts than there are in print versions. It is often possible to exercise judgement about such matters, however. If, for example, you are not required to base your essay on a particular edition of Darwin's *Origin of Species* but may find your own, you will be far better off using the text you will find on the reputable Project Gutenberg site than you will using a text you might find on a site such as "Manybooks.com."

When there is no date for a source, include *n.d.*, as in the first example below. When there is no date for an online source, include your access date.

1. Thomas Gray, *Gray's Letters*, vol. 1 (London: John Sharpe, n.d.), 60.

2. Don LePan, *Skyscraper Art*, accessed February 10, 2020, http://www.donlepan.com/Skyscraper_Art.html.

Gray, Thomas. *Gray's Letters*. Vol. 1. London: John Sharpe, n.d.
LePan, Don. *Skyscraper Art*. Accessed February 10, 2020. http://www.donlepan.com/Skyscraper_Art.html.

two or more dates for a work: Note that in the Darwin example above both the date of the original publication and the date of the modern edition are provided. If you are citing work in a form that has been revised by the author, however, you should cite the date of the revised publication, not the original, and use the abbreviation *rev. ed.* to indicate that the work has been revised.

1. Robert Mutti, *Making Up Your Mind*, rev. ed. (Peterborough, ON: Broadview Press, 2014), 150.

Mutti, Robert. *Making Up Your Mind*. Rev. ed. Peterborough, ON: Broadview Press, 2014.

two or three authors: If there are two or three authors, they should be identified as follows in the footnote and in the bibliography. Pay attention to where commas do and do not appear, and note that in the bibliography entry, only the first author's name is inverted. Put the names of the authors in the order in which they appear in the work itself.

1. Joerg Fingerhut and Jesse J. Prinz, "Aesthetic Emotions Reconsidered," *The Monist* 103, no. 2 (April 2020): 223, https://doi.org/10.1093/monist/onz037.

Fingerhut, Joerg, and Jesse J. Prinz. "Aesthetic Emotions Reconsidered." *The Monist* 103, no. 2 (April 2020): 223–29. https://doi.org/10.1093/monist/onz037.

four or more authors: In the footnote name only the first author, and use the phrase *et al.*, an abbreviation of the Latin *et alia*, meaning *and others*. In the bibliography name all authors, as below:

11. Victoria Fromkin et al., *An Introduction to Language*, 4th Canadian ed. (Toronto: Nelson, 2010), 113.

Fromkin, Victoria, Robert Rodman, Nina Hyams, and Kirsten M. Hummel. *An Introduction to Language*. 4th Canadian ed. Toronto: Nelson, 2010.

organization as author/reference work/government document: Identify by the organization if known, and otherwise by the title of the work. Unsigned newspaper articles or dictionary and encyclopedia entries are usually not listed in the bibliography. In notes, unsigned dictionary or encyclopedia entries are identified by the title of the reference work, e.g., Wikipedia, and unsigned newspaper articles are listed by the title of the article.

6. Major League Baseball, *2021 Regular Season Standings*, accessed June 9, 2021, https://www.mlb.com/standings.

7. "Argentina's President Calls on UK Prime Minister to Relinquish Control of Falkland Islands," *Vancouver Sun*, January 3, 2013, A9.

8. Broadview Press, "Broadview's 2020 Recycled Paper Usage and Charitable Donations," accessed May 3, 2021, https://broadviewpress.com/broadviews-2020-recycled-paper-usage-and-charitable-donations/.

9. Commonwealth Corporation of Massachusetts, *Resources for Individuals & Communities in Response to Coronavirus (COVID-19)*, 2020, accessed January 12, 2021, https://

archives.lib.state.ma.us/bitstream/handle/2452/831037
/on1178881472.pdf?sequence=1&isAllowed=y.

10. Wikipedia, s.v. "Mary Wollstonecraft," last modified May 19, 2021, 11:46, https://en.wikipedia.org/w/index
.php?title=Mary_Wollstonecraft&oldid=1023975388.

11. *OED Online*, s.v. "aesthetic, n.1," last modified March 2021, accessed May 25, 2021, https://www-oed-com./view/Ent
ry/3237?rskey=49BHJn&result=1&isAdvanced=false.

The following are the bibliography entries for the preceding notes (notice that, because unsigned newspaper articles and articles from well-known reference works are not usually included in Chicago Style bibliographies, the Wikipedia, *Oxford English Dictionary*, and *Vancouver Sun* articles are not included). Ignore initial articles (*the*, *a*, *an*) when alphabetizing.

Broadview Press. "Broadview's 2020 Recycled Paper Usage and Charitable Donations." Accessed May 3, 2021. https://
broadviewpress.com/broadviews-2020-recycled-paper
-usage-and-charitable-donations/.

Commonwealth Corporation of Massachusetts. *Resources for Individuals & Communities in Response to Coronavirus (COVID-19)*. 2020. Accessed January 12, 2021. https://
archives.lib.state.ma.us/bitstream/handle/2452/831037
/on1178881472.pdf?sequence=1&isAllowed=y.

Major League Baseball. *2021 Regular Season Standings*. Accessed June 9, 2021. https://www.mlb.com/standings.

works from a collection of readings or anthology: In the citation for a work in an anthology or collection of essays, use the name of the author of the work you are citing. If the work is reprinted in one source but was first published elsewhere, include the details of the original publication in the bibliography.

6. Eric Hobsbawm, "Peasant Land Occupations," in *Uncommon People: Resistance and Rebellion* (London: Weidenfeld & Nicolson, 1998), 167.

7. Daniel Heath Justice, "The Necessity of Nationhood: Affirming the Sovereignty of Indigenous National Literatures,"

in *Introduction to Indigenous Literary Criticism in Canada*, ed. Heather Macfarlane and Armand Garnet Ruffo (Peterborough, ON: Broadview Press, 2015), 245.

Hobsbawm, Eric. "Peasant Land Occupations." In *Uncommon People: Resistance and Rebellion*, 166–90. London: Weidenfeld & Nicolson, 1998. Originally published in *Past and Present* 62 (1974): 120–52.

Justice, Daniel Heath. "The Necessity of Nationhood: Affirming the Sovereignty of Indigenous National Literatures." In *Introduction to Indigenous Literary Criticism in Canada*, edited by Heather Macfarlane and Armand Garnet Ruffo, 241–55. Peterborough, ON: Broadview Press, 2015. Originally published in *Moveable Margins*, edited by Chelva Kanaganayakam. Toronto: TSAR Publications, 2005.

indirect source: If you are citing a source from a reference other than the original source itself, you should include information about both sources, supplying as much information as you are able to about the original source.

- In de Beauvoir's famous phrase, "one is not born a woman, one becomes one."[1]

1. Simone de Beauvoir, *The Second Sex* (London: Heinemann, 1966), 44, quoted in Ann Levey, "Feminist Philosophy Today," *Philosophy Now*, par. 8, accessed October 8, 2020, http://www.ucalgary.ca.philosophy.nowsite675.html.

de Beauvoir, Simone. *The Second Sex*. London: Heinemann, 1966. Quoted in Ann Levey, "Feminist Philosophy Today," *Philosophy Now*. Accessed October 8, 2020. http://www.ucalgary.ca.philosophy.nowsite675.html.

two or more works by the same author: After the first entry in the bibliography, use three hyphens to begin subsequent entries of works by the same author (rather than repeat the author's name). Entries for multiple works by the same author are normally arranged alphabetically by title.

Menand, Louis. "Bad Comma: Lynne Truss's Strange Grammar." *The New Yorker*, June 28, 2004. http://www.newyorker.com/critics/books/?040628crbo_books1.

---. *The Metaphysical Club: A Story of Ideas in America.* New York: Knopf, 2002.

edited works: Entries for edited works include the abbreviation *ed.* or *eds.* Note that when *ed.* appears after a title, it means "edited by."

> 5. Roberto Frega and Steven Levine, eds., *John Dewey's Ethical Theory: The 1932 Ethics* (London: Routledge, 2021), 256.
> 6. Mary Shelley, *Frankenstein*, 3rd ed., ed. Lorne Macdonald and Kathleen Scherf, Broadview Editions (Peterborough, ON: Broadview Press, 2012), 89.

Frega, Roberto, and Steven Levine, eds. *John Dewey's Ethical Theory: The 1932 Ethics.* London: Routledge, 2021.
Shelley, Mary. *Frankenstein.* 3rd ed. Edited by Lorne Macdonald and Kathleen Scherf. Broadview Editions. Peterborough, ON: Broadview Press, 2012.

translated works: The name of the translator follows the work's title. Notice that, in the first example below, the work's author is unknown; begin with the author's name if it is known.

> 1. *Beowulf*, trans. R.M. Liuzza, 2nd ed. (Peterborough, ON: Broadview Press, 2012), 91.
> 2. Franz Kafka, "A Hunger Artist," *The Metamorphosis and Other Stories*, trans. Ian Johnston (Peterborough, ON: Broadview Press, 2015), 112.

Beowulf. Translated by R. M. Liuzza. 2nd ed. Peterborough, ON: Broadview Press, 2012.
Kafka, Franz. "A Hunger Artist." *The Metamorphosis and Other Stories.* Translated by Ian Johnston. Peterborough, ON: Broadview Press, 2015.

e-books: Electronic books come in several formats. The first of the two sample citations below is for a book found online; the second is for a book downloaded onto an e-reader.

4. Mary Roberts Rinehart, *Tish* (1916; Project Gutenberg, 2005), chap. 2, http://www.gutenberg.org/catalog/world/readfile?fk_files=1452441.

5. Lao Tzu, *Tao Te Ching: A Book about the Way and the Power of the Way*, trans. Ursula K. Le Guin (Boston: Shambhala, 2011), verse 12, iBooks.

Lao Tzu. *Tao Te Ching: A Book about the Way and the Power of the Way*. Translated by Ursula K. Le Guin. Boston: Shambhala, 2011. iBooks.

Rinehart, Mary Roberts. *Tish*. 1916. Project Gutenberg, 2005. http://www.gutenberg.org/catalog/world/readfile?fk_files=1452441.

magazine articles: The titles of articles appear in quotation marks. If no authorship is attributed, list the title of the article as the "author" in the footnote, and, if a bibliography entry is deemed necessary, the magazine title may be listed there as "author." Specific page references should be included in notes, but page ranges for magazine articles may be omitted from the bibliography.

2. Ferdinand Mount, "Ruthless and Truthless," *London Review of Books*, May 6, 2021, 7.

3. "The Impact of Green Investors," *Economist*, March 27, 2021, https://www.economist.com/finance-and-economics/2021/03/27/the-impact-of-green-investors.

4. Alec MacGillis, "The Union Battle at Amazon Is Far from Over," *New Yorker*, April 13, 2021, https://www.newyorker.com/news/news-desk/the-union-battle-at-amazon-is-far-from-over.

Economist. "The Impact of Green Investors." March 27, 2021. https://www.economist.com/finance-and-economics/2021/03/27/the-impact-of-green-investors.

MacGillis, Alec. "The Union Battle at Amazon Is Far from Over." *New Yorker*, April 13, 2021. https://www.newyorker.com/news/news-desk/the-union-battle-at-amazon-is-far-from-over.

Mount, Ferdinand. "Ruthless and Truthless." *London Review of Books*, May 6, 2021.

Chicago Style

newspaper articles: The basic principles to follow with newspaper articles or editorials are the same as with magazine articles (see above). Give page numbers in the note if your source is a hard copy rather than an electronic version, but indicate section designation alone in the bibliography entry.

1. Konrad Yakabuski, "Many Looking for Meaning in Vice-Presidential Debate," *The Globe and Mail*, October 12, 2012, A3.

2. Emma Graney and Jeffrey Jones, "Big Oil Loses Carbon Emissions Showdown in Landmark Case," *Globe and Mail*, May 26, 2021, https://www.theglobeandmail .com/business/article-canadas-oil-industry-on-watch-after -dutch-court-orders-shell-to-cut/.

Graney, Emma, and Jeffrey Jones. "Big Oil Loses Carbon Emissions Showdown in Landmark Case." *Globe and Mail*, May 26, 2021. https://www.theglobeandmail .com/business/article-canadas-oil-industry-on-watch -after-dutch-court-orders-shell-to-cut/.

Yakabuski, Konrad. "Many Looking for Meaning in Vice-Presidential Debate." *The Globe and Mail*, October 12, 2012, sec. A.

journal articles: The basic principles are the same as with magazine articles, but volume number, and issue number (if the journal is published more than once a year), should be included as well as the date. Give page numbers or e-locator numbers where available. For online journal articles, provide the DOI, if available, rather than the URL.

1. Amy Y. Li, "The Weight of the Metric: Performance Funding and the Retention of Historically Underserved Students," *The Journal of Higher Education* 90, no. 6 (April 2019): 970–71, https://doi.org/10.1080/00221546.2019.1602391.

2. Amanda L. Griffith and Veronica Sovero, "Under Pressure: How Faculty Gender and Contract Uncertainty Impact Students' Grades," *Economics of Education Review* 83 (May 2021): 6, e102126, https://doi.org/10.1016/j.econedurev.2021.102126.

3. Esteban M. Aucejo et al., "The Impact of COVID-19 on Student Experiences and Expectations: Evidence from a Survey," *Journal of Public Economics* 191 (November 2020): 2–3, e104271, https://doi.org/10.1016/j.jpubeco.2020.104271.

Aucejo, Esteban M., Jacob French, Maria Paola Ugalde Araya, and Basil Zafar. "The Impact of COVID-19 on Student Experiences and Expectations: Evidence from a Survey." *Journal of Public Economics* 191 (November 2020): e104271. https://doi.org/10.1016/j.jpubeco.2020.104271.

Griffith, Amanda L., and Veronica Sovero. "Under Pressure: How Faculty Gender and Contract Uncertainty Impact Students' Grades." *Economics of Education Review* 83 (May 2021): e102126. https://doi.org/10.1016/j.econedurev.2021.102126.

Li, Amy Y. "The Weight of the Metric: Performance Funding and the Retention of Historically Underserved Students." *The Journal of Higher Education* 90, no. 6 (April 2019): 965–91. https://doi.org/10.1080/00221546.2019.1602391.

films and video recordings: Include the director's name, the city of production, the production company, and date. Depending on the context, you may wish to add further details (actors, writers, producers) to the author section of the citation. Add the medium of publication if the film is recorded on DVD or videocassette; if it is streamed online, add the air date and URL.

1. *The Birds,* directed by Alfred Hitchcock (1963; Los Angeles: Universal Studios Home Entertainment, 2005), DVD.

2. *Nomadland,* directed by Chloé Zhao, featuring Frances McDormand (Los Angeles: Searchlight Pictures, 2020), on Hulu, https://www.hulu.com/nomadland-movie.

Hitchcock, Alfred, dir. *The Birds*. 1963; Los Angeles: Universal Studios Home Entertainment, 2005. DVD.

Zhao, Chloé, dir. *Nomadland*. Featuring Frances McDormand. Los Angeles: Searchlight Pictures, 2020, on Hulu. https://www.hulu.com/nomadland-movie.

television broadcasts: To cite an episode, start with the title of the show; then give the episode number, broadcast date, and network. Include the names of the relevant contributors. The bibliography entry should be listed under the director's name.

1. *Little Fires Everywhere*, season 1, episode 1, "The Spark," directed by Lynn Shelton, written by Liz Tigelaar, aired March 18, 2020, on Hulu, https://www.hulu.com/series/little-fires -everywhere-bce24897-1a74-48a3-95e8-6cdd530dde4c.

Shelton, Lynn, dir. *Little Fires Everywhere*. Season 1, episode 1, "The Spark." Written by Liz Tigelaar. Aired March 18, 2020, on Hulu. https://www.hulu.com/series/little-fires -everywhere-bce24897-1a74-48a3-95e8-6cdd530dde4c.

sound recordings: Include the original date of recording if it is different from the recording release date, as well as the recording number and medium.

1. Glenn Gould, performance of *Goldberg Variations*, by Johann Sebastian Bach, recorded 1981, CBS MK 37779, 1982, compact disc.

Gould, Glenn. Performance of *Goldberg Variations*. By Johann Sebastian Bach. Recorded 1981. CBS MK 37779, 1982, compact disc.

interviews and personal communications: Notes and bibliography entries begin with the name of the person interviewed. Only interviews that are broadcast, published, or available online appear in the bibliography.

7. Claudia Rankine, "The Art of Poetry No. 102," interview by David L. Ulin, *Paris Review*, no. 219 (Winter 2016), accessed February 20, 2021, https://www.theparisreview.org /interviews/6905/the-art-of-poetry-no-102-claudia-rankine.

8. Patricia Lockwood, "Patricia Lockwood Is a Good Reason to Never Log Off," interview by Gabriella Paiella, *GQ*, February 15, 2021, accessed April 2, 2021, https://www.gq.com/story /patricia-lockwood-book-interview.

9. Willie Nelson, "The Silver-Headed Stranger," interview by Andrew Goldman, *New York Times Magazine*, December 16, 2012, 12.

10. Herbert Rosengarten, telephone interview by author, January 17, 2020.

Lockwood, Patricia. "Patricia Lockwood Is a Good Reason to Never Log Off." Interview by Gabriella Paiella. *GQ*, February 15, 2021. Accessed April 2, 2021. https://www.gq.com/story/patricia-lockwood-book-interview.

Nelson, Willie. "The Silver-Headed Stranger." Interview by Andrew Goldman. *New York Times Magazine*, December 16, 2012, 12.

Rankine, Claudia. "The Art of Poetry No. 102." Interview by David L. Ulin. *Paris Review*, no. 219 (Winter 2016). Accessed February 20, 2021. https://www.theparisreview.org/interviews/6905/the-art-of-poetry-no-102-claudia-rankine.

book reviews: The name of the reviewer (if it has been provided) should come first, as shown below:

1. Brian Leiter and Michael Weisberg, "Do You Only Have a Brain? On Thomas Nagel," review of *Why the Materialist Neo-Darwinian Conception of Nature Is Almost Certainly False*, by Thomas Nagel, *The Nation*, October 22, 2012, http://www.thenation.com/article/170334/do-you-only-have-brain-thomas-nagel.

Leiter, Brian, and Michael Weisberg. "Do You Only Have a Brain? On Thomas Nagel." Review of *Why the Materialist Neo-Darwinian Conception of Nature Is Almost Certainly False*, by Thomas Nagel. *The Nation*, October 22, 2012. http://www.thenation.com/article/170334/do-you-only-have-brain-thomas-nagel.

blog posts: Begin with the author's name, if there is one.

1. Tom Clayton, "York School Crowdfunds for 'Magical' Reading Cottage," *MobyLives* (blog), May 18, 2021, https://www.mhpbooks.com/york-school-crowdfunds-for-magical-reading-cottage/.

Clayton, Tom. "York School Crowdfunds for 'Magical' Reading Cottage." *MobyLives* (blog), May 18, 2021. https://www.mhpbooks.com/york-school-crowdfunds-for-magical-reading-cottage/.

websites: Unless the website title is also that of a book or periodical, do not put the site's title in italics. If possible, indicate when the site was last updated; otherwise, include your date of access.

1. The Camelot Project, University of Rochester, last modified December 21, 2012, http://www.lib.rochester.edu/camelot/cphome.stm.

The Camelot Project. University of Rochester. Last modified December 21, 2012. http://www.lib.rochester.edu/camelot/cphome.stm.

online videos: Include the author or principal performer, length of the video, and date of posting, if available, as well as the medium and its source.

1. Anindya Kundu, "The 'Opportunity Gap' in US Public Education," TED video, January 23, 2020, 5:33, https://www.youtube.com/watch?v=wRG5_-9eE4w.

Kundu, Anindya. "The 'Opportunity Gap' in US Public Education." TED video. January 23, 2020. https://www.youtube.com/watch?v=wRG5_-9eE4w.

tweets: Chicago Style recommends that a tweet be transcribed (up to 160 characters). This can happen in your note or in the text of your essay (see the examples below). If you include the tweet and citation information in the body of your essay, you may omit a note. In most cases, you need not include a bibliography entry for a tweet, but if you are citing the tweet more than once, or if it is an extended thread, then you may wish to create an entry. Note that, like all websites that don't have a print counterpart, Twitter is not italicized; note also that time stamps should be included in both the note and bibliography entry.

- On May 17, 2021, Stephen King tweeted about the elusive nature of artistic inspiration: "Good writing is a delight to those who read it and a mystery to those who write it."[1]

    1. Stephen King (@StephenKing), "Good writing is a delight to those who read it and a mystery to those who write it," Twitter, May 17, 2021, 9:10 p.m., https://twitter.com/StephenKing/status/1394460364549627906.

    King, Stephen (@StephenKing). "Good writing is a delight to those who read it and a mystery to those who write it." Twitter, May 17, 2021, 9:10 p.m. https://twitter.com/StephenKing/status/1394460364549627906.

39b. Chicago Style Sample Essay Pages

A sample of text with citations in Chicago Style appears below. Note that a full sample essay in Chicago Style appears on the adjunct website associated with this book.

Urban renewal is as much a matter of psychology as it is of bricks and mortar. As Paul Goldberger has described, there have been many plans to revitalize Havana.[1] But both that city and the community of Cuban exiles in Florida remain haunted by a sense of absence and separation. As Lourdes Casal reminds us,

> Exile
>
> is living where there is no house whatever in
> which we were ever children …[2]

The psychology of outsiders also makes a difference. Part of the reason Americans have not much noticed the dire plight of their fifth-largest city is that it does not "stir the national imagination."[3] Conversely, there has been far more concern over the state of cities such as New Orleans and Quebec City, whose history and architecture excite the romantic imagination. As Nora Phelps has discussed, the past is in itself a key trigger for romantic notions, and it is no doubt inevitable that cities whose history is particularly visible will engender passionate attachments.[4] And as Stephanie Wright and Carole King have detailed

---

1. Paul Goldberger, "Annals of Preservation: Bringing Back Havana," *The New Republic*, January 2004, 54, accessed March 4, 2020, http://www.findarticles.comgoldberg.p65.jn.htm.

2. Lourdes Casal, "Definition," trans. Elizabeth Macklin, *The New Yorker*, January 26, 1998, 79.

3. Witold Rybczynski, "The Fifth City," review of *A Prayer for the City*, by Buzz Bissinger, *New York Review of Books*, February 5, 1998, 13.

4. Nora Phelps, "Pastness and the Foundations of Romanticism," *Romanticism on the Net* 11 (May 2001): par. 14, accessed March 4, 2020, http://users.ox.ac.uk/~scato385/phelpsmws.htm.

in an important case study,[1] almost all French-speaking Quebecers feel their heritage to be bound up with that of Quebec City. (Richard Ford's character Frank Bascombe has suggested that "New Orleans defeats itself" by longing "for a mystery it doesn't have and never will, if it ever did,"[2] but this remains a minority view.)

In addition to the roles history and memory play in shaping our approach to urban renewal, new research also points to the crucial impact of nature experience on psychological health. This has prompted urban designers, city planners, and psychologists to prioritize access to green and blue spaces in their design plans for cities. One important dimension of this emergent research is environmental justice; as one study of Los Angeles's San Fernando Valley concludes, "We find that low-income neighborhoods … have higher traffic volumes, fewer shade trees, and street environments that are less clean and well maintained compared to high-income areas and that similar disparities exist between ethnic minority and white communities."[3] …

1. Stephanie Wright and Carole King, *Quebec: A History*, 2 vols. (Montreal: McGill-Queen's University Press, 2012).

2. Richard Ford, *The Sportswriter*, 2nd ed. (New York: Random House, 1995), 48.

3. Alessandro Rigolon, Zeynep Toker, and Nara Gasparian, "Who Has More Walkable Routes to Parks? An Environmental Justice Study of Safe Routes to Parks in Neighborhoods of Los Angeles," *Journal of Urban Affairs* 40, no. 4 (2018): 576, https://doi.org/10.1080/07352166.2017.1360740.

The bibliography relating to the above text would be as follows:

Bibliography

Casal, Lourdes. "Definition." Translated by Elizabeth Macklin. *The New Yorker*, January 26, 1998, 79.

Ford, Richard. *The Sportswriter*. 2nd ed. New York: Random House, 1995.

Goldberger, Paul. "Annals of Preservation: Bringing Back Havana." *The New Republic*, January 2004, 50–62. Accessed March 4, 2020. http://www.findarticles.com.goldberg.p65 .jn.htm.

Phelps, Nora. "Pastness and the Foundations of Romanticism." *Romanticism on the Net* 11 (May 2001). Accessed March 4, 2020. http://users.ox.ac.uk/~scat0385/phelpsmws.htm.

Rigolon, Alessandro, Zeynep Toker, and Nara Gasparian. "Who Has More Walkable Routes to Parks? An Environmental Justice Study of Safe Routes to Parks in Neighborhoods of Los Angeles." *Journal of Urban Affairs* 40, no. 4 (2018): 576–91. https://doi.org/10.1080/07352166.2017 .1360740.

Rybczynski, Witold. "The Fifth City." Review of *A Prayer for the City*, by Buzz Bissinger. *New York Review of Books*, February 5, 1998, 12–14.

Wright, Stephanie, and Carole King. *Quebec: A History*. 2 vols. Montreal: McGill-Queen's University Press, 2012.

Among the details to notice in this reference system:

- Where two or more works by the same author are included in the bibliography, they are normally arranged alphabetically by title.

- All major words in titles and subtitles are capitalized.

- Date of publication must appear, where known. Provision of access dates for electronic materials is recommended for sources that are likely to change over time.

- Commas are used to separate elements within a footnote, and, in many circumstances, periods separate these same elements in the bibliographic entry.

- When a work has appeared in an edited collection, information on the editors must be included in both the first note and the bibliographic reference.

- First author's first and last names are reversed in the bibliography.

- Translators must be noted both in footnotes and in the bibliography.

- Publisher as well as city of publication should be given.

- Months and publisher names are not abbreviated.

- The day of the month comes after the name of the month.

- Online references should include a publication date, if available, and/or a revision date. You may also include both: "Published June 10, 2019; last modified February 3, 2021." If neither date is available, you may include the date of access: "Accessed March 2, 2022."

GLOSSARY OF USAGE

accept/except: *Accept* is a verb meaning to receive something favourably; *except* is a conjunction meaning *not including* or *but*. ("All the members of the Security Council except China voted to accept the proposal.")

advice/advise: *Advice* is the noun, *advise* is the verb. ("We advised them to proceed, but they did not take our advice.")

affect/effect: *Effect* is normally used as a noun meaning result. *Affect* is normally a verb meaning *cause a result*. ("There is no visible effect; perhaps nothing we can do will affect it.") Note, however, that *effect* may also be used as a verb meaning *put into effect*, as in "The changes were effected by the committee."

all right: Two words.

allusion: See *illusion*.

a lot: Two words.

already/all ready: When used as an adverb, *already* is one word. ("They were all ready to do the job, but he had already done it.")

alternately/alternatively: *Alternately* means *happening in turn, first one and then the other*; *alternatively* means *instead of*. Be careful as well with the adjectives *alternate* and *alternative*.

altogether/all together: One word when used as an adverb to mean *completely* or *entirely*. ("He is not altogether happy with the result." "They were all together for the picnic.")

among: See *between*.

amoral/immoral: An *amoral* act is one to which moral standards do not apply; an *immoral* act, on the other hand, is one that goes against a moral standard.

anybody/anyone: See pages 128–29.

anyone: One word unless it is followed by *of*.

anyways/anywheres: There is never a need for the *s*.

assure/ensure/insure: To *assure* someone of something is to tell them with confidence or certainty; to *insure* (or *ensure*) that something will happen is to make sure that it does; to *insure* something is to purchase insurance on it so as to protect yourself in case of loss.

because of the following reasons: See page 22.

beg the question: To *beg the question* is to take for granted the very thing to be argued about. In recent years the phrase has been widely used to mean *invite the question*.

between/among: Use *among* if it's among three or more.

can/may: *Can* is used to refer to ability, *may* to refer to permission. ("He asked if he might leave the room.")

capital/capitol: *Capitol* refers to an American legislative building or a Roman temple; *capital* can refer to wealth, to the city from which a government operates, or to the top of a pillar; it may also be used as an adjective to mean *most important* or *principal*.

change: You <u>make</u> a *change* (not *do* a change).

childish/childlike: The first is a term of censure, the second a term of praise.

classic/classical: As adjectives, *classic* means of such high quality that it has lasted or will last for a long time, and *classical* means *pertaining to ancient Greece and Rome* or, particularly when speaking of music, *written in a traditional style*. ("Sophocles was a great classical author; his plays are acknowledged classics.")

climatic/climactic: Weather is not the most exciting part. ("Climatic projections concerning average temperature are often inaccurate." "He spilled his drink at the most climactic moment in the movie.")

compliment/complement: To *compliment* people is to praise them, and a *compliment* is the praise; to *complement* something is to add to it to make it better or complete, and a *complement* is the number or amount needed to make it complete. ("None of the divisions had its full complement of troops, and the troops were complimented on the good job they had done despite being short-staffed.")

comprise/compose: The whole *comprises* or includes the various parts; the parts *compose* the whole.

conscience/conscious/consciousness: To be *conscious* is to be awake and aware of what is happening, whereas *conscience* is a part of our minds that tells us what is right or wrong to do. ("Her conscience told her not to steal the chocolate bar.")

continual/continuous: If something is *continuous* it never stops; something *continual* is frequently repeated but not unceasing. ("He has been phoning me continually for the past two weeks.")

could of: A corruption of *could have*.

council/counsel; councillor/counsellor: A *council* is a group of officials, and a *councillor* is a member of that group. *Counsel* is advice or, in the special case of a lawyer, the person offering advice. In other situations the person offering *counsel* is a *counsellor*.

couple: The phrase *a couple of* should be avoided in formal writing. In informal English, be sure to include *of* after *couple*.

definite/definitive: If something is *definite* then there is no uncertainty about it; a *definitive* version of something fixes it in its final or permanent form.

deny/refute: To *deny* something is to assert that it is not true; to *refute* it is to prove conclusively that it is not true. ("After weeks of denying the allegations he was finally able to produce evidence to refute them.")

discrete/discreet: *Discrete* means separate or distinct, whereas *discreet* means prudent and tactful; unwilling to give away secrets. ("The Queen was renowned for being discreet.")

disinterested/uninterested: A *disinterested* person is unbiased; uninfluenced by self-interest, especially of a monetary sort. If one is *uninterested* in something, one is bored by it.

each: See pages 128–29.

effect: See *affect.*

e.g./i.e.: The abbreviation *e.g.* is short for *exemplum gratia* ("example given"; or, in the plural *exempli gratia*, "examples given"). It is sometimes confused with the abbreviation *i.e.*, which is short for *id est* ("that is to say").

elicit/illicit: *Elicit* is a verb; one elicits information about something. *Illicit* is an adjective meaning illegal or not approved.

emigrate/immigrate: To *emigrate* is to leave a country; to *immigrate* is to move to it. ("More than 10,000 emigrants from the United States became immigrants to Canada last year.")

enthuse/enthusiastic: *Enthuse* is a verb; *enthused* is its past participle. The adjective is *enthusiastic*. ("Everyone was enthusiastic about the movie.")

everybody/everyone: See pages 128–29.

everyday/every day: One word when used as an adjective to mean "daily," but two words when used to mean "each day." ("Brushing your teeth should be part of your everyday routine." "She comes here every day.")

everyone: One word unless it is followed by *of.*

explicit/implicit: Something *explicit* is stated in precise terms, not merely suggested or implied. By contrast, something *implicit* is not stated overtly.

farther/further: *Farther* refers to physical distance, *further* to time or degree. ("We do not have much farther to go." "The plan needed further study.")

flaunt/flout: To *flout* is to disobey or show disrespect for; to *flaunt* is to display very openly. ("The demonstrators openly flouted the law.")

forget: To *forget* something is to fail to remember it, not to leave it somewhere. ("I left my book at home" or "I forgot to bring my book" but not "I forgot my book at home.")

forward/foreword: You find a *foreword* before the other words in a book.

good/well: The most common of the adjective-for-adverb mistakes. ("He pitched very well today.") See pages 100–01, 131–32.

hardly: *Hardly* acts as a negative; there is thus no need to add a second negative. ("They claim that you can hardly tell the difference.")

historic/historical: *Historic* means *of sufficient importance that it is likely to become famous in history* (a historic occasion). *Historical* means *having to do with history* (historical research).

hopefully: Traditionalists argue that the correct meaning of the adverb *hopefully* is *filled with hope,* and that the use of the word to mean *it is to be hoped that* is therefore incorrect. Others argue, plausibly, that many other adverbs may function as independent comments at the beginning of a sentence ("Finally, ..." "Clearly, ..." "Obviously, ...") and that there is no good reason for treating *hopefully* differently. Using *hopefully* to mean *it is to be hoped that* should not be regarded as a grievous error—but it is a form of English usage that will upset some instructors.

illusion/allusion: An *allusion* is an indirect reference to something; an *illusion* is something falsely supposed to exist. ("Her poem makes many allusions to Shakespeare.") Also, when you make an *allusion*, you are alluding to something.

in/into/throughout/within: Whereas *in* typically indicates a particular location, *into* implies motion, and *throughout* implies omnipresence. *Within* and *in* are not interchangeable; *within* should be used only in certain contexts involving extent, duration, or enclosure.

increase: Numbers can be *increased* or *decreased*, as can such things as production and population (nouns which refer to certain types of numbers or quantities). Things such as *houses*, however, or *books* (nouns which do not refer to numbers or quantities) cannot be *increased*; only the number of houses, books, etc. can be *increased* or *decreased*, *raised* or *lowered*.

infer/imply: To *imply* something is to suggest it without stating it directly; the other person will have to *infer* your meaning. ("This sentence implies that the character is not to be trusted.")

irregardless/regardless: There is no need for the extra syllable; use *regardless*.

is when/is where: Avoid these expressions when defining something. ("Osmosis occurs when ...," not "Osmosis is when....")

its/it's: *Its* is an adjective meaning *belonging to it*. *It's* is a contraction of *it is*—a pronoun plus a verb. ("It's true that a coniferous tree continually sheds its leaves.")

later/latter: *Later* means afterwards in time, whereas the *latter* is the last mentioned of two things.

lay/lie: You *lay* something on the table, and a hen *lays* eggs, but you *lie* down to sleep. In other words, *lie* is an intransitive verb; it should not be followed by a direct object. *Lay*, by contrast, is transitive. ("That old thing has been lying around for years.")

lend/loan: In formal English *loan* should be used only as a noun; *lend* is the verb. ("He was unwilling to lend his sister any money.")

less/fewer: Use *less* only with non-count nouns; use *fewer* with anything that can be counted. ("This checkout is for people buying fewer than twelve items.")

liable/likely: Do not use *liable* unless you are referring to possible undesirable consequences. ("It is liable to explode at any moment.")

like/as: In formal writing use the conjunction *as* to introduce a clause—not the preposition *like*. ("He looks like his father." "He looks as his father did at his age.")

literally: A *literal* meaning is the opposite of a figurative or metaphorical meaning. Do not use *literally* simply to emphasize what you are saying.

loose/lose: *Loose* is normally used as an adjective meaning *not tight*; *lose* is always a verb. ("The rope has come loose." "He began to lose control of himself.")

may be/maybe: One word when used as an adverb to mean *possibly*, but two words when used as a verb. ("Maybe he will arrive later tonight." "He may be here later tonight.")

may of: A corruption of *may have*.

might of: A corruption of *might have*.

mitigate/militate: To *mitigate* something is to make it less harsh or severe ("mitigating circumstances"); to *militate* against something is to act as a strong influence against it.

must of: A corruption of *must have*.

neither: See pages 104–05, 128–29.

none: See pages 104–05, 128–29.

nor: Use in combination with *neither*, not in combination with *not*. When using *not* use *or* instead of *nor*. ("She does not drink or smoke." "She neither drinks nor smokes.")

nothing/nobody/nowhere: These words should not be used with another negative word such as *not*. With *not* use *anything*, *anybody*, *anywhere*. ("He could not do anything about it.")

novel: A novel is an extended work of prose fiction. Extended works of non-fiction—of history or philosophy or political theory or science, for example—are not works of fiction, so they cannot be novels. ("Darwin's groundbreaking work, *On the Origin of Species*, appeared in 1859"—not "Darwin's groundbreaking novel….")

passed/past: "She *passed* me on the street," and "I *passed* her a note," but "that was all in the *past*."

per cent/percentage: If you use *per cent* (or *percent*), you must give the number. Otherwise use *percentage*. ("The percentage of people who responded was very small.")

persuade: If one does not succeed in making people believe or do what one wants, then one has not *persuaded* or convinced them, but only *tried* to persuade them.

precede/proceed: To *precede* is to come before; to *proceed* is to go forward. ("Once the students understood that *G* precedes *H* in the alphabet, they proceeded with the lesson.")

prescribe/proscribe: To *prescribe* something is to recommend or order its use; to *proscribe* something is to forbid its use.

principal/principle: *Principal* can be either a noun or an adjective. As a noun it means *the person in the highest position of authority in an organization* (e.g., a school principal) or *an amount of money*, as distinguished from the interest on it. As an adjective it means *first in rank or importance.* ("The principal city of northern Nigeria is Kano.") *Principle* is always a noun; a principle is *a basic truth or doctrine, a code of conduct*, or *a law describing how something works.* ("We feel this is a matter of principle.")

protest: You *protest* something (not protest against it).

quote/quotation: *Quote* is the verb, *quotation* the noun. ("The following quotation illustrates the point.")

real/really: *Real* is the adjective, *really* the adverb. ("She was really happy.")

reason is because: Use *that* instead of *because* to avoid redundancy. ("The reason may have been that they were uncertain of the ally's intentions.")

relatable: The problem with *relatable* is not that it shouldn't ever be used; it's that many people use it too often to mean too many different things. If you're going to write that something is *relatable*, it may be useful to ask yourself before you do so *who* is likely to find that thing easy to relate to, and *why* they may be likely to find it easy to relate to. It will sharpen what you write if you can be more specific. ("That's a feeling that any low-wage worker in twenty-first-century North America is likely to be able to relate to." "This is a book that people of colour are particularly likely to find relatable—but it's also a book that may help white people to better understand the challenges that people of colour face.")

respectively/respectfully: *Respectively* means *in the order mentioned*; *respectfully* means *done with respect*. ("Green Bay, Denver, and San Francisco are, respectively, the three best teams in the league.")

sensory/sensuous/sensual: Advertising and pornography have dulled the distinction among these three adjectives; *sensual* is the one relating to sexual pleasure.

set/sit: *Set* means *to place something somewhere*.

short/scarce: If people are *short* of something, that thing is *scarce*. ("Food is now extremely scarce throughout the country.")

should of: A corruption of *should have*.

since (1): As a time word, *since* is used to refer to the <u>point</u> at which a period of time began ("since six o'clock," "since 2008"). *For* is used to refer to the <u>amount</u> of time that has passed ("for two years," "for centuries"). ("He has been with us for three weeks" or "He has been with us since three weeks ago.")

since (2): Watch for ambiguity involving *since* meaning *because*, and *since* meaning *from the time that*; "Since he crashed his car he has been travelling very little" could mean either "Because he crashed his car ..." or "From the time that he crashed his car...."

so: *So* should not be used in formal writing as an intensifier in the way that *very* is used. ("He looked very handsome," not "He looked so handsome.")

some/someone: With negatives (*not, never*, etc.) *any* is used in place of *some*. ("He never gives me any help.")

somebody/someone: See pages 128–29.

stationary/stationery: *Stationary* means not moving; *stationery* is what you write on. ("The cars were stationary.")

suppose/supposed: Be sure to add the *d* in the expression *supposed to*. ("We are supposed to be there now.")

sure and: In formal writing always use *sure to*, not *sure and*.

than/that: *Than* is the one used for comparative statements ("more than we had expected").

than/then: *Than* is used in comparisons, whereas *then* denotes time.

thankful/grateful: We are *thankful* that something has happened and *grateful* for something we have received. ("I am very grateful for the kind thoughts expressed in your letter.")

that/which: See pages 163–64.

they/there/their/they're: Four words that are confused perhaps more frequently than any others. *They* is a pronoun used to replace any plural noun (e.g., books, people, numbers). *There* can be used to mean *in* (or *at*) *that place*, or can be used as an introductory word before various forms of the verb *to be* (*There is, There had been*, etc.). *Their* is a possessive adjective meaning *belonging to them*. Beware in particular of substituting *they* for *there*. ("There were many people in the crowd," not "They were many people in the crowd.")

tiring/tiresome: Something that is *tiring* makes you feel tired, though you may have enjoyed it very much. Something that is *tiresome* is tedious and unpleasant.

to/too/two: *Too* can mean *also* or be used to indicate excess (*too many, too heavy*); *two* is of course the number. ("She seemed to feel that there was too much to do.")

try and: In formal writing always use *try to*, not *try and*. ("He had agreed not to try to convert them.")

unexceptional/unexceptionable: *Unexceptional* means *ordinary, not an exception*; if something is *unexceptionable*, then you do not object (or *take exception*) to the thing in question.

unique/universal/perfect/complete/correct: None of these can be a matter of degree. Something is either unique or not unique, perfect or imperfect, and so on, never *very unique* or *quite perfect*.

use/used: Be sure to add the *d* in the expression *used to*. ("This neighbourhood used to be very different.")

valid/true/accurate: An *accurate* statement is one that is factually correct. A combination of *accurate* facts may not always give a *true* picture, however. *Valid* is often used carelessly and as a consequence may seem fuzzy in its meaning. Properly used it can mean *legally acceptable*, or *sound in reasoning*; do not use it to mean *accurate*, *reasonable*, *true*, or *well-founded*.

weather/whether: *Whether* the *weather* will be good or bad is hard to predict.

were/where: *Were* is of course a past tense form of the verb *to be*, while *where* refers to place.

where: Do not use *where* for *that* (as in *I read in the paper where the parties are tied in popularity*).

whose/who's: *Whose* means *belonging to whom*; *who's* is a contraction of *who is*.

would of: A corruption of *would have*.

your/you're: *Your* shows possession, *you're* is a contraction of *you are*.

Additional Material Online

Exercises on words that may cause confusion and on other points of usage may be found at
sites.broadviewpress.com/writingcdn.
Click on **Exercises** and go to **M2, Usage.**

CORRECTION KEY

Correction Key

abbr	Abbreviation error (183–84)
adj	Adjective used improperly (100–01, 131–32)
adv	Adverb used improperly (100–01, 131–32)
agr	Agreement issue with subject & verb (25–26, 112–14)
amb	Ambiguity (22–23)
appr	Appropriateness of language issue (69–92)
awk	Awkward expression or construction
cap	Capitalization faulty (182–83)
⌒	Close up
dang	Dangling construction, dangling modifier (123–26)
ℓ	Delete
dict	Diction faulty (12, 346–56)
frag	Fragment (incomplete sentence) (132–48)
∧	Insert
ital	Italics (185)
lc	Lowercase should be used (182–83)
¶	Paragraph: begin a new paragraph here (17–18)
no ¶	Paragraph: do not begin a new paragraph here (17–18)
//	Parallelism faulty or lacking (25–26, 27–32, 104–05)
pass	Passive voice (15–17, 62–63, 116–17)

pron	Pronoun reference error (129–30)
	Punctuation error (162–79)
	Apostrophe (or single quotation mark) needed (170–71)
	Comma needed (132–48, 162–64)
	Period needed (132–48, 162)
	Quotation marks needed (171–73)
rep	Repetition
run-on	Run-on sentence (fused sentence or comma splice) (132–48)
ss	Sentence structure faulty
sl	Slang or overly informal language (68–69)
#	Space should be added
sp	Spelling error (185–96)
t	Tense of verb wrong (112–23)
tr	Transition faulty or insufficient (19–21)
	Transposed elements
v	Verb form wrong (112–23, 155)
	Wordiness (12–14)

INDEX

INDEX

Entries in **bold** are to words, not topics.

DVDs (digital versatile discs),
citing as sources, 245 (MLA); 336
(Chicago)

each, 95
EAL (English as an Additional
Language), 149–61: articles (and
other determiners), 150–53;
conditional, 156–58; continuous
verb tenses, 155; non-count nouns
(list), 153–54; omission or repetition of the subject, 155–56; useful
information about, 149–50; word
order, 158–60
e-books, citing as sources, 261
(MLA), 333–34 (Chicago)
effect/affect, 346
e.g., 184
e.g./i.e., 349
elicit/illicit, 349
ellipses, 178–79, 218–19
email, 66–68
email messages, citing as sources,
296 (APA)
emigrate/immigrate, 349
ensure/assure/insure, 346
enthuse/enthusiastic, 349
ESL: *See* EAL (English as an Additional Language), 149–61
*Essays and Arguments: A Handbook
on Writing* (Johnston), 43
et al./et alia, 184
etc./et cetera, 184
ethnicity, 74, 75–80
everybody/everyone, 129
everyday/every day, 349
everyone, 349
exclamation mark, 166
explicit/implicit, 349

factor, 14
FANBOYS, 102. *See also*
conjunctions
farther/further, 349
fewer/less, 351
films and video recordings, citing as
sources, 307 (APA); 336 (Chicago)

**First Nations/Indian/Indigenous/
Aboriginal,** 77–79
First Peoples, Inuit, Métis, 78
flaunt/flout, 349
forget, 349
for the most part, 36
forward/foreword, 350
fragments, sentence, 132–33,
142–48
from my point of view, 14
fused sentence, 136
future perfect tense, 116
future perfect continuous tense, 116
future progressive tense, 116

gay/homosexual, 84–85
gender, 69–73: non-sexist language,
69–71; pronouns, 71
good/well, 100, 131, 350
Google Scholar, 199
government documents, citing as
sources, 330–31 (Chicago)
Graff, Gerald, and Cathy Birkenstein, *They Say / I Say,* 44, 45
graphic narratives, citing as sources,
258 (MLA)
grammar: adjectives, 97–99;
adverbs, 100–01; articles, 96,
150–53; comma splices, 133,
134, 136–37, 138, 167; conjunctions, 101–04, 136–37, 140–41;
dangling constructions, 123–26;
incomplete sentences, 132–35;
participles, 119–26; prepositions,
101; pronouns, 94–99, 128–31,
176–77; run-on sentences,
135–42; sentence fragments,
132–33, 142–48; verbs, 132–33,
142–48
grammar-check, 186
grammatical structure: parallelism,
29–32
grateful/thankful, 355

hardly, 350
he/she, 71–72
he/she/it, 87–88

The Authors

Doug Babington was for many years Director of the Writing Centre at Queen's University; he is co-author of *Writing Analytically with Readings* (2012) and also author of a book of bilingual poems, *News from the Recent Quake* (2015).

Corey Frost, an Associate Professor in the English Department at The City University of New Jersey, has published widely on poetry and poetics, orality, and digital pedagogy; his *A Prescription for Zombies: A Critical Approach to English Grammar and Usage* is forthcoming from Broadview Press.

Don LePan's other books include *The Broadview Pocket Glossary of Literary Terms* (2013), *Animals: A Novel* (2010), and *Lucy and Bonbon: A Novel* (2022); he is a general editor of *The Broadview Anthology of British Literature* and Co-Managing Editor of *The Broadview Anthology of American Literature*.

Maureen Okun, for many years a professor in both the English and the Liberal Studies Departments at Vancouver Island University, is the author, co-author, or editor of several books, among them Sir Thomas Malory's *Le Morte Darthur: Selections* (2014).

Nora Ruddock is co-author of *The Broadview Pocket Guide to Citation and Documentation* and co-editor of *The Broadview Anthology of Expository Prose* and of *Popular Culture: A Broadview Topics Reader*.

Karen Weingarten, Associate Chair of the English Department at Queens College, CUNY, is the author of *Abortion in the American Imagination: Before Life and Choice, 1880–1940* (2014); her book *Pregnancy Test* is scheduled for 2023 publication in Bloomsbury's Object Lessons series.

This book is made of paper from well-managed FSC® - certified forests, recycled materials, and other controlled sources.